THE COMPLETE SOMATIC THERAPY & POLYVAGAL THEORY TOOLBOX

Y.D. GARDENS

THE EMERALD
SOCIETY

A SPECIAL GIFT TO MY READERS

Visit emeraldsocpublishing.com to
download your FREE copy!

CONTENTS

VOLUME 1

VOLUME 2

VOLUME ONE

LEAVE A REVIEW

Don't forget to share the love and **leave your**
Amazon review for:

The Somatic Therapy Handbook

PREFACE

Iɴ ᴛʜᴇ ᴠᴀsᴛ expanse of human emotion and experience, it is the quiet moments of connection between mind, body, and soul that often go unnoticed. Yet, these often imperceptible time lapses hold the key to our most profound healing and understanding.

After a few years of taking a deep dive into shadow work, I felt compelled to create this complete somatics toolkit. This is my way of extending a heartfelt invitation to women like yourself to embark on the most significant journey you will ever undertake—the journey inward. Somatic healing has come to be not only an important addition to my work exploring inner child wounds and shadow webs; it is now clearly an inevitable component of this holistic healing journey.

You see, my own path to discovering the power of somatic therapy began in a place of darkness, a period when the weight of unspoken trauma seemed to cloud every aspect of my existence. It was a time when anxiety was a constant companion, whispering doubts and fears into my ear, chaining me to memories and sensations I felt powerless to escape. The turning point came unexpectedly, through the gentle guidance of a wonderful therapist and several holistic healers, who taught me the transformative power of tuning into my body's wisdom. Little by little, I learned to listen to the subtle cues my body was giving me—tension, breath, heartbeat—and to respond with compassion rather than fear.

The true turning point, however, was learning to connect these physiological sensations to my thoughts, thus to my perceptions and reactions.

One particularly profound moment stands out. During a therapy session a few years ago, I was asked to close my eyes and, as I pictured a triggering past event in my mind, I was told to notice the sensations in my body, without judgment. It was uncomfortable at first, to say the least. But as I continued to focus and breathe into spaces of tension, I instinctively released a tightly held breath I didn't even know I was holding. In that moment, a surge of emotion overwhelmed me, and tears began flowing freely not from pain, but from a deep sense of release. It was as if my body was finally allowed to speak its truth, and in doing so, began the process of letting go of years of stored trauma. This experience was a game changer, illuminating the next steps of my path toward healing and wholeness.

Drawing from these deeply personal encounters with somatic healing, this all in one guide-journal-workbook is designed to be a compassionate companion on your journey. Each page is crafted with the intention of guiding you gently toward discovering your own body's wisdom, providing tools to release stored trauma, and offering practices to cultivate a harmonious connection between your mind, body, and soul.

As you engage with the information, exercises and reflections within these pages, remember that the journey of healing is not linear. There will be moments of challenge and resistance, but also moments of profound insight and liberation. Also, you should know that this is not a race to the finish line - in fact, there is no ending. I therefore encourage you to respect the ebb and flow of your own life story, and to be gentle with yourself as you go through this work. This workbook is here to support you through it all, offering a safe space to explore, heal, and grow.

I hope this guide serves as hope and a testament to the resilience of the human spirit. My deepest wish is that through these practices, you too will experience the transformative power of connecting with your body's innate wisdom.

Here's to your journey of healing, discovery, and ultimately, tapping into that delicious space of inner peace.

WELCOME to the beginning of a new chapter.

INTRODUCTION

Have you ever stood at the edge of the ocean, toes buried in the sand, watching the waves wash away your footprints with effortless ease? There is a profound lesson in this simple act of nature: just as the water smooths the sands of time, somatic therapy holds the power to gently cleanse our being, releasing us from the grip of past traumas and anxiety. You should know that the journey toward healing and self-discovery can be as transformative as the ocean's relentless reshaping of the shoreline. This book is your invitation to explore the depths of somatic therapy, a practice that has not only changed lives but has also provided a healing path for many - myself included.

My dedication to the realm of women's mental health and wellness is not just a professional choice; it is a calling that has shaped my life's work. Through years of experience and a deeply rooted passion for guiding women through their emotional barricades, I have come to understand the intricate dance of mind, body, and soul. My belief in the transformative power of integrating these aspects of our being is what led me to somatic therapy—a path that promises harmonious balance that beckons inner peace.

This book was crafted with you in mind. Whether you are new to the concept of somatic therapy or looking to deepen your practice, this guide is designed to be your best companion. Picking up this book is already a testament to the strength within you, ready to be discovered and nurtured. Here, you will find a blend of information, advice, practical tools, and heartfelt wisdom, all aimed at guiding you towards holistic healing.

As you have probably already noticed, the tone of this book is much like a supportive friend—compassionate, encouraging, and filled with hope. My aim was to create a space where jargon does not hinder understanding, and the complex becomes accessible, no matter your experience. You will soon discover that this unique approach combines informational content with practical workbook activities and journaling prompts, encouraging you to not just read or listen, but engage, reflect, and grow. This was designed to ensure a comprehensive understanding of somatic therapy principles, whilst empowering you to actively engage and apply these learnings immediately in your daily life.

Perhaps you've already begun your journey of inner work and know that it is as profound as it is personal. I firmly believe that the release from anxiety, recovery from trauma, and a deepened connection between your mind, body, and soul is the greatest gift you can offer yourself. This promise of finding inner peace and achieving a state of harmonious balance that once may have seemed out of reach is absolutely life-changing.

So, I now invite you to dive in with an open heart and mind, ready to explore the depths of your being. Take as much time as is needed to digest the informational content. Engage fully with the exercises and reflections provided, for the path to healing and inner peace begins with this very step. Let us navigate these waters together, with the promise that on the other side, a renewed sense of self awaits.

Somatics:

A field within bodywork and movement studies which emphasizes internal physical perception and experience.

ONE

SOMATICS: THE ORIGINS

In the midst of a world brimming with rapid advancements and technological marvels, we often find our essence tethered to the past, weighed down by experiences that shape our present yet remain untouched and unexplored. It's within this complexity of human experience that somatic therapy emerges, not as a mere method of healing but as a profound dialogue between body and soul. This chapter unfolds the mosaic of somatic therapy, tracing its lineage from ancient wisdom to contemporary practice, and shedding light on its transformative power.

The Origins of Somatic Therapy: A Historical Overview

The roots of somatic therapy stretch deep into the soil of human history, intertwined with the earliest practices of healing and spirituality. Long before the advent of modern medicine, ancient civilizations understood the inseparable connection between the body and the mind. In the healing temples of Egypt, the therapeutic baths of Rome, and the yogic traditions of India, we find the precursors to somatic therapy. These cultures recognized that physical ailments often have emotional and spiritual components, a concept that forms the cornerstone of somatic therapy today.

Wilhelm Reich, a student of Freud, laid the groundwork for what would become somatic therapy in the early 20th century. Reich proposed that psychological trauma manifests physically as "body armors", constricting the flow of vital energy. His revolutionary ideas paved the way for further exploration into the mind-body connection. Peter Levine, another pivotal figure, expanded on this foundation with his development of Somatic Experiencing® in the latter part of the century. Drawing from observations of how animals process stress and trauma, Levine's work offered a new perspective on human trauma recovery, emphasizing the body's inherent ability to heal itself.

The influence of diverse cultures on somatic practices cannot be understated. From the mindfulness of Buddhist meditation to the rhythmic movements of African dance, global traditions have enriched the fabric of somatic therapy, introducing a variety of techniques that cater to the multifaceted nature of human healing. This integration of perspectives underscores the universal truth that healing transcends cultural boundaries, resonating with the core of our shared humanity.

As somatic therapy gained traction, its applications broadened, touching the lives of people seeking relief from the vestiges of trauma, stress, and disconnection. Today, somatic therapy enjoys a revered place in healing and wellness communities, highlighting its effectiveness and holistic approach. Far from a one-size-fits-all solution, it offers a personalized path to wellness, acknowledging the unique stories etched in our bodies and spirits.

In a coffee shop, a place seemingly distant from the quiet introspection of therapy, one might observe a microcosm of somatic principles at play. Notice how a deep breath and a moment of mindfulness can cut through the noise of a busy day, grounding us in the present. This simple act, a practice deeply rooted in somatic therapy, illustrates the profound impact of reconnecting with our bodily sensations, offering a momentary respite from the whirlwind of thoughts and emotions. It's in these everyday moments that the essence of somatics comes to life, bridging the ancient and the modern in the quest for healing and balance.

The journey of somatics, from its ancient origins to its current prominence, reflects a growing recognition of the body's wisdom and the healing power of mindful presence. As we continue to explore and expand upon these practices, we'll draw closer to a more integrated and holistic understanding of health and well-being, one that honors the intricate dance between body, mind, and spirit.

Within somatic therapy, the threads of mind, body, and spirit weave together, supporting holistic healing that is both intricate and profound. This fusion is foundational, asserting that these elements are not separate entities but deeply interconnected aspects of our being. This recognition shifts the focus from treating isolated symptoms to nurturing the whole person, a perspective that is both revolutionary and as ancient as humanity itself.

Interconnectedness

The principle of interconnectedness lies at the heart of somatic therapy. It posits that the mind influences the body just as the body influences the mind, with the spirit acting as the bridge between the two. This triad forms a complex system where changes in one aspect invariably affect the others. For instance, a prolonged state of stress can lead not only to mental health issues like anxiety but also to physical symptoms such as tension headaches or digestive problems, reflecting the body's distress. Similarly, a chronic physical condition can lead to depression or anxiety, demonstrating the body's impact on the mind. The spirit, in this context, encompasses our sense of self, purpose, and connection to something greater than ourselves, influencing and being influenced by the state of our mind and body.

Holistic Health

The concept of holistic health emerges naturally from the interconnectedness of mind, body, and spirit. It advocates for a comprehensive approach to well-being that considers all aspects of the individual. In practice, this means addressing more than physical symptoms by also exploring emotional, psychological, and spiritual dimensions. This approach promotes deep, lasting healing and transformation, as it acknowledges and addresses the root causes of imbalance rather than merely alleviating symptoms. For those navigating the challenges of stress and trauma, this holistic approach offers a path to recovery that is both thorough and empathetic, recognizing the individual as a complex, multifaceted being.

The Impact of Stress and Trauma

Stress and trauma, often seen as primarily psychological issues, reverberate through the mind, body, and spirit, highlighting the necessity of a holistic healing approach. The physical manifestations of stress and trauma can range from tense muscles and headaches to more severe conditions like fibromyalgia or chronic fatigue syndrome. Psychologically, they can lead to anxiety, depression, and PTSD, affecting one's sense of self and place in the world. Spiritually, trauma can leave individuals feeling disconnected, lost, or without purpose. Somatic therapy, with its holistic lens, recognizes these intricate connections and addresses the multifaceted impact of stress and trauma, facilitating healing on all levels.

The Path to Wellness

Somatic therapy charts a course towards wellness that honors and nurtures the connection between mind, body, and spirit. It employs a variety of techniques, from mindful body scanning and breathing exercises to movement and expressive arts, each designed to foster awareness, release stored trauma, and promote integration and healing. This path is not linear but is tailored to the individual's unique experiences, needs, and pacing.

Consider, for example, the practice of mindful body scanning. This technique encourages us to tune into our body, noticing sensations without judgment. This simple act creates a deeper connection with our physical self, revealing areas of tension or numbness that may be holding emotional pain. By bringing awareness to these areas and gently exploring their emotional context, we can begin to release and heal trauma wounds stored within our body.

Breathing exercises offer another powerful tool for reconnecting the mind, body, and spirit. Controlled breathing not only calms the mind and reduces stress but also helps to regulate the body's physiological response to stress. On a spiritual level, breathwork can be a meditative practice that promotes inner peace and connectedness.

Movement practices, whether through yoga, dance, or simple stretching, allow individuals to express and release emotions physically, facilitating psychological healing. These also strengthen the body-mind connection, enhancing physical health and a general feeling of wholeness.

For those navigating the aftermath of trauma, techniques like Somatic Experiencing® offer a structured approach to processing and integrating traumatic experiences. By focusing on bodily sensations and employing titration to gradually work through trauma, this method allows for safe, controlled healing, addressing the impact of trauma on the mind, body, and spirit.

The path to wellness offered by somatic therapy is a journey of self-discovery, healing, and transformation. It recognizes the individual as a whole, honoring the complex interplay between mind, body, and spirit. Through a combination of awareness, expression, and integration, somatic therapy provides a path to a more balanced, peaceful, and fulfilling life.

Principles of Somatic Therapy: Core Beliefs and Practices

Somatic therapy operates on foundational principles that distinguish it from other therapeutic modalities. These principles guide the practice, ensuring that healing is not only effective but also holistic and empowering.

Body as the Primary Focus

Central to somatic therapy is the recognition of the body as both the repository of trauma and the vehicle for healing. This view challenges conventional approaches that prioritize the mind in understanding and treating psychological distress. Instead, somatic therapy posits that the body holds onto traumatic experiences, manifesting them through various physical symptoms and patterns. By focusing on the body, somatic therapy engages directly with the source of trauma, offering a pathway to release and heal these deep-seated wounds.

This principle is evident in the way somatic therapy approaches the treatment of anxiety, for instance. Traditional therapy might explore the thoughts and beliefs contributing to anxiety, offering cognitive strategies to manage it. Somatic therapy, while not dismissing the value of under-standing the mind's role, dives deeper into the bodily sensations associated with anxiety. It explores how anxiety is experienced in the body—

the tightness in the chest, the quickening of the breath, the tension in the shoulders—and uses this awareness as a starting point for healing.

The Wisdom of the Body

Somatic therapy teaches that the body possesses an intrinsic wisdom, capable of guiding us towards understanding and healing. This wisdom speaks through the language of sensations, impulses, and movements, communicating needs, boundaries, and unresolved emotions. Learning to listen and interpret these signals is a fundamental aspect of somatic therapy. It requires cultivating a deep sense of body awareness, a process that can be both challenging and liberating.

For example, consider the experience of feeling a knot in the stomach when faced with a difficult decision. This physical sensation is the body's way of signaling stress or fear, perhaps pointing to underlying concerns or doubts. Somatic therapy encourages us to explore these sensations with curiosity, allowing them to unfold and reveal the emotions and memories they contain. This is a process which helps develop self-awareness whilst supporting emotional processing and resolution.

Integration of Experiences

Similar to aspects of shadow work, the key aim of somatic therapy is the integration of traumatic experiences, facilitating a process of healing that is both comprehensive and sustainable. As we know, integration involves acknowledging and processing traumatic memories, rather than simply reliving them - a distinction that is crucial to understand. Integrating traumatic experiences involves a gentle and controlled exploration of the trauma, guided by the body's wisdom and, if possible, a therapist's support.

Integration sees traumatic experiences as fragmented pieces of the self that have been disowned or disconnected due to their overwhelming nature. Through somatic therapy, these pieces are gradually acknowledged, felt, and understood within the safety of the therapeutic relationship. This process allows for a reconnection with these disowned parts, leading to a sense of wholeness and coherence. The integration of traumatic experiences transforms how these memories are held within the body and the mind, moving from sources of distress to aspects of the self that have been healed and reclaimed.

Empowerment through Self-Regulation

At its core, somatic therapy is about empowerment. It will equip you with skills for self-regulation, enhancing your ability to manage your emotional and physiological states. Self-regulation is vital in navigating the stresses and challenges of life, promoting resilience and a sense of agency. As you'll soon discover, somatic therapy offers practical tools and exercises that strengthen the capacity for self-regulation, such as meditative practices, grounding techniques, and intuitive movement.

Mindful breathing, for instance, is a simple yet powerful tool for self-regulation. By focusing on the breath and consciously slowing it down, individuals can directly influence their nervous system, shifting from a state of alertness and stress to one of calm and relaxation. This ability to regulate one's state is empowering, offering a way to manage anxiety, stress, and emotional overwhelm independently.

Grounding techniques serve a similar purpose, helping us anchor in the present moment when faced with distressing emotions or memories. These techniques, which often involve engaging the senses or focusing on physical sensations, provide a means to stabilize and center ourselves. Whether it's feeling the texture of a fabric, focusing on the sensation of feet touching the ground, or listening to the sounds in our environment, grounding techniques help make us feel safe and in control.

Also, movement practices, from yoga and dance to simple stretching exercises, play a key role in self-regulation. They allow for the expression and release of pent-up emotions, facilitating emotional equilibrium. Movement connects the mind and body, promoting an integrated experience of self-awareness and emotional processing.

The empowerment that comes from mastering self-regulation skills is transformative. It shifts the narrative from one of victimhood or helplessness to one of strength and agency. We can learn to trust in our ability to navigate our internal world, managing emotional and physiological states with confidence and skill. This empowerment shows the capacity for resilience and healing inherent in each person, one that somatic therapy seeks to awaken and nurture.

The dance between our physical experiences and psychological states finds a compelling explanation within the realm of neurobiology, particularly when examining the impact of trauma. Trauma, often perceived through a purely psychological lens, leaves indelible marks on both the brain and nervous system, illustrating the profound interconnectedness of our mental and physical wellbeing.

If you're ready, we will briefly dive into some of the scientific underpinnings of somatic therapy. The purpose here is to shed light on its effectiveness in healing trauma by bridging the gap between body and mind, so that we can better understand the 'what' and 'how' before jumping into practice.

Neurobiology of Trauma

Recent advancements in neuroscience have provided invaluable insights into how traumatic events alter the brain's structure and function. Trauma can dysregulate the brain's fear circuitry, particularly the amygdala, hippocampus, and prefrontal cortex, leading to heightened states of anxiety and an impaired ability to process emotions. The amygdala, responsible for detecting threats, becomes overly reactive, while the hippocampus, crucial for memory consolidation, may shrink, impacting an individual's ability to contextualize fear. Conversely, the prefrontal cortex, which governs reasoning and impulse control, may show reduced activity, making it challenging to regulate emotions and responses to perceived threats. This dysregulation contributes to the persistent feeling of being "stuck" that many trauma survivors experience, unable to move past the traumatic event.

The Role of the Nervous System

Central to somatic therapy is an understanding of the autonomic nervous system (ANS), which regulates involuntary bodily functions, including heartbeat, digestion, and respiratory rate. The ANS comprises two main branches: the sympathetic nervous system (SNS), which triggers the "fight or flight" response during perceived threats, and the parasympathetic nervous system (PNS), which promotes "rest and digest" functions, restoring calm and balance after the threat has passed. Trauma can lead to an imbalance, with the SNS remaining in a hyperactivated state, leaving us in a constant state of alertness and tension.

Here's what you need to remember: Somatic therapy aims to restore balance within the autonomic nervous system. To do this, we employ techniques that activate the parasympathetic nervous system to counteract this hyperarousal (stress) and facilitate a state of relaxation and safety.

Body-Brain Feedback Loop

The relationship between the body and the brain is not unidirectional but rather a continuous feedback loop, where bodily sensations affect mental states and vice versa. This loop is crucial in understanding somatic therapy. For instance, the act of taking slow, deep breaths—a common somatic practice—can signal the brain to lower stress levels, demonstrating how physical actions can influence psychological wellbeing. Similarly, adopting a posture of confidence can not only reflect but also generate feelings of self-assuredness. Somatic therapy leverages this feedback loop, using physical sensations and movements to influence emotional and mental states, creating an environment where healing can occur from the inside out.

Evidence-Based Practices

The effectiveness of somatic therapy in treating trauma is supported by a growing body of research. Studies have shown that somatic practices, such as mindful movement and breathwork, can significantly reduce symptoms of PTSD, anxiety, and depression. These practices help reduce symptoms of hyperarousal and increase feelings of safety and grounding. Furthermore, neuroimaging research has revealed that somatic therapy can lead to changes in brain areas impacted by trauma, such as increased hippocampal volume and reduced amygdala reactivity, pointing to its potential in facilitating not only psychological but also neurological healing.

One compelling study observed the effects of Somatic Experiencing on individuals with PTSD. Participants reported significant reductions in PTSD symptoms, including flashbacks, anxiety, and sleep disturbances. These findings were mirrored in physiological measures, with participants showing decreased heart rate and increased heart rate variability, indicators of a more balanced ANS. These results demonstrate the potential of somatic therapy to address the root causes of trauma, offering a holistic approach to healing that encompasses both mind and body.

As you are now well aware, understanding the science of somatics allows us to demystify the mechanisms through which somatic therapy facilitates healing from trauma. By addressing the neurobiological and physiological impacts of trauma, somatic therapy offers a comprehensive approach that honors the intricate connection between the brain and the body. As you continue to move through these chapters, you'll discover targeted practices that engage this connection and will lead you on a path of healing, moving beyond the shadows of your past and towards a future marked by balance, resilience, and well-being.

Somatic Therapy vs. Traditional Therapy

In the area of therapeutic practices, the distinction between somatic therapy and traditional therapeutic modalities is as profound as it is pivotal. This differentiation is not only academic but touches the very essence of how healing is approached, experienced, and integrated by those who seek relief from the shadows cast by trauma.

Approach to Trauma

At the heart of somatic therapy lies an emphasis on bodily sensations and experiences as the gateway to understanding and healing trauma. This contrasts with the cognitive or talk therapy focus, which predominantly navigates thoughts, beliefs, and narratives. While traditional therapy often seeks to untangle the cognitive webs surrounding traumatic experiences, somatic therapy plunges directly into the body's memory of the event, exploring the non-verbal cues and sensations that are frequently bypassed in verbal recounting. This approach acknowledges that trauma often resides deeper than words can reach, manifesting in physical symptoms like tension, breathlessness, or numbness. By tuning into these bodily signals, somatic therapy facilitates a direct engagement with the trauma, offering a pathway to release and healing that circumvents the sometimes-limiting framework of language.

The Role of the Therapist

The role of the therapist in somatic therapy diverges significantly from traditional approaches, embodying a facilitative rather than directive presence. Somatic therapists act as guides, helping individuals to cultivate awareness of their bodily sensations and to interpret these signals as meaningful narratives about their experiences and traumas. This contrasts with the more directive role often assumed by traditional therapists, who may steer conversations, interpret psychological patterns, or suggest cognitive strategies for coping with distress.

In somatic therapy, the therapist and client embark on a collaborative journey, with the therapist supporting the client's exploration of their internal landscape. This partnership is predicated on trust, with the therapist providing a safe and non-judgmental space for the client to reconnect with their body's wisdom and capacity for self-healing.

Treatment Outcomes

Considering treatment outcomes, somatic therapy offers distinctive benefits, particularly in addressing deep-seated trauma. Traditional therapy has been instrumental in providing insights into the psychological dimensions of trauma, offering strategies for managing symptoms and reshaping cognitive narratives. However, for some, this may not fully address the somatic imprint of trauma, which can linger in the body's memory, manifesting as chronic pain, tension, or dysregulated arousal states.

Somatic therapy, by focusing on the body's role in trauma and healing, provides a complementary pathway to wellness. It allows for the release of stored trauma and the reintegration of the self, leading to outcomes that encompass mental and emotional healing, as well as physical relief and a renewed sense of embodiment. Somatic practitioners often report a greater sense of connection to their bodies, improved emotional regulation, and a decrease in physiological symptoms associated with trauma.

Accessibility and Inclusivity

One of the most compelling aspects of somatic therapy is its accessibility and inclusivity. Traditional therapy, with its reliance on verbal communication, can inadvertently exclude those who may find it difficult to articulate their experiences or emotions, such as individuals with certain disabilities, young children, or those for whom language is a barrier. Somatic therapy, with its non-verbal approach, opens the door to healing for a broader spectrum of individuals. It transcends linguistic and cognitive limitations, making it particularly valuable for diverse populations. This inclusivity extends to cultural considerations as well. The somatic healing focus on universal bodily experiences allows it to bridge cultural gaps, providing a form of healing that resonates on a fundamentally human level, irrespective of an individual's background or language.

IN SUM, the landscape of therapeutic practices is rich and varied, with each approach offering its unique pathways to healing. With its focus on the body's wisdom and capacity for healing, somatic therapy offers a distinctive and valuable complement to traditional therapeutic modalities. By engaging directly with the body's memory of trauma and facilitating a deep, non-verbal process of healing, somatic therapy expands the possibilities for recovery and wellness. It emphasizes a collaborative and facilitative approach, empowering us to become active participants in our healing journey. Furthermore, its accessibility and inclusivity make it a vital resource for individuals across a broad spectrum of experiences and backgrounds, underscoring its importance in the field of mental health and wellness.

MIND & BODY

The body is our gauge of truth, our inner oracle - and when we're disconnected from it, we're disconnected from our innate intuitive strengths and our primal gut instincts.

ALETHEIA LUNA

TWO

THE BODY'S TALE

Your body is like a vast library - each cell a book, each muscle a tome of memories. Within this library, stories of joy and sorrow, pleasure and pain are archived, not always consciously accessed but ever-present.

I'm offering this perspective for you to consider how deeply your experiences, particularly traumatic ones, are embedded within your physical self. It's not just about scars seen by the eye but about those felt only when you tune into the silent whispers of your body.

In this exploration, we turn our focus to understanding trauma's impact on the body. The aim is to shed light on the often-overlooked somatic symptoms of trauma, guiding us through recognizing these signs and gently releasing the stories they hold. This understanding acknowledges the presence of trauma and empowers us with knowledge and techniques to navigate through its somatic expressions towards healing.

Physiological Effects of Trauma

Trauma has a profound impact on the body, often triggering a chronic stress response. This is not merely a psychological state but a physiological one, where the body is perpetually in a "fight or flight" mode. Such constant vigilance can manifest as tension in the muscles, a rapid heartbeat, or even disrupted digestive and immune systems. Over time, these responses, meant to protect us in moments of danger, can become our default state, leading to a range of physical health issues from chronic pain to autoimmune diseases.

Somatization

Somatization is a phenomenon where emotional distress is expressed through physical pain. When trauma is not processed or expressed emotionally, the body becomes a vessel for this unspoken pain, manifesting symptoms without a clear medical cause. For instance, someone might experience severe stomach aches during periods of stress or headaches when recalling a traumatic event. These are not just random occurrences and should not be reduced to regular bodily functions: They are the body's way of signaling unresolved emotional turmoil.

The Concept of 'Body Memory'

The idea that our bodies remember traumatic events, even when our minds may not fully recall them, is central to understanding somatization and the physiological effects of trauma. This 'body memory' can surface through sudden, unexplained physical reactions to certain people, places, or situations that are reminiscent of the trauma. It's as if the body has its own alarm system, alerting us to potential danger based on past experiences. Recognizing these reactions as memories rather than immediate threats is a crucial step in the healing process.

Releasing Trauma

Facilitating the release of trauma stored in the body is a delicate process, requiring patience, compassion, and often guided support. Techniques vary, but the goal is the same: to allow the body to express and let go of the trauma it holds. This can be achieved through:

- Mindful Movement: Practices like yoga or tai chi encourage attentiveness to bodily sensations, creating a space for the body to communicate its stored traumas and begin the process of releasing them.
- Breath Work: Controlled breathing exercises can help regulate the body's stress response, creating a sense of safety that allows for the release of tension and trauma.
- Body Scanning: By mentally scanning the body and noticing areas of tension or discomfort, individuals can begin to identify where trauma might be stored and approach these areas with gentle awareness and curiosity.

As we continue, we will explore these further and learn how incorporating these techniques into daily routines can significantly impact how trauma is held and processed in the body. For example, starting the day with a few moments of deep, mindful breathing can set a tone of calm and presence. Similarly, integrating gentle stretches or yoga poses into breaks throughout the day can help release physical tension and remind us to stay connected with our bodies.

The Language of the Body: Learning to Listen and Respond

Our bodies communicate with us constantly, sending signals about our physical and emotional well-being through a language of sensations, pulses, and movements. This form of communication is subtle, often overlooked in the noise of daily life, yet it holds insights into our inner world. This section aims to illuminate the process of tuning into the body's language, interpreting its messages, and responding with care and compassion.

Developing Body Awareness

Increasing awareness of bodily sensations is akin to tuning an instrument, refining our ability to detect the subtle nuances of our internal experience. Here are several strategies designed to heighten this awareness:

- Scheduled Check-ins: Set aside specific times each day to pause and scan your body. Notice any areas of tension, discomfort, or ease without trying to change anything. This practice helps in cultivating a habit of listening to your body.
- Mindfulness Meditation: Engage in mindfulness meditation, focusing your attention on different parts of your body. Observe the sensations without judgment, allowing yourself to become more attuned to your body's language.
- Movement Exploration: I have a soft spot for this one, as it is certainly one of my favorite ways to reconnect with my breath and body. I recommend experimenting with different forms of movement, such as stretching, dancing, or walking. Pay attention to how each movement feels and what it reveals about your body's state.

Interpreting Signals

Our body's signals are messages about our needs, boundaries, and unresolved issues. Learning to interpret these signals involves a deep attunement to our physical sensations and the emotions they evoke. Here are three ways in which to decipher the body's communications.

1. Connecting Sensations to Emotions: When you notice a physical sensation, such as a tight chest or clenched jaw, ask yourself what emotion might be linked to this sensation. Is it anxiety, anger, or perhaps something else?

2. Historical Context: Reflect on whether the sensation is familiar or linked to a specific event or period in your life. Understanding the historical context can provide clues about unresolved issues or traumas. This is also very useful for inner child healing.

3. Somatic Journaling: Keep a journal of bodily sensations and their possible meanings. Over time, patterns may emerge that offer deeper insights into your emotional world.

Case Studies

To illustrate the transformative power of listening to and responding to your body's language, I've decided to share four short stories. Although I've left out some details about each person's journey, I'm hoping that these may shed some light on how somatics can support you on your own path to reconnecting with yourself.

Case 1: Anna's Journey of Reconnection

After years of chronic tension headaches, Anna began practicing daily body check-ins, discovering a link between her headaches and unexpressed anger. Through somatic therapy and mindfulness practices, she learned to acknowledge and express her emotions in healthy ways, leading to a significant reduction in her headaches.

Case 2: Mark's Path to Emotional Freedom

Mark experienced sudden panic attacks with no apparent trigger. Through somatic experiencing® therapy, he uncovered that certain physical sensations were triggering memories of a car accident he had been in years before. By working through these body memories in a safe and supportive environment, Mark was able to process the trauma, leading to a cessation of his panic attacks.

Case 3: Lily's Discovery of Boundaries

Lily often found herself feeling drained after social interactions. Through mindful movement and body scanning, she realized that her energy levels dropped significantly in certain company. This awareness helped her set healthier boundaries in her relationships, improving her energy and emotional well-being.

These three case studies, although briefly summarized, show aspects of the healing process that become possible when we attune to our body's language, interpret its messages, and respond with compassion and intention.

Checklist of Somatic Symptoms

Trauma can manifest physically in various ways, often without a direct or immediate connection to the traumatic event itself. This is a comprehensive checklist of somatic symptoms that can be useful in identifying potential signs of unprocessed trauma.

Physical Sensations and Pain

- Chronic pain in muscles and joints
- Stomach pain and digestive issues
- Sudden, unexplained headaches
- Pervasive fatigue or exhaustion
- Extreme sensitivity to cold and heat

Cardiovascular and Respiratory Symptoms

- Rapid heartbeat or palpitations
- Difficulty breathing or shortness of breath
- Feelings of pressure or tightness in the chest

Immune System and Health Changes

- Frequent illnesses or infections
- Changes in appetite, significant weight loss or gain
- Sleep disturbances, insomnia, or oversleeping

Neurological and Sensory Symptoms

- Hyperarousal or hypervigilance
- Numbness or tingling in different parts of the body
- Heightened sensitivity to light, sound, or touch

Motor Functions

- Tremors or uncontrollable shaking
- Difficulty coordinating movements or clumsiness
- Startle response more pronounced or easily triggered

Other Physical Symptoms

- Dizziness or feeling faint
- Skin issues (e.g., rashes, eczema triggered by stress)
- Sexual dysfunction or loss of libido

Emotional Responses Connected to Physical Symptoms

- Physical symptoms that worsen with stress or emotional distress
- Somatic symptoms that flare up around anniversaries of traumatic events or in specific situations that remind you of trauma
- Physical reactions or panic attacks triggered by memories or reminders of the traumatic event

This checklist can be a starting point for recognizing the physical manifestations of trauma. It's important to note that having one or more of these symptoms does not necessarily mean you have experienced trauma - however, if these symptoms are persistent and significantly impact your quality of life, it might be beneficial to seek professional help. Consulting with a healthcare provider can also help determine the cause of these symptoms and develop an appropriate treatment plan.

Body Awareness: The First Step Towards Healing

In the realm of somatic therapy, developing an acute awareness of one's physical self is the foundation upon which the path to healing is built. This awareness guides us through the fog of disconnection that trauma often casts over the body. It is here, in the quiet observation of our physical sensations, that we begin to unlock the door to deeper understanding and, ultimately, transformation.

Starting the Journey

The initiation into body awareness is at once an exercise and a reacquaintance with the self. For many, trauma creates a rift between the mind and body, leading to a life lived more in the head than in the flesh.

This disconnection serves as a survival mechanism, a way to avoid the pain and discomfort that the body holds. However, it also keeps us from fully experiencing the present and can inhibit healing. By re-establishing this connection, by simply noticing, we start to mend the rift, acknowledging our physical selves with curiosity and without judgment.

Practical Exercises

Several exercises stand out for their effectiveness in cultivating body awareness. These practices invite us to slow down and tune into the whispers of our bodies:

- Mindful Breathing: This involves focusing on the breath, observing its rhythm, depth, and the sensations it creates in the body. It's an anchor to the present moment, drawing our attention away from the clutter of thoughts and into the physical self.
- Body Scanning: Lying down in a comfortable position, direct your attention gradually through each part of the body, from the toes to the top of the head. Notice sensations such as warmth, tightness, or tingling, without trying to change them. This scan illuminates areas of tension and relaxation, mapping the landscape of our physical selves.
- Sensory Engagement: Engage intentionally with the senses —touch, taste, sight, sound, and smell—to anchor in the present and cultivate an acute awareness of the body's interaction with its environment. This can be as simple as feeling the texture of fabric under your fingertips or noticing the nuances of flavor and texture in a bite of food.

Challenges and Strategies

As with any new skill, developing body awareness can present challenges. Some common hurdles include:

- Distraction: Our minds wander, pulled by thoughts of the past or future. When you notice your attention drifting, gently bring it back to the sensation you were focusing on, without self-criticism.

- Discomfort: Tuning into the body can sometimes reveal discomfort or pain, leading to avoidance. Approach these sensations with kindness, allowing them to be felt and heard. If they become overwhelming, shift your focus to a neutral part of the body and return later, perhaps with a lesser intensity.
- Impatience: The desire for quick progress can lead to frustration. Remember, this is a process of relearning and reconnection that unfolds in its unique time.

To navigate these challenges, it helps to set realistic expectations through understanding that body awareness is a skill that deepens over time. Celebrate your small victories and progress! Furthermore, incorporating practices into your daily routine to make them part of your regular self-care will be very helpful. Consistency is key.

The Role of Patience and Persistence

Patience and persistence are vital allies on this journey. The road to reconnection with one's body is not linear; it is marked by ebbs and flows, moments of insight, and periods of seeming stillness. Each step forward, no matter how small, is a triumph, a reclaiming of territory long ignored or forgotten. It is through persistent, gentle attention that we begin to decode the language of our bodies, learning to inhabit ourselves fully once again. This process of cultivation, of patiently tending to our physical selves, allows for a blooming of awareness that can transform how we live and heal.

The Power of Breath: Breathing Techniques for Relaxation and Awareness

Within the moments of our lives that are stitched together by the rhythm of our breaths lies a simple yet profound tool for healing and awareness. Breathing, an act as natural as the ocean's tides, holds the key to calming the storm within us, gently guiding us back to tranquility and clarity.

This section illuminates the transformative potential of breath work, guiding you through techniques that not only soothe but also awaken a deeper connection with the self.

The Science of Breathing

The act of breathing does more than fill our lungs with air; it communicates with the nervous system, whispering signals of calm or alert depending on its pattern. When we engage in controlled breathing, we send a message to the nervous system to shift gears, moving from the often overactive sympathetic state to the calming embrace of the parasympathetic state. This transition is a crucial physiological recalibration that lowers heart rate, reduces blood pressure, and decreases stress hormone levels, leaving you in a state of peace and readiness for healing.

Breathing Exercises

When exploring breath work, we find a variety of exercises, each with its unique rhythm and purpose. Let's explore a few that have been proven time and again to promote relaxation and awareness:

- Diaphragmatic Breathing: By placing a hand on the abdomen and focusing on deep, slow breaths that expand the diaphragm rather than the chest, this technique encourages full oxygen exchange and engages the parasympathetic nervous system.
- 4-7-8 Breathing: Inhale through the nose for four counts, hold the breath for seven counts, and exhale through the mouth for eight counts. This pattern, repeated for a few cycles, acts as a natural tranquilizer for the nervous system.
- Alternate Nostril Breathing: This is a practice borrowed from ancient yoga traditions, where you gently close one nostril, inhale through the other, and then switch nostrils for the exhale. This dance of breath balances the body's energy channels and harmonizes the hemispheres of the brain.

Incorporating Breathing into Daily Life

The beauty of breath work lies in its simplicity and accessibility, making it possible to include these practices into our daily routines. Here are three simple yet powerful ways to integrate mindful breathing into your day.

1. Morning Intentions: Begin your day with a few minutes of diaphragmatic breathing, setting a calm and centered tone for the hours ahead.

2. Transitional Breaths: Use moments of transition, such as finishing a task or arriving home, to practice a few cycles of 4-7-8 breathing, marking the end of one activity and the beginning of another with a clear, calm mind.

3. Mindful Moments: Throughout the day, take short "breath breaks," pausing for a minute or two of alternate nostril breathing, to reset and recharge, especially during moments of stress or fatigue.

The Benefits of Breath Work

The realm of breath work is rich with benefits that impact our emotional, physical, and mental well-being. For one thing, it offers a direct pathway to emotional regulation, soothing emotional turmoil, providing a tool to navigate anxiety, anger, and sadness with greater ease. There is also no doubt that it enhances physical health as, beyond immediate relaxation, regular breath work can improve respiratory function, invigorate circulation, and boost immune system resilience. Additionally, mindful breathing practices are known to sharpen mental clarity and focus. By calming the mind's chatter, breath work clears the mental fog, facilitating a state of presence and attentiveness.

The practice of controlled breathing connects aspects of our existence - body, mind, and spirit - in harmony. It reflects the body's inherent wisdom and capacity for self-regulation, a reminder that within each breath lies the potential for healing, transformation, and awakening. Let's remember the power of our breath, a gentle force that shapes our experience and existence, moment by moment, inhale through exhale.

Our muscles hold memories, encapsulating emotional experiences just as vividly as any thought or image our minds might conjure. This muscle memory isn't just about repetitive physical actions becoming second nature, but also our emotional history being written into the very fabric of our physical selves. When we experience trauma, our muscles contract, sometimes holding onto that tension long after the initial event has passed. This tension is a silent witness to our past, a holder of unspoken stories waiting to be acknowledged and released.

Exploring Muscle Memory

Muscle memory, in the context of trauma and emotional experiences, is an involuntary physical response to a feeling or memory. For instance, shoulders might tense up in situations that subconsciously remind us of a time when we felt burdened or stressed. This reaction is the body's way of preparing to deal with a perceived threat, a remnant of our instinctual fight or flight response. However, when these muscular reactions become chronic, they can lead to discomfort, pain, and even mobility issues, signaling a need for release.

The Process of Releasing

Techniques for releasing the emotional and physical tension stored in our muscles are varied, each offering a unique path to relief and healing. Here are a few of my favorites:

Massage

Deep tissue and therapeutic massage can help to loosen the tightness held in muscles, encouraging a release of both physical and emotional tension. What is incredibly special (and less often mentioned) when it comes to touch therapy or massages is that these practices often carry us into a state somewhere between wakefulness and sleep, which enhances the production of theta brain waves. This promotes a connection between our conscious and unconscious minds, which is a central aspect of shadow, inner child, and somatic healing.

Stretching

Gentle stretching exercises can increase flexibility and circulation, gradually easing the muscle's grip on past traumas. It also usually involves mindful breathing, which is an important part of releasing emotional blockages. Moreover, including this in your daily routine may allow you to systematically rest, ground, and regroup.

Movement

Activities that incorporate rhythm, such as drumming, dance, or even walking, can have a soothing effect on the nervous system. The predictability and structure of rhythmic movement can help regulate the body's stress response systems and promote a state of calm. Other activities like yoga, running, and tai chi allow for expressive movement that can unlock and release the emotional stories etched into our muscles. This is often where stress and trauma are physically held in the body. By engaging in movement, muscles can relax, reducing stiffness and pain, which can be physical manifestations of emotional stress.

Moreover, physical activity is well-known to influence the brain's chemistry by increasing the production of endorphins, which are chemicals that improve mood and reduce pain. Movement can also decrease the production of stress hormones like cortisol. This biochemical change can help alleviate both emotional and physical tension.

Through these three main techniques, we can develop outlets for emotional release and encourage our bodies to let go of the past. Doing more than alleviating physical discomfort, they offer an opportunity to acknowledge and honor our emotional histories by allowing them to surface and then move through us, leaving us lighter and more present.

The Importance of Safety and Trust

Creating a safe and trusting environment is crucial for the process of releasing muscle memory. This safety can be physical, ensuring that the space in which we engage in these practices is comfortable and secure. More importantly, it must be emotional, fostering an atmosphere where vulnerability is met with compassion and understanding. Whether working with a therapist, a trusted instructor, or on our own, the feeling of being supported and safe in our explorations and expressions of stored trauma is vital. It is within this cocoon of security that true release and healing can occur, as the body and mind learn to trust in the process and in their capacity for resilience.

Transformative Effects

The effects of releasing muscle memory are profound, impacting both our emotional well-being and our physical health. Individuals often report a sense of lightness and liberation following the release of chronic muscular tension, describing it as a shedding of weight they didn't know they were carrying. Physically, the reduction in muscle tightness can lead to improved posture, increased mobility, and a decrease in pain and discomfort.

But the benefits extend beyond the physical. Emotionally, releasing muscle memory can lead to significant shifts in how we relate to our past traumas. By letting go of the physical reminders of our pain, we open ourselves up to a deeper level of healing, one that acknowledges the interconnectedness of body and mind. This process can lead to increased emotional resilience, a greater sense of peace, and a renewed capacity to engage with life in a more present and meaningful way.

In essence, the act of releasing muscle memory is a powerful step toward reclaiming our bodies and our stories. It allows us to move forward, not by forgetting the past, but by integrating and transcending it.

THREE
MINDFUL AWARENESS THROUGH BODY SCANNING

IMAGINE that you're sitting in a quiet room.

The only sound is the rhythm of your breath. You're about to listen to a symphony that's played not by instruments, but by your body. Sure, you will notice the obvious - a cramped neck from too much screen time or the soreness in your back from gardening yesterday. However, this precious moment is your chance to tune into your body's subtle cues: the warmth of your hands, the weight of your feet on the floor, perhaps even the flutter of your heartbeat.

This is the essence of body scanning, a practice that turns inward to explore the body's landscape, discovering its places of ease and tension. It's a method that invites us to meet ourselves right where we are, with kindness and curiosity.

Body Scanning: The Basics

Body scanning is essentially a mindfulness exercise that encourages us to pay meticulous attention to different parts of our body in a sequential manner, usually from head to toe or vice versa. It's about observing without the intention to change anything. Think of it as being a curious observer of your own body, noticing each part as if for the first time. This practice helps us tune into our bodily sensations, recognizing areas of tension, discomfort, or relaxation without judgment.

Origins and development

Drawing from ancient mindfulness traditions, body scanning has been an integral part of various healing and meditative practices for centuries. Its formal introduction into Western therapeutic practices is largely credited to Jon Kabat-Zinn and the Mindfulness-Based Stress Reduction (MBSR) program. Kabat-Zinn's work in integrating mindfulness into stress reduction and pain management has highlighted body scanning as a key tool for promoting deep bodily awareness and healing.

Benefits for healing

Engaging in body scanning offers numerous benefits, particularly in the realm of mental health and somatic therapy.

Stress Reduction: By focusing on the present moment and bodily sensations, body scanning can significantly lower stress levels, offering a peaceful break from the hustle of daily life.

Pain Management: It provides insights into how pain is experienced in the body, often leading to a reduction in pain perception as one learns to observe discomfort with detachment.

Emotional Release: As we become more attuned to our bodies, we might uncover emotional blockages manifested as physical tension, paving the way for emotional processing and release.

Increased Body Awareness: Regular practice enhances our connection with our bodies, helping us recognize signs of stress or illness early on.

It's important to approach body scanning with a mindset open to whatever arises, without expecting instant relaxation or insights. Patience is key. Some days you might find the practice deeply calming; other days, it might feel challenging to stay focused. Both experiences are valuable. Body scanning is not about achieving a particular state but about cultivating an attitude of curiosity and non-judgment towards our bodily experiences.

Body Scanning Checklist

Engaging in a body scanning practice can be a deeply restorative and insightful experience, offering a moment to connect with oneself on a profound level. This checklist is designed to ensure you maximize the benefits of this practice.

Find a Quiet, Comfortable Space: Choose an environment where inter-ruptions are minimal. This space should feel safe and serene to you, allowing for a sense of peace and the ability to focus without external distractions.

Choose Your Position Wisely: Your physical comfort is paramount in a body scanning session. Decide whether lying down, sitting, or slowly walking suits your current state and preference best. Each position offers a unique perspective and experience, so select the one that feels most conducive to introspection and relaxation.

Set a Gentle Intention: Before beginning, take a moment to mentally articulate your intention for the practice. This could be as simple as saying to yourself, "I am here to notice, not to fix." Such an intention sets a tone of non-judgment and openness, reminding you that the goal is to observe and be present with whatever arises.

Embrace a Patient Mindset: It's natural for the mind to wander during a body scanning practice. When you notice your thoughts drifting, gently acknowledge this without criticism and redirect your focus back to your body sensations. Remember, wandering thoughts are not failures but opportunities to practice patience and gently return to the moment.

By keeping this checklist in mind, you're setting the stage for a mean-ingful and enriching body scanning practice. Each step is designed to help you enter a state of deep awareness and connection with your body, enabling a profound exploration of the physical and emotional land-scapes within.

Body scanning involves paying attention to parts of the body and bodily sensations in a gradual sequence from feet to head. As you know, by tuning into your body, you can promote relaxation and enhance your mind-body connection. Just below is an overview of the body scanning process. Additionally, at the end of this book, you will find a beautiful guided body scan meditation.

Step-by-Step Flow

1. Find a Quiet Space: Choose a calm and comfortable setting where you won't be disturbed.
2. Choose Your Position: Lie down on your back or sit comfortably, ensuring your posture is relaxed yet attentive.
3. Breathe Deeply: Close your eyes and take several deep breaths, inhaling through your nose and exhaling through your mouth to settle into the moment.
4. Scan Your Body: Begin at your feet and slowly move your attention up through your body. Notice each part of your body from your toes to your head. Acknowledge any sensations, pain, or discomfort you might feel, without judgment. If you encounter areas of tension, imagine your breath flowing to these areas, gently enveloping them in warmth and care.
5. Acknowledge and Release: As you notice sensations, acknowledge them, and imagine each breath flowing to and from that part of the body, releasing tension with each exhale.
6. Conclude Your Practice: Once you've scanned all the way to the top of your head, take a few more deep breaths and slowly open your eyes. Take a moment to notice how your body feels as a whole and carry that awareness with you.

TRYING a new method of tapping into your inner world can bring its lot of challenges. As you begin to include this practice into your regular self-care routine, please remember to:

- **Redirect**: When your mind wanders, acknowledge the distraction gently without judgment and guide your attention back to the body part you were focusing on.
- **Use Guided Recordings**: Especially in the beginning, following along with guided body scan meditations can help keep you on track.
- **Establish a Routine**: Practicing at the same time each day can help body scanning become a habit, making it easier to maintain focus.
- **Embrace Distractions**: Understand that distractions are part of the process. They're opportunities to practice returning your focus to the present.

Finally, by incorporating body scanning into your daily routine, you can enjoy the numerous benefits it brings to both your mental and physical health. Whether you're new to mindfulness or looking to deepen your practice, body scanning is a simple yet powerful tool to help you reach your wellness goals.

Interpreting Body Scans: What is Your Body Telling You?

In a world brimming with constant stimulation, our bodies often whisper secrets of our deepest emotions and states of being, secrets that we, in our perpetual busyness, might overlook. These whispers, if listened to during a body scan, can reveal the tales of tension, discomfort, or even unexpected ease within us.

This section peels back the layers of our physical sensations to uncover what they might signify about our emotional well-being and how we might process and integrate these discoveries into our broader healing practices. Moreover, it sheds light on recognizing when additional support could be beneficial in navigating the sometimes-ravelled messages of our bodies.

Recognizing Physical Sensations

Throughout your body scan, a variety of sensations might come to the surface. Here's a look at some of the most common ones and their potential implications.

Tightness or Tension: Often found in the shoulders, neck, or back, tightness can signify stress or burden. It might indicate areas where we metaphorically "carry the weight of the world".

Warmth or Heat: Sensations of warmth, especially in the hands or chest, might reflect feelings of love, compassion, or healing.

Coldness or Numbness: Feeling cold or numb in certain body parts can sometimes point to avoidance or disconnection from certain emotions or experiences.

Fluttering or Tingling: These sensations, perhaps in the stomach or limbs, might signal anticipation, anxiety, or the reawakening of parts of ourselves we've neglected.

By paying attention to these sensations without judgment, we can start to decode the body's language, gaining insights into our emotional landscapes.

Emotional Responses to Body Scanning

As we direct our attention inward during a body scan, we might encounter a spectrum of emotions. Discovering areas of relaxation can elicit feelings of relief, a sign of unburdening or letting go. Acknowledging areas of tension or discomfort can sometimes release pent-up emotions, leading to a sense of sadness as we connect with past hurts. Also, focusing on the body might initially heighten feelings of anxiety for some, especially if the body scan brings attention to previously ignored areas of tension.

These emotional responses are natural and valuable. They offer clues to our internal states, encouraging us to explore and heal underlying issues. When emotions surface, acknowledging them and allowing them to be present without forcing a change can be a powerful step in processing these feelings.

Making Sense of the Body's Messages

Interpreting the body's signals requires patience and openness, allowing for a nuanced understanding of our physical and emotional states. Here are some strategies for making sense of the body's messages.

Pattern Recognition: Over time, you might notice certain sensations recur under specific circumstances. Mapping these patterns can provide insights into how your body reacts to stress, joy, or other emotional states.

Emotion-Sensation Link: Try to connect physical sensations with emotional states. For instance, tightness in the chest might be linked to feelings of anxiety or sadness.

Mindful Reflection: After a body scan, spend a few moments reflecting on the experience. Consider journaling about the sensations and emotions observed, exploring their potential meanings and connections to your life.

When to Seek Further Guidance

While body scanning is a powerful tool for self-awareness and healing, there are instances when professional support can be invaluable. If certain physical sensations persistently cause discomfort or are linked to unexplained pain, consulting a healthcare provider or a somatic therapist can help address these issues more deeply. Should emotions become overwhelming or lead to distress, a mental health professional skilled in somatic practices can offer support, helping to navigate and process these feelings in a safe and structured environment. Furthermore, the desire to explore the body's messages more deeply or to integrate somatic practices into healing from trauma might prompt seeking a therapist.

Listening to our bodies through the practice of body scanning opens up a dialogue with ourselves that is both revealing and healing. It teaches us to meet our physical sensations and emotional responses with curiosity and compassion. As we learn to interpret and integrate these messages, we cultivate a more harmonious balance between body and mind, moving closer to a state of well-being that embraces the totality of our experiences.

Integrating Body Scans into Daily Life for Continuous Awareness

The essence of mindfulness lies not in the grand gestures of retreats or hour-long meditations but in weaving moments of awareness into our daily lives. This is particularly true with body scanning, a practice that, when integrated regularly, can become a touchstone for self-awareness and a means to gracefully navigate through the day's stresses and strains.

Making body scanning a part of your daily routine invites a constant stream of mindfulness into your life, transforming mundane moments into opportunities for self-discovery and stress relief. Consider the following to seamlessly include body scanning in your day.

Morning: Start your day by spending a few minutes in bed, conducting a brief body scan before rising. This can help set a tone of awareness and presence for the day ahead.

Work Breaks: Use short breaks at work to conduct mini body scans, even if it's just focusing on your hands, feet, or breath. These brief pauses can reduce stress and increase productivity by refocusing and re-energizing your mind.

Evening: End your day with a more thorough body scan, perhaps before sleep. This can aid in releasing the day's tensions and transitioning into restful sleep.

For those moments when time is scarce, short-form body scanning can be a powerful tool. These abbreviated versions focus on one part of the body or even just the breath and can be done anywhere, anytime. Here are two examples:

1. Hand Awareness: Focus on the sensations in your hands — the temperature, textures, and any tingling or pulsing. It's a simple yet effective way to ground yourself in the present.
2. Foot Grounding: Pay attention to your feet on the ground, feeling the solidity of the earth beneath you. This can be particularly calming in moments of anxiety or overwhelm.

Another important aspect of body scanning is that it can be particularly potent when applied to specific emotional states or situations. Here are some ways in which you can use it as a self-soothing technique:

- In stressful moments, a quick body scan can help identify areas of tension. Once recognized, directing your breath to these areas can facilitate relaxation and release.
- During anxious episodes, focusing on grounding parts of the body, like the feet or seat, can help stabilize your emotions, anchoring you back to a sense of safety.
- When emotions flood in, conducting a body scan with an emphasis on the heart and stomach (areas often affected by strong emotions) can help in acknowledging and gently navigating these feelings.

The beauty of integrating body scanning into daily routines lies in the cumulative effect it has on well-being. Consistency in practice deepens the connection with one's body, enhancing the ability to detect nuances of sensation and emotional states.

Enhanced Stress Management: Regular body scanning fosters a more resilient response to stress, enabling you to meet challenges with a calm and centered presence.

Improved Physical Well-being: By regularly tuning into the body, you're more likely to notice early signs of physical discomfort or illness, allowing for timely care and attention.

Deeper Emotional Insight: Continuous practice cultivates a nuanced understanding of how emotions manifest in the body, providing valuable insights for emotional processing and healing.

Increased Mindfulness: The habit of body scanning reinforces a broader mindfulness practice, encouraging a more attentive, present, and compassionate approach to life's experiences.

Through regular engagement, this practice becomes less of an activity and more of a way of being.

Navigating through the practice of body scanning, one might encounter hurdles that can seem to obscure the path to deeper self-awareness and healing. Recognizing and addressing these challenges head-on will help maintain a nourishing and effective practice.

Distraction and Restlessness

The mind's tendency to wander and the body's inclination towards restlessness can disrupt the flow of a body scan, making it difficult to maintain focus. Here are strategies to gently recalibrate your attention:

- Anchor in Sound: Incorporate ambient sounds or gentle music as a background to your practice. This auditory cue can help anchor your mind, providing a gentle return point for wandering thoughts.
- Guided Visualizations: Integrate visualizations into your body scan. Imagining a wave of light or warmth moving through your body can keep both mind and body engaged in the practice.
- Incremental Sessions: Start with shorter sessions, gradually increasing the duration as your concentration improves. This builds your focus muscle without overwhelming it.

Dealing with Discomfort or Emotional Pain

Body scanning can sometimes surface discomfort or emotional pain, which may deter one from continuing the practice. Here's how to navigate this:

- Gentle Acknowledgment: Recognize and acknowledge the discomfort or pain without forcing it away. This acceptance can often lessen its intensity.
- Shift the Focus: If certain areas bring significant discomfort, allow yourself to shift focus to a part of the body that feels neutral or pleasant, balancing the experience with positive sensations.

- Breathing Through: Use your breath as a tool to surround areas of discomfort with care. Imagine breathing into and out from the discomfort, envisioning a softening or release with each breath.

Building a Consistent Practice

Consistency is key to reaping the full benefits of body scanning, yet establishing a regular practice can be challenging. Here are tips to create a sustainable routine:

- Schedule It: Treat your body scanning time as you would any important appointment, scheduling it into your day with reminders to ensure it's a priority.
- Flexible Timing: Find the time of day that works best for you, whether it's morning to start your day centered or evening to unwind and reflect.
- Variety in Practice: Keep the practice fresh by varying your approach, perhaps trying different postures or integrating new visualization techniques.

As we continue to explore somatics, remember that each practice and insight adds to the richness of your journey. Let's make sure we remain open to exploring new dimensions of the powerful body-mind connection, with an eagerness to uncover the deeper ties and transformations that await.

FOUR

ANCHORING IN THE NOW

In somatic therapy, mindfulness guides us to experience our body and emotions in their purest form, without the weight of past traumas or future anxieties. The essence of mindfulness is a state of being fully present and engaged in the now, aware yet detached from judgment.

It is here, in the realm of the present, that healing finds fertile ground.

Mindfulness in Somatic Therapy: The Role of Present Moment Awareness

Mindfulness, at its core, is about paying attention. When applied to healing, it is a tool that brings us into direct contact with our experiences, allowing us to observe our physical sensations, thoughts, and emotions from a place of curiosity rather than judgment. This observational stance is crucial in somatic therapy. It shifts our focus from trying to "fix" what we perceive as problems to simply being with what is. This shift is transformative, offering a path to healing that embraces acceptance and presence, turning our attention to the richness of each moment and what it can teach us about ourselves.

Practices to Enhance Mindfulness

Mindfulness in somatic therapy can take various forms, each of which invites a deeper connection with the present moment.

Mindful Eating: This practice involves paying close attention to the process of eating—observing the colors, textures, and smells of food, chewing slowly, and noting the flavors and sensations in each bite. It turns a daily activity into an exercise in presence, promoting a greater appreciation for nourishment and the act of eating.

Mindful Walking: Here, walking becomes a deliberate act of mindfulness. Notice each step, the feel of the ground beneath your feet, the rhythm of your breath, and the sensations in your body as you move. It's a way to ground yourself in the now, turning a simple walk into a profound exercise in awareness.

Mindful Listening: Engage fully in the act of listening, whether to sounds in your environment or to another person. Notice the nuances in sounds, the rise and fall of voices, and the spaces between sounds. This practice cultivates a deep sense of presence and can enhance communication and relationships through authentic engagement.

The Benefits of a Mindful Approach

The inclusion of mindfulness in somatic therapy offers a range of benefits, touching every aspect of our being. These practices have been shown to lower levels of cortisol, the stress hormone, promoting a sense of calm and reducing anxiety. Regular mindfulness practice can also lower blood pressure, improve sleep, and enhance overall physical health and well-being.

Seeing mindfulness as more than just a series of practices - as a way of life - can transform our relationship with our body and emotions. It invites us to approach every moment with freshness and curiosity, whether we're washing dishes, taking a shower, or simply breathing. This attitude of presence enriches our daily experiences, turning routine activities into opportunities for discovery and connection. It's a way of moving through life where each step, each breath, is an intentional act that brings us closer to the essence of who we are.

Mindfulness Integration Checklist

Setting Intentions

- Reflect on your current state: Take a moment to note how you're feeling physically, emotionally, and mentally.
- Set a clear intention for your mindfulness practice today: Consider what you wish to cultivate or release (e.g., peace, clarity, healing of emotional pain).
- Write down your intention: Keep it somewhere you can see throughout the day to remind you of your focus.

Choosing Mindfulness Practices

MARK THE PRACTICES you feel drawn to and would like to incorporate into your daily routine.

o **Breath Awareness:** Dedicate 5-10 minutes to observe your breath, noting the rise and fall of your chest or the sensation of air at your nostrils.

o **Body Scan:** Spend 10-15 minutes scanning through each part of your body, observing without judgment any sensations, tensions, or emotions that arise.

o **Walking Meditation:** Incorporate a 10-20 minute mindful walk into your day, paying attention to the sensation of each step and the environment around you.

o **Mindful Eating:** Choose one meal or snack to eat mindfully, observing the flavors, textures, and sensations of eating without distraction.

o **Journaling:** Spend 5-10 minutes writing about your experiences, thoughts, and feelings during your mindfulness practices or throughout the day.

Daily Practice Schedule

Schedule a consistent time for your mindfulness practice, or a combination that suits your lifestyle:

o Morning

o Midday

o Evening

o Other: _____

Set Gentle Reminders:

o Sticky notes

o Phone alarms or Apps to remind you of your practice times

o Other: _____

Approaching Activities with Curiosity and Non-Judgment

- Embrace a beginner's mind: Approach each practice as if it's your first time, even if it's familiar.
- Notice judgment and let it go: When you catch yourself judging your experience or progress, acknowledge it and then return to your practice without self-criticism.
- Cultivate curiosity: Each day, try to notice something new in your practice or how it affects you differently.

Reflection and Adjustment

- Weekly reflection: Spend 10-15 minutes at the end of the week reviewing your journal entries and experiences. What did you learn? What surprised you?
- Adjust practices as needed: Based on your reflection, decide if you need to try different practices, adjust the time spent, or focus on different intentions.
- Celebrate progress: Acknowledge your commitment to your practice and any shifts you've noticed in your well-being, no matter how small.

Additional Tips:

1. If possible, designate a quiet and comfortable area in your home for mindfulness practices.

2. Consider connecting with a mindfulness group or online community for support and shared experiences.
3. Be patient and kind with yourself: Remember that mindfulness is a practice, not a destination. Some days will be easier than others, and that's perfectly okay.

If possible, keep your checklist in a visible place to guide and remind you of your journey toward integrating mindfulness into your daily life. Adjust it as you go along to fit your evolving needs and preferences.

Mindful Moment Prompts

Incorporate these Mindful Moment Prompts into your day to cultivate a continuous practice of mindfulness, enhancing your somatic and shadow work. Each prompt is designed to be a gentle nudge back to the present moment, helping you create a deeper connection with your inner self and the world around you. Whether you're new to mindfulness or looking to deepen your practice, these simple activities can be seamlessly integrated into your daily life.

Prompts for Spontaneous Mindfulness:

One-Minute Breath Focus: Pause for one minute, close your eyes if possible, and focus solely on your breath. Notice the sensation of air entering and exiting your nostrils, and observe the rise and fall of your chest.

Sensory Engagement with Your Morning Beverage: While drinking your morning coffee or tea, engage all your senses. Observe its color, smell its aroma, feel the warmth of the cup, and taste each sip. Be fully present in the experience.

Mindful Listening: Spend a few minutes listening to the sounds around you, whether you're indoors or outdoors. Try to identify as many sounds as you can, listening without judgment or analysis.

Gratitude Touch Points: Identify three things you're grateful for at this moment. They can be as simple as the sunlight streaming through a window, a comfortable chair, or having a meal. Feel the gratitude in your heart.

Mindful Movement Stretch: Stand up and engage in a slow, mindful stretch. Pay attention to the sensations in your muscles and joints. Breathe deeply and notice how your body feels during and after the stretch.

Texture Exploration: Touch something nearby and focus on its texture. It could be the fabric of your clothes, the surface of your desk, or a natural object like a plant. Notice the details with your fingertips.

Aroma Awareness: Take a moment to notice any smells in your environment. If you have a fragrance source nearby, like a flower or a cup of coffee, close your eyes and take a deep inhale, fully experiencing the aroma.

Visual Mindfulness: Look around you and choose an object to focus on for a few moments. Observe it as if you're seeing it for the first time, noticing its colors, shapes, and any details you might usually overlook.

Mindful Eating Snack: Choose a small snack and eat it mindfully. Pay attention to the process of chewing and the flavors and textures of the food. How does it feel in your mouth? What sensations do you notice?

Heartbeat Check-In: Place your hand over your heart and focus on your heartbeat for a few moments. Feel the rhythm and notice any sensations in your body. Use this time to connect with yourself.

How to Use These Prompts

1. Set random alarms throughout the day as prompts for a mindful moment. When the alarm goes off, choose one to practice.

2. Use a prompt as a transition between tasks or activities to reset and refocus your attention.

3. Share a prompt with a friend, family member, or coworker, and practice together, either in person or virtually, to deepen the sense of connection and presence.

Incorporating these Mindful Moment Prompts into your daily life can serve as a powerful tool in your somatic healing and shadow work journey, offering regular opportunities to reconnect with the present.

Grounding Techniques: Staying Anchored During Emotional Storms

In navigating the highs and lows of emotional experiences, grounding emerges as a foundation for stability. Imagine yourself in the midst of an emotional tempest, where thoughts and feelings whirl around with dizzying intensity. Grounding is the anchor that helps you find your footing, offering a return to a place of calm and clarity. It's a practice rooted in the present, a deliberate focus on the here and now that can dissipate the fog of overwhelm, anxiety, or dissociation.

Grounding is particularly effective because it shifts your focus from the storm of internal experiences to the solid reality of the external world. This transition is not about ignoring emotions but providing a safe platform from which to observe and manage them.

Simple Grounding Exercises

The beauty of grounding lies in its simplicity and accessibility. Here are exercises that can be woven into any moment, requiring nothing more than your intention and attention.

5-4-3-2-1 Technique: Engage all five senses to bring your awareness into the present. Identify five things you can see, four you can touch, three you can hear, two you can smell, and one you can taste. This practice is especially useful for halting the spiral of anxious thoughts and rooting yourself in the environment around you.

Focused Object Observation: Choose any object in your vicinity —a pen, a cup, a plant—and spend a few minutes observing it in detail. Notice its color, texture, weight, and any other characteristics. This concentration on a single point draws your attention away from distressing emotions and into a state of focused calm.

Grounding Through Movement: Simple movements like stretching your arms, gripping your chair, or slowly tapping your feet on the ground can help reconnect with your body and the physical space you occupy. Movement acts as a gentle reminder of your physical presence in the world, anchoring you firmly to the present.

The Role of the Senses

Utilizing the five senses is a cornerstone of effective grounding techniques. Sensory experiences provide immediate, tangible points of focus that can easily be accessed at any moment. Here's how each sense can play a role in grounding:

Sight: Observing the details in your environment or focusing on a specific color can redirect your attention outward.

Touch: Feeling the texture of an object, the fabric of your clothes, or the ground beneath your feet can help you reconnect with the present.

Hearing: Listening to ambient sounds, music, or your own breathing can calm the mind and reduce feelings of anxiety.

Smell: Inhaling a comforting scent, whether from a cup of tea, a scented candle, or fresh air, can have an immediate soothing effect.

Taste: Savoring a piece of fruit, a mint, or even a sip of water can be a simple yet effective way to ground yourself.

Personalizing Grounding Practices

While grounding techniques share the common goal of returning you to a state of calm, their effectiveness can vary from person to person. Personalizing your approach ensures that your grounding practices resonate with your needs and preferences. Here are four elements to consider when tailoring your practice to reflect your individuality.

1. Experiment with Different Techniques: Explore a variety of grounding exercises to discover which ones feel most effective for you. You might find that certain practices work better in specific situations or that your preferences change over time.

2. Create a Grounding Plan: Once you've identified the techniques that work best for you, create a personalized grounding plan. This plan can include a list of preferred exercises and when to use them, such as specific techniques

for quick grounding in public spaces or more involved practices for deeper emotional work at home.

3. Incorporate Grounding into Your Routine: Look for opportunities to integrate grounding exercises into your daily routine. This could mean starting your day with a grounding meditation, using focused object observation during work breaks, or ending your day with a sensory grounding practice.

4. Adapt and Adjust: Be open to adjusting your grounding practices as your needs evolve. What works for you today might change, and that's okay. The key is to stay attuned to your body and emotions, adapting your techniques to support your well-being in the moment.

Grounding stands as a testament to the power of presence, a practice that gently but firmly guides you back to a place of stability and clarity amidst emotional chaos. Through focused attention on the present and the deliberate engagement of the senses, grounding techniques create tranquility and balance, accessible anytime and anywhere.

Breathing as Grounding: Simple Yet Effective Techniques

Within our daily lives, as every moment flows into the next, breath stands as a constant companion, a silent witness to our experiences. This act of breathing, so innate and automatic, hides within it a potent tool for grounding and calming. Through breathwork, we tap into this well-spring of tranquility, guiding our nervous system back to a state of balance and presence.

Here, we will explore the foundational aspects of using breath as a primary resource for grounding, along with practical exercises and the integration of mindfulness to enhance the practice. We will also uncover the science that underscores the efficacy of breathwork in somatic therapy, shedding light on how something as simple as breathing can be transformative.

Breathwork Basics

At its heart, breathwork involves conscious control over our breathing patterns to influence our mental, emotional, and physical states. It's a bridge connecting the conscious with the subconscious, the body with the mind, leading us to a place of deeper self-awareness and calm. As we discovered in previous chapters, by focusing on and manipulating our breath, we can signal our nervous system to shift from a state of alertness to one of relaxation, a transition that is both subtle and profound.

To begin, let's consider two foundational aspects of breathwork:

1. Observation: Start by simply observing your breath without any intention to change it. Notice its rhythm, depth, and the sensations it evokes in your body. This awareness is the first step toward harnessing the power of your breath.
2. Regulation: Once you're attuned to your natural breathing pattern, you can start experimenting with regulating your breath. This might involve deepening your inhales and exhales, introducing pauses, or finding a rhythm that feels soothing and grounding.

Guided Breathing Exercises

Engaging in guided breathing exercises can dramatically enhance your ability to ground and center yourself. Here are a few techniques to try:

- Equal Breathing: Inhale slowly through your nose for a count of four, then exhale through your nose for the same count. This balanced breathing helps harmonize the nervous system.
- Box Breathing: Visualize a box as you breathe in for a count of four, hold your breath for four, exhale for four, and hold again for four. This practice is excellent for moments when you need to reset and focus.
- Progressive Relaxation Breath: Inhale deeply, filling your lungs completely. As you exhale, consciously release tension from your body, starting from your head and moving down to your toes. With each breath, feel yourself becoming more relaxed and grounded.

Combining breathwork with mindfulness practices amplifies the grounding effect, creating a holistic approach to calming the mind and body. Here are ways to integrate these practices.

Mindful Awareness of Breath: As you engage in breathwork, bring a mindful awareness to the experience, noticing the sensations of air moving in and out of your body, the rise and fall of your chest, and any thoughts or emotions that arise, observing them without attachment.

Breathing in Nature: If you have access to an outdoor space, try practicing your breathwork surrounded by nature. The fresh air and natural beauty enhance mindfulness and the grounding effect of your breathwork.

Incorporating Mindful Pauses: Throughout your day, take short "breath breaks" to practice mindfulness and breathwork simultaneously. Even a few deep, mindful breaths can serve as a powerful grounding technique in the midst of a hectic schedule.

The Science Behind Breathwork

The transformative power of breathwork is not just a matter of subjective experience; it is grounded in science. When we engage in controlled breathing, we directly impact our autonomic nervous system, which regulates our stress response. Research has shown that breathwork can:

- Activate the Parasympathetic Nervous System: Slow, deep breathing activates the vagus nerve, a key component of the parasympathetic nervous system, signaling the body to relax and de-escalate the stress response.
- Reduce Cortisol Levels: Regular breathwork practice has been linked to lower levels of cortisol, the body's primary stress hormone, contributing to a state of calm and reducing anxiety.

- Enhance Brain Function: Controlled breathing can increase coherence between different parts of the brain, improving focus, emotional regulation, and cognitive performance.
- Improve Respiratory and Cardiovascular Health: By optimizing our breathing patterns, we can enhance oxygen exchange, lower blood pressure, and improve overall cardiovascular health.

Breathwork, with its roots in ancient practices and its efficacy validated by modern science, creates a profound connection between breath, body, and mind. Through the simple act of breathing with intention, we can access a state of grounded presence, finding calm in the midst of chaos and clarity within complexity.

Nature as a Healer: Using Outdoor Spaces for Grounding

The natural world has long been recognized for its restorative properties, offering a sanctuary where the mind and body can find balance and peace. Recent studies underscore the profound impact that immersion in nature has on our well-being, highlighting reductions in stress, enhanced mood, and even improved cognitive function. This connection to the earth underpins many grounding practices, providing a powerful antidote to the disconnection and overstimulation of modern life.

The Therapeutic Effects of Nature

Within the canopy of a forest or the expanse of a desert, nature engages us in a dialogue that transcends words, speaking directly to our primal selves. The simple act of being in natural surroundings can lower blood pressure, decrease levels of cortisol, and elevate our mood. This is not merely anecdotal; research in the field of ecotherapy provides compelling evidence of these effects. For instance, a study published in the "International Journal of Environmental Research and Public Health" found that participants who engaged in walks within green spaces reported significantly lower stress levels and improved mental health outcomes compared to those in urban settings.

Practical Ways to Connect with Nature

Engaging with the natural world doesn't require grand adventures; even small acts can deepen our connection to the earth and its rhythms.

- Forest Bathing: Originating from Japan, forest bathing, or Shinrin-yoku, involves immersive walks in forested areas, focusing on the sensory experiences the environment offers.
- Gardening: Tending to plants, whether in a backyard garden or a container garden on a balcony, can be a meditative practice, fostering a sense of care and connection to the cycle of life.
- Nature Walks in Urban Parks: For those in urban environments, local parks offer green spaces for leisurely walks or simply sitting and observing nature's nuances.
- Beach Combing or River Walking: This is my absolute favorite. If you're near water, walking along a beach or riverbank provides a rhythmic, meditative experience, enhanced by the calming presence of water.

Overcoming Barriers to Outdoor Access

Access to natural spaces can be limited by urban living, mobility issues, or time constraints. However, with creativity, the benefits of nature can still be found.

- Indoor Plants and Herb Gardens: Bringing nature indoors through houseplants or a small herb garden can offer daily touchpoints with the natural world.
- Virtual Nature Experiences: Technology offers virtual walks through forests, mountains, and beaches, providing visual and auditory experiences of nature.
- Natural Elements in Home Decor: Incorporating elements like wood, stones, or water features into home décor can create a more natural, grounding environment.
- Nature Sounds: Listening to recordings of nature sounds, such as rain, birdsong, or ocean waves, can have a soothing,

grounding effect, especially when outdoor access is challenging.

Nature-Inspired Mindfulness Practices

Incorporating mindfulness into outdoor activities amplifies the grounding effects of nature, creating a synergy that enhances both practices.

Mindful Observation: Choose an outdoor spot and spend time observing the details around you—the shape of leaves, the pattern of bark on a tree, the way light filters through branches. This focused observation brings you into the present moment, deepening your connection to the environment.

Sensory Walks: On a walk, engage each of your senses sequentially to fully experience your surroundings. Note what you see, then focus on what you can hear, followed by what you can smell, and finally, what you can feel. This practice not only grounds you but also enriches your experience of nature.

Breathing with Nature: Find a quiet spot outdoors to sit comfortably. Close your eyes and synchronize your breathing with the natural sounds around you, such as the wind or waves. This harmonization of your breath with the rhythms of nature fosters a deep sense of peace and belonging.

Gratitude Moments: While in nature, take a few moments to reflect on what you're grateful for, focusing on the elements of the natural world that nurture and sustain us. This gratitude practice not only grounds you but also fosters a positive, appreciative mindset.

Reconnecting with nature grounds us and rekindles our sense of wonder, reminding us of the beauty that surrounds us and resides within. Through intentional engagement with the outdoors—whether by immersing ourselves in forest canopies, tending to plants, or simply pausing to breathe in sync with the natural world—we can rediscover our intrinsic connection to the earth.

Building a Personal Toolkit: Customizing Techniques for Your Needs

Navigating mindfulness and grounding techniques can feel like standing at the edge of an ocean, contemplating its depth and expanse. The key is not to plunge into its depths all at once but to wade in gently, selecting the practices that resonate with your unique rhythm and flow. This process of selection and customization lies at the heart of creating a personal toolkit that aligns with your needs and preferences whilst evolving with you over time.

Assessing Personal Needs and Preferences

Initiating this process begins with a reflection on your current state and what you hope to achieve through mindfulness and grounding practices. Consider your daily routine, the challenges you face, and where you feel most disconnected. Are you seeking calm in a storm of anxiety? Or perhaps looking for moments of clarity amid confusion? Understanding these needs provides a compass for selecting practices that truly resonate with you.

Next, explore your preferences. Do you find solace in silence or comfort in the rhythmic sounds of nature? Does your body crave movement, or do you prefer stillness? If you're like me, you may find that every day your body requests something different. These questions are not meant to confine but to guide you towards practices that feel nurturing and right for you. So, listen to what your body is telling you and allow your intuition to show you the way.

Creating a Personalized Toolkit

Once you've gained a clearer understanding of your needs and preferences, it'll be time to assemble your toolkit. This process is both creative and intuitive, encouraging you to listen deeply to yourself and choose practices that feel like a balm to your soul. Here's a three-step framework to get you started.

First, from the list of mindfulness practices you've been introduced to, select two or three that you feel drawn to. This could be anything from mindful eating to focused object observation.

Next, choose a couple of grounding exercises that you feel will be most beneficial, especially in moments of emotional overwhelm. This could include the 5-4-3-2-1 technique or focused object observation.

Finally, incorporate one or two breathing exercises that you can call upon to center yourself. Equal breathing and box breathing are excellent places to start.

Remember, this toolkit is not static but a living collection that grows and changes as you do. Record any adjustments you make in your journal.

Flexibility and Adaptation

Staying open to experimentation will make a difference in your somatic therapy journey. As you practice, you might find that certain techniques don't resonate as you thought they would, or you may stumble upon new ones that feel like a perfect fit. This fluidity is natural and it is even encouraged. It reflects your growth and deepening understanding of yourself. Periodically review your toolkit, adding new techniques that you discover and letting go of those that no longer serve you.

Sharing and Community

While the practice of mindfulness and grounding is deeply personal, sharing your experiences and techniques with others can enrich your journey. It creates a space for mutual learning and support, offering new perspectives and insights.

Again, you may want to consider joining a mindfulness group or participating in forums where you can exchange ideas and practices. Also, teaching a friend or family member a technique that has been particularly impactful for you not only deepens your understanding but also fosters a shared experience of growth and healing. This exchange of knowledge and experience with others will broaden your own practice and contribute to a collective well-being.

As we conclude this exploration of building a personalized toolkit, remember that the essence of this process lies in tuning into your inner space, selecting practices that nurture and support you, and remaining open to the journey of discovery as it unfolds.

REDISCOVERING BALANCE THROUGH MOVEMENT

Here you are.

Standing in the middle of a room, feeling the weight of the world on your shoulders.

Slowly, you begin to sway gently from side to side. With each movement, the weight begins to lift, leaving a sense of freedom in its wake.

I'm not just talking about physical motion. Movement is powerful - it can stir the stagnant parts of our lives, bringing a fresh flow of energy and emotion.

In this chapter, we will explore movement as a powerful tool for healing, offering a path to release trauma and restore emotional balance.

Movement as Medicine

From the moment we wake, our bodies are in constant motion, a silent language expressing our inner states. When words fall short, our bodies speak volumes. Movement therapy taps into this language, using physical activity to address and heal emotional pain. This is a process that acknowledges the body's role in storing and releasing trauma. Think of it like this: just as laughter can be a release valve for stress, physical movement offers a way to release emotional tension, transforming it into something manageable, even healing.

Varieties of Therapeutic Movement

Movement therapy encompasses a broad spectrum of activities, each with unique benefits. A few popular ones are yoga, dance, and martial arts. More than just poses and choreographies, these activities offer a mindful practice that connects breath with movement, promoting self-awareness and inner calm. They assist in freeing the body to express what's within, whether it's joy, sorrow, or something in between. Some combine slow, deliberate movements with deep breathing, enhancing physical and mental balance.

The Science Behind Movement Therapy

Recent studies shed light on how movement affects our brains and bodies, especially concerning trauma. One key finding is that physical activity, especially rhythmic, repetitive motions, can help regulate the nervous system, disrupted by traumatic experiences. Movement therapy has been shown to decrease symptoms of anxiety and depression, improve sleep, and even enhance cognitive functions like memory and attention. The body's physical movement can help "reprogram" the brain's response to stress, creating new pathways to emotional resilience.

Movement in Daily Life

Integrating therapeutic movement into your routine doesn't have to mean a complete overhaul of your day. Small shifts can lead to significant benefits. Here are some suggestions:

1. Morning Stretch: Begin your day by stretching your body, reaching your arms above your head, and gently swaying from side to side. It's a simple way to wake up your body and mind.
2. Walks: Take short walks during breaks at work or in the evening. Focus on the sensation of your feet touching the ground and the rhythm of your steps.
3. Breath and Movement: Pair deep breathing with simple movements like arm raises or shoulder rolls. It's a quick way to center yourself, especially during stressful moments.

Types of Therapeutic Movement and Their Benefits

The following are various movement activities used for somatic healing. This table highlights the key benefits of each activity so that you can explore and find the type that best resonates with your healing needs.

Type of Movement	Key Benefits
Yoga	- Stress relief - Improved flexibility and balance - Enhanced mental clarity and calmness
Dance	- Improved mood and emotional regulation - Increased physical fitness - Enhanced creativity
Martial Arts	- Enhanced focus and discipline - Improved physical strength and coordination - Stress reduction
Tai Chi	- Reduced anxiety and depression - Improved balance and motor function - Enhanced mindfulness and relaxation
Pilates	- Strengthened core muscles - Improved posture and alignment - Increased body awareness
Swimming	- Low-impact whole-body workout - Improved cardiovascular health - Relaxation and stress relief
Walking/ Nature Walks	- Enhanced mood through exposure to nature - Improved cardiovascular health - Stress relief and mental clarity
Cycling	- Increased physical endurance - Stress relief - Improved joint mobility and flexibility

Remember to choose activities that most resonate with you. These can sometimes be challenging, but they should always feel fulfilling and beneficial to your physical and mental well-being.

Create a Personalized Daily Movement Plan

Creating a personalized daily movement plan is a great way to incorporate physical activity into your routine in a way that feels enjoyable and sustainable. You can track your routines and record any emotional/physical changes or insights in your journal or movement diary. Here's a step-by-step guide to help you get started.

Step 1: Identifying Preferences

Explore Different Types of Movement: Experiment with various activities to find what you enjoy. This could include dance, yoga, martial arts, walking, cycling, or swimming. Pay attention to how each activity makes you feel during and after.

Listen to Your Body: Notice which movements feel good and which do not. Your preferences might change daily based on your body's needs, so stay flexible in your approach.

Consider Accessibility: Think about what activities are most accessible to you based on your current lifestyle, location, and resources. Choosing activities that are easy to incorporate into your life will increase your chances of sticking with them.

Step 2: Setting Realistic Goals

Assess Your Schedule: Look at your daily and weekly schedule to determine how much time you realistically have to dedicate to movement. It's better to start with a small, manageable goals.

Set Clear, Achievable Goals: Decide on specific, realistic goals.

This could be as simple as dedicating 5 minutes each morning to stretching or taking a 15-minute walk during your lunch break.

Be Flexible: Allow for flexibility in your goals. If a 15-minute walk is too much some days, consider a shorter duration or a different activity that feels more doable.

Step 3: Integrating Movement into Your Routine

Identify Opportunities for Movement: Look for pockets of time in your routine where movement can fit naturally. This might include walking or biking to work, stretching while watching TV, or doing yoga before bed.

Make It Convenient: Prepare for your chosen activities in advance. If you plan to walk during lunch, consider keeping a pair of comfortable shoes at your workplace. If you enjoy yoga, set up a quiet, comfortable space in your home.

Track Your Progress: Keep a log of your activities and how they make you feel. This can help you adjust your plan based on what works best for you and provide motivation to keep going.

Be Consistent but Kind to Yourself: Aim for consistency in your movement plan, but be kind to yourself on days when it doesn't happen. The goal is to build a positive, sustainable relationship with movement.

Step 4: Review and Adjust

Evaluate Your Plan Regularly: Every few weeks, take some time to review your movement plan. Assess what's working and what isn't, and adjust your activities and goals as needed.

Seek Inspiration: Stay motivated by trying new types of movement,

joining community classes, or partnering with a friend for joint
activities.

BY FOLLOWING THESE STEPS, you can create a personalized daily
movement plan that fits your preferences, goals, and lifestyle. This will
help you to enjoy the benefits of physical activity in a way that feels
right for you and that promotes somatic healing through emotional regulation and release.

Yoga for Somatic Healing: Poses and Practices

Yoga, with its ancient roots, offers a unique blend of physical postures,
breath control, and meditation that specifically caters to healing both the
mind and body. It stands out in somatic therapy for its gentle approach
to unraveling the layers of trauma stored within our bodies.

Through mindful movement and focused breathing, yoga invites a
dialogue between the body and mind, facilitating a release of deeply
rooted tensions and promoting a state of balanced well-being.

Yoga's Role in Somatic Therapy

At the heart of yoga's integration into somatic therapy is its ability to
cultivate an increased body awareness. This awareness is critical in identifying and subsequently releasing the physical manifestations of
emotional trauma. For instance, a forward bend does not merely stretch
the hamstrings and lower back but also offers an opportunity to bow
down, symbolically letting go of burdens. In this way, yoga postures, or
asanas, serve as metaphors for emotional states, providing a safe space
for us to explore and express feelings that might be difficult to articulate
verbally.

Yoga also emphasizes staying present during practice, which can
help break free from the grip of past traumas and anxieties about the
future. This presence—anchored in each breath and movement—allows
for a deeper connection with the self and healing from within.

Guided Yoga Sequences

For those seeking to release trauma and regulate emotions through yoga, specific sequences can be particularly beneficial.

Restorative Yoga Sequence

This involves a series of poses held for longer durations with the support of props like blankets and bolsters. The aim is to create a physical and mental state of relaxation, allowing the body to release tension naturally. Poses such as Supported Child's Pose and Legs-Up-The-Wall encourage a gentle opening and relaxation of the body's stress points.

Gentle Flow Sequence

A series of fluid movements synchronized with the breath, designed to build a gentle heat in the body and encourage emotional release. Cat-Cow stretches, for example, promote spinal flexibility while facilitating an emotional connection with the heart and belly, areas often affected by trauma.

Breath and Movement Synergy

Integrating breathwork with yoga poses amplifies their healing potential. Each inhale in yoga can symbolize an acceptance and opening up to new experiences, while each exhale represents a release of what no longer serves us. For instance, in a pose like Warrior II, a deep inhale helps to expand the chest and open the heart, embodying courage and strength, whereas the exhale aids in grounding and stabilization. This synergy between breath and movement not only deepens the practice but also teaches individuals how to regulate their emotional responses, promoting resilience and emotional flexibility.

Adapting Yoga for All Bodies

Yoga is not a one-size-fits-all practice. It honors the uniqueness of each body and its capabilities. Here are ways to ensure yoga remains accessible and beneficial for everyone:

1. Modifications: Use props like blocks, straps, and chairs to modify poses, making them accessible for individuals with physical limitations or those new to yoga. For example, a block can bring the ground closer in a forward fold, reducing strain on the back and hamstrings.
2. Chair Yoga: This form of yoga is performed with the aid of a chair, either by sitting on it or using it for support in standing poses. It is ideal for those of us with mobility issues or seniors, allowing everyone to experience the benefits of yoga without having to get down on the floor.
3. Personalized Sequences: Tailoring yoga sequences to meet your individual needs can be extremely beneficial, especially if you are dealing with specific traumas or health conditions. A personalized approach ensures the practice addresses our unique healing journey, creating a sense of safety and progression.

Yoga's integration into somatic healing underscores the profound connection between our physical postures and emotional well-being. Through mindful practice, yoga allows us to explore the depths of our being, releasing the emotional blockages that inhibit our growth, embracing the present moment and a future where we are free to move and live without the weight of our past experiences.

Dancing Out Trauma: How Rhythmic Movement Can Heal

Within therapeutic practices, dance therapy emerges as a game changing healing method. Through combining rhythmic patterns of movement with the emotional landscape of the self, this form of therapy transcends conventional boundaries, allowing for a profound expression and processing of emotions through the body's natural movements. At its core, dance therapy acknowledges that our bodies hold stories and traumas that words alone cannot fully capture or release. Through dance, individuals are invited to communicate these narratives, engaging in a physical dialogue that drives emotional liberation.

Dance Therapy Fundamentals

Dance therapy, grounded in the principle that body and mind are interrelated, utilizes movement as a means of achieving emotional, cognitive, physical, and social integration. It operates on the understanding that changes in movement can affect total functioning, facilitating a pathway to discover, explore, and express one's deepest concerns and feelings. Certified dance therapists guide participants through this journey, employing both structured and improvised dance activities designed to mirror or express emotions, thus promoting insight, integration, and recovery.

Structured vs. Freeform Dance

The spectrum of dance therapy encompasses both structured and freeform dance, each offering unique benefits.

Structured dance involves specific choreography or sequences that aim to target certain emotions or physical states. This format can provide a sense of safety and containment for individuals, offering clear guidance and a structured outlet for expression. It can be particularly helpful for those who may feel overwhelmed by the openness of freeform dance, providing a scaffolded approach to exploring movement and emotion.

Freeform or intuitive dance encourages spontaneous movement, guided by the individual's internal rhythms and emotions. This unscripted approach allows for a direct and unfiltered expression of feelings, fostering a deep sense of freedom and personal exploration. It can be especially transformative for those feeling restricted or confined by their trauma, offering a space to explore and release emotions without the constraints of specific steps or patterns.

Creating a Safe Space for Dance

For dance therapy to be effective, creating a supportive and judgment-free environment is paramount. Such a space encourages participants to fully engage with their emotions and movements without fear of critique or embarrassment.

Here are some key considerations to create a positive and effective environment:

- Physical Safety: Ensure the space is free from obstacles and hazards, providing ample room for movement. Comfortable flooring and a private or semi-private setting can make us feel more at ease to express ourselves freely.
- Emotional Safety: Establish ground rules that emphasize respect, confidentiality, and non-judgment. Encouraging an atmosphere of openness and empathy allows us to feel supported and understood.
- Guidance and Support: Having a skilled facilitator or therapist present to guide the session and provide emotional support is quite important. Their role is to guide and support us through the process, usually by offering prompts or interventions as needed, while ensuring a safe emotional space for all.

Shaking and Vibrational Practices

In the realm of healing, the practice of shaking and vibrational movements emerges as a profound method to address and release the physical manifestations of trauma embedded within our bodies. This method, both ancient and modern, serves as a powerful means to liberate those often ineffable emotions held in our physical form, facilitating a process of renewal and release.

Cultural and Historical Context

The use of shaking as a form of emotional release and healing is a concept deeply rooted in various cultures around the world. Many indigenous traditions recognize the therapeutic value of rhythmic movement and vibration, incorporating them into rituals and ceremonies aimed at physical and emotional purification. For example, the Kalahari Bushmen of Africa engage in trance dances, where intense shaking is a key component, believed to activate healing energies and foster community connection. Similarly, in the practices of Qigong and Tai Chi from China, subtle vibrations and shaking movements are used to unblock energy pathways and promote health.

The Science of Shaking

Shaking practices, when examined through the lens of physiology and psychology, reveal a fascinating interplay between our physical actions and emotional states. The act of shaking or engaging in vibrational movements activates the body's natural relaxation response, a counterbalance to the fight-or-flight mechanism triggered by stress or trauma. This activation is facilitated through the stimulation of the vagus nerve, a critical component of the parasympathetic nervous system, which helps to lower heart rate, reduce blood pressure, and initiate a state of calm throughout the body. Additionally, shaking has been shown to disrupt the body's chronic stress patterns, effectively 'resetting' the nervous system to a more balanced state. This physiological shift not only alleviates symptoms of anxiety and tension but also paves the way for emotional release and healing.

Neurochemical Release: Engaging in shaking practices has been correlated with the release of neurochemicals such as dopamine and serotonin, which play key roles in mood regulation and a sense of well-being.

Muscle Relaxation: The rhythmic contraction and release inherent in shaking help to alleviate muscle tension, a common physical byproduct of emotional stress or trauma.

Guided Shaking Exercises

If you are looking to add shaking to your healing regimen, here are some step-by-step instructions for a simple yet effective shaking exercise:

1. Find a Comfortable Space: Choose a spot where you feel safe and won't be disturbed. Standing with your feet shoulder-width apart, take a few deep breaths to center yourself.
2. Begin with Gentle Movement: Start by gently bouncing your knees, letting your arms hang loosely by your sides. Allow the movement to extend naturally through your body, from your legs to your torso, arms, and head.

3. Intensify the Shaking: Gradually let your movements become more vigorous. Shake your hands, wiggle your fingers, and let your whole body move freely. If comfortable, close your eyes to enhance your inward focus.
4. Use Breath as an Anchor: Maintain deep, rhythmic breathing throughout the exercise. This helps to support the release of tension and promotes a deeper sense of relaxation.
5. Wind Down Gradually: After several minutes, begin to slow your movements, transitioning from shaking to gentle swaying. Finally, come to a standstill, taking a moment to feel the sensations throughout your body.

This practice can be performed alone or in a group setting, with each offering its unique benefits. Group sessions, guided by a trained facilitator, can create a collective energy that enhances the experience of release and renewal.

Integrating Shaking with Other Therapies

Incorporating shaking and vibrational practices into a holistic healing approach can significantly enhance the process of recovery from trauma. Here are some ways shaking can complement other therapeutic modalities:

- Combination with Breathwork: Integrating shaking exercises with focused breathing techniques can amplify the relaxation response, deepening the sense of calm and facilitating a more profound release of trauma.
- Sequencing with Yoga or Dance: Starting a therapeutic session with shaking can serve to release initial layers of tension, making the body more receptive to the deeper stretches in yoga or the expressive movements in dance therapy.
- Incorporation into Psychotherapy: Shaking practices can be a valuable tool to physically release the emotions unearthed during counseling sessions, bridging the gap between cognitive understanding and somatic experience.

In the pursuit of emotional and physical healing through movement, the environment in which we practice holds significant influence over our experience. A space that radiates warmth, privacy, and tranquility can become a sanctuary for those seeking solace and strength through movement. This section is dedicated to crafting such an environment, whether in the solitude of your home or within the collective energy of a group setting.

Importance of a Nurturing Environment

The ambiance of a space can deeply affect our ability to connect with our bodies and emotions during movement practices. A nurturing environment acts as a supportive embrace, encouraging openness and vulnerability. It's in these settings that movement transcends mere physical activity, becoming a profound dialogue with our inner selves.

Elements of a Healing Space

Creating a personal space that supports healing through movement involves several key elements. Ensure your space offers privacy, a corner where the outside world's demands and judgments are momentarily kept at bay. This could mean using a room with a door you can close or setting up a screen in a part of a larger room. The physical comfort of your space is also vital. Ample room to move without restriction, a floor that supports your body, and the right temperature all contribute to a sense of well-being. Additionally, lighting plays a crucial role in setting the mood. Soft, gentle light can calm the mind, while brighter settings can energize. Consider using dimmable lights or candles. The inclusion of plants or elements of nature can also enhance the calming effect of your environment.

Make your space as unique as you are by infusing it with objects that hold meaning to you. These might be photographs, inspirational quotes, or anything that reminds you of peace, strength and healing.

Navigating Shared Spaces

For those without the luxury of a dedicated movement space, here are strategies to maintain a sense of safety and boundary:

- Timing: Choose times when the space is least likely to be needed by others, perhaps early morning or late evening.
- Portable Elements: Create a mobile kit of items that make a space feel personal and healing, such as a small rug, a cushion, or a scarf. These can be set up quickly and packed away after your practice.
- Communication: If you share your living space, communicate the importance of this practice to you and negotiate times or areas where you can have the privacy you need.

As we wrap up our exploration of setting up a nurturing environment for movement, the takeaway is clear: the space in which we engage in therapeutic movement deeply influences our healing process. Use this knowledge to optimize your surroundings, thus influencing your inner space.

SIX
CRAFTING YOUR SOMATIC SELF-CARE SANCTUARY

Just as life brings forward continuous changes, your healing process is not static; it evolves, adapts, and grows with you. Your journey through somatic therapy and self-care requires attention, nurturing, and a routine that respects the seasons of your life. In this chapter, we will explore how creating a structured yet flexible routine can be your sanctuary, a space where healing flourishes.

The Importance of Routine in Healing

Creating a routine is like laying down a map for a road trip. It gives you a sense of direction, spots to visit, and where you might need to refuel. Similarly, a well-thought-out routine in healing provides structure, ensuring that the practices necessary to your well-being are not left by the wayside in the hustle of daily life.

Building structure for healing

Imagine waking up each day knowing you have a set time for meditation, a moment carved out for journaling, or a specific hour for your body scan practice. This structure acts as a scaffold, supporting your healing process and ensuring that self-care becomes as natural as your morning cup of coffee.

Routine as a grounding tool

On days when life feels like a whirlwind, your routine can be the calm eye of the storm. For instance, no matter how chaotic a day gets, taking those ten minutes to breathe deeply or stretch can anchor you, providing a sense of normalcy and grounding.

The role of rituals

When somatic practices become rituals, they transcend mere activities, becoming sacred moments of connection with yourself. Lighting a candle before meditation or setting up a cozy corner for journaling can elevate these practices, imbuing them with deeper significance and enhancing their therapeutic effect.

Consistency and safety

For anyone healing from trauma, predictability can be soothing. A routine offers just that—a reliable framework within which you can explore, heal, and grow. It tells you, "Here, at this time, you are safe to focus on your well-being."

THE FOLLOWING checklist is designed to guide you through creating a somatic healing routine tailored to your unique needs and lifestyle. By reflecting on your preferences, commitments, and rhythms, you can build a practice that nurtures your body, mind, and spirit.

1. Choose Somatic Practices to Include

- Yoga
- Meditation
- Tai Chi or Qigong
- Breathwork
- Dancing
- Nature Walks
- Body Scans

- Journaling
- Other: _____

2. **Determine the Best Times for These Practices**

Reflect on your daily and weekly schedule, your energy levels throughout the day, and how these practices can fit into your lifestyle seamlessly.

- Early morning practices for energizing and setting intentions.
- Midday sessions to refresh and refocus.
- Evening routines for relaxation and unwinding.
- Specific times that align with your natural rhythms

3. **Identify Simple Rituals to Elevate These Practices**

Rituals can transform your practices from routine to sacred, enhancing their impact.

- Lighting a candle or incense to signify the beginning of your practice.
- Creating a dedicated space filled with items that inspire tranquility.
- Playing soothing music or nature sounds.
- Using aromatherapy or essential oils.
- Starting with a short gratitude practice.
- Custom rituals: _____

4. **Plan for Consistency While Allowing Flexibility**

A flexible approach ensures your routine is sustainable and adaptable to life's inevitable changes.

- Set a goal for the frequency of your practice (daily, several times a week).
- Choose a primary practice but have 1-2 alternatives for variety or when time is limited.

- Remember the principle of gentleness: If you miss a session, simply resume the next day without self-criticism.
- Regularly assess and adjust your routine as needed.

5. **Final Steps**

- **Integrate**: Once you've completed this checklist, take some time to integrate your choices into a coherent routine. Sketch out a weekly schedule as a starting point.
- **Commit**: Commit to your routine for a set period (e.g., one month) before making any adjustments, allowing habits to form.
- **Reflect and Adjust**: At the end of your commitment period, reflect on what worked and what didn't. Adjust your routine accordingly, and set a new commitment period.

Remember, your personal checklist is not only a plan but a living document to your journey toward somatic healing. Regular reflection and adaptation will keep your practice aligned with your evolving needs and circumstances. This balance ensures that your healing practices are not just another task on your to-do list, but a cherished sanctuary. These moments of self-care are a precious reminder of your commitment to nurturing your well-being - of your commitment to yourself.

Building Your Somatic Self-Care Plan: A Step-by-Step Guide

When you first set out to create a personal somatic self-care plan, keep in mind that it should be a reflection of what *you* truly need in order to flourish. Here's a detailed guide to help you come up with a plan that supports your unique well-being and healing goals.

Assessing Individual Needs

The first step in this process involves a deep and honest look at what your needs actually are. It's about listening to your body and mind to understand where you're at and where you'd like to be. Start by asking yourself a series of questions:

When do I feel most at peace?

When do I feel most fulfilled and in alignment with my higher self?

What areas of my life (physical, emotional, mental) feel out of balance?

When do I feel most disconnected from myself?

What physical sensations or emotions arise regularly that I would like to address?

Reflecting on these questions helps pinpoint areas where somatic practices will bring you the most benefits. It's also useful to consider how external factors, such as work or relationships, impact your well-being. This holistic view forms the foundation of your self-care plan.

Selecting Somatic Techniques

With a clearer understanding of your needs, the next step is to explore somatic techniques that resonate with you. As we've already seen, there is a vast array of practices available, each offering unique benefits. When choosing techniques, think about what feels most appealing and manageable to you. It might be helpful to try a few different practices initially to see what best suits your needs.

Creating a Balanced Plan

A well-rounded self-care plan includes a variety of practices that address multiple aspects of well-being. To achieve this balance, it is vital to consider all three of the following:

- Physical: Incorporate activities that engage the body, like stretching or walking, to improve physical health and bodily awareness.
- Emotional: Choose practices that allow for emotional expression and processing, such as journaling or dance therapy.

- Mental: Include techniques focused on calming the mind, like meditation or breathwork, to reduce stress and enhance mental clarity.

Think about how these practices can fit into your daily and weekly routines. It might be helpful to designate certain activities for the morning to energize and prepare for the day, while others could be reserved for the evening to unwind and reflect.

Flexibility Within Structure

While having a structured plan is beneficial, it's equally important to remain flexible. Life is unpredictable, and your needs will inevitably change over time. Here are some tips for maintaining flexibility in your self-care routine.

1. Listen to Your Body and Mind: Regularly check in with yourself to assess how your chosen practices are serving you. If something doesn't feel right, be open to trying something new.
2. Adjust According to Life's Demands: If you find yourself going through a particularly busy or stressful period, it might be necessary to modify your plan to make it more manageable.
3. Be Open to Experimentation: As you evolve, so too will your self-care needs. Allow yourself the freedom to explore new techniques and practices that might better support your journey at any given time.

Tips for Staying Consistent with Your Practice

Establishing and maintaining a somatic healing routine is a process that can sometimes be challenging. The following are strategies designed to nurture your commitment, ensuring that these practices continue to support and grow with you throughout life.

Setting Realistic Goals

When we talk about goals, it's easy to aim high, often offering an ephemeral illusion of success. Yet, the key to creating a sustainable practice lies in setting targets that feel within your grasp. This approach encourages consistency whilst shielding you from the weight of discouragement that can creep in when goals seem too lofty.

Begin by identifying what you realistically can commit to each day or week. If ten minutes is all you have, let that be your starting point.

Break down larger aspirations into smaller, actionable steps. For instance, if your goal is to integrate body scanning into your routine, start with shorter sessions and gradually increase the duration as it becomes a more natural part of your day.

Remember, the aim is progress, not perfection. Allow your goals to adapt and evolve with your growing confidence and changing circumstances.

Incorporating Practices into Daily Life

Weaving somatic exercises into your everyday routine ensures they become as familiar and essential as your morning coffee or evening unwind time.

Identify activities where somatic practices can seamlessly fit. For example, performing a few mindful stretches during your morning shower or practicing deep breathing while waiting for your computer to boot up can turn idle moments into opportunities for self-care.

Use the transitions between different parts of your day as reminders. Shifting from work to home life, for example, can be an excellent time for a brief grounding exercise, helping to clear your mind and reset your energy.

Get creative with integration. Cooking dinner? Use the time to focus deeply on the sensations of the ingredients. Watching TV? Dedicate breaks to quick mindfulness or body awareness exercises.

Accountability Strategies

Staying on track with your somatic self-care routine can sometimes require a nudge. Employing strategies to keep yourself accountable ensures that your practice remains front and center.

1. Track Your Practices: Use a journal or an app to log your daily somatic activities. Visually seeing your progress can be a powerful motivator and a tool for reflection.
2. Set Reminders: Leverage technology by setting alarms or calendar reminders for your somatic practices. These little prompts can be the gentle push needed to prioritize your self-care.
3. Partner with a Friend: Sharing your journey with a friend can significantly boost your accountability. Schedule check-ins to share experiences, challenges, and successes. This shared commitment can reinforce your motivation and provide support when it wanes.

Celebrating Progress

Recognizing and celebrating each step forward fuels your journey, turning even the smallest achievements into milestones. This practice of acknowledgment serves as a reminder of how far you've come and the growth you're cultivating each day.

- Take time to reflect on your progress, noting changes in your physical sensations, emotional state, and overall well-being since integrating somatic practices into your life.
- Celebrate the wins, no matter their size. Did you remember to take deep, mindful breaths during a stressful moment? Acknowledge it. Managed to keep up with your body scanning routine for a week? Reward yourself with something that enhances your practice, like a new journal or a comfortable meditation cushion.
- Share your victories with someone who understands and supports your journey. Sometimes, just voicing your progress can amplify its significance and motivate you to keep going.

Life seldom remains static. Changes, both subtle and significant, ripple through our existence, prompting us to reevaluate and adjust our sails. Amidst this flux, maintaining your healthy routines can feel like navigating uncharted waters. That's why I propose that we explore strategies for adapting your somatic practices to life's inevitable transitions, ensuring that your commitment to self-care remains steadfast.

Life Transitions

Transition periods are inevitable. Be they joyful or challenging, they often disrupt our established routines. Whether it's a new job, a move to a different city, or a change in relationship status, these shifts can upend the familiar, leaving us searching for solid ground. Therefore, adapting your somatic practices during these times will need to involve a few key steps.

1. Identify Core Practices: Pinpoint one or two somatic exercises that form the cornerstone of your routine. These should be practices that you can lean on, no matter the circumstances, offering a sense of continuity and stability.
2. Simplify: During times of transition, simplifying your routine can help maintain its essence without overwhelming you. If your usual practice spans an hour, consider how you can condense it into a 15-minute session that still captures its core benefits.
3. Portable Practices: Cultivate a set of exercises that don't rely on specific locations or equipment. Practices like mindful breathing, simple yoga poses, or short meditations can be performed anywhere, ensuring you can maintain your routine, no matter where life takes you.

Flexibility for Busy Times

Even without major life changes, daily pressures can sometimes leave little room for extensive self-care routines. For these busy periods, having a repertoire of quick, adaptable somatic exercises ensures that self-care doesn't fall by the wayside. You can fall back on integrating micro-practices into your day. These are brief exercises, such as a two-minute deep breathing session or a series of gentle neck stretches, that can be done even during short breaks. Also, incorporating small doses of movement - movement snacks - throughout your day will allow you to keep looking after yourself when time is scarce. A series of squats while waiting for the kettle to boil or discreetly practicing foot grounding techniques under your desk can invigorate your body without needing dedicated time.

Emotional and Physical Shifts

Our bodies and minds are in a constant state of flux, influenced by internal and external factors. Emotional upheavals, hormonal changes, or physical injuries require us to listen closely to our bodies and adapt our practices accordingly.

Listening and Responding
Tune into your body's signals. If you're experiencing heightened emotional stress, prioritize practices that promote relaxation and grounding. Conversely, during periods of low energy or sadness, energizing movements might be more beneficial.

Modifying Practices
Adapt exercises to accommodate physical limitations. For instance, if you're recovering from an injury, modify yoga poses to avoid strain, or focus on seated meditation if movement is currently challenging. As a general guideline for somatics, make sure to pause often and listen to your body. Tuning in to your needs and respecting your limits is a vital component of this work.

Emotional Alignment
Align your practices with your emotional state. On days filled with anxiety, grounding techniques can provide calm. In contrast, on days where you feel disconnected or numb, engaging in more dynamic movements can awaken your senses and emotions.

Re-evaluating Needs

As I keep mentioning, the only constant in life is change. As we evolve, so do our somatic needs. Regularly taking stock of where you are in your healing process and how your needs have shifted is crucial for maintaining a routine that serves you.

Set aside time each week or month to reflect on your current somatic routine. Periodic check-ins allow you to reflect on what's working, what isn't, and why. This can help identify areas that need adjustment.

Be open to experimenting with new practices or revisiting ones you might have previously set aside. As your body and circumstances change, you might find different techniques resonate more strongly with you. If possible, seek feedback from a trusted therapist, coach, or fellow practitioners can provide new insights into how your routine might be refined to better support your growth. Our own perceptions can be limited and hinder our personal growth.

Tracking Progress and Making Adjustments

In the endeavor of nurturing oneself through somatic self-care, the act of journaling emerges as a pivotal ally. This practice acts as a mirror reflecting the nuances of your healing path, capturing shifts that might otherwise go unnoticed. By diligently jotting down thoughts, feelings, and bodily sensations associated with each somatic practice, you can create a tangible record of our journey.

Journaling as a Tool

Your journal is your trusted confidant, a safe space where every observation, no matter how small, is worthy of note. When you are ready, begin by recording the date, the somatic practices you engaged in, the duration, and any specific intentions set for each session. Afterward, reflect on and jot down the immediate physical sensations experienced during the practice, as well as any emotions or thoughts that surfaced. Over time, these entries compile into a comprehensive overview, unveiling the practices that resonate deeply with you and those that might require tweaking or replacement.

The feedback your body and mind offer is invaluable. As you pore over your journal entries, look for cues—perhaps a certain practice consistently evokes a sense of calm, or another leaves you feeling unsettled. Use these insights to fine-tune your somatic self-care plan. If a particular technique consistently aligns with feelings of peace and restoration, consider making it a more central part of your routine. Conversely, if another practice consistently stirs discomfort or dissonance, it might be time to explore alternatives that better suit your current state.

There are moments on this path where the guidance of a seasoned practitioner can be illuminating. If your journal reflections reveal persistent challenges or plateaus in your progress, reaching out for professional advice can offer new perspectives and strategies. A therapist or somatic coach can provide tailored suggestions based on your documented experiences, helping refine your practices to better align with your goals. They can also introduce you to new techniques that you might not have considered, enriching your self-care repertoire.

I hope this chapter has left you with the understanding that self-care is a dynamic, responsive practice. Throughout, we've uncovered the importance of attentive observation, the wisdom in our body's and mind's feedback, and the value of seeking external guidance when needed. We've explored the importance of patience, a reminder to be kind and compassionate toward ourselves, as healing unfolds in its own time.

SEVEN

SOMATIC SOLUTIONS FOR ANXIETY

ANXIETY IS like having an alarm system in your body that's a bit too sensitive—it goes off even when there's no real danger. Imagine you're walking in a quiet street and suddenly a leaf rustles. Instead of just noticing and moving on, your body reacts as if a lion jumped out—it's trying to protect you, but it's overdoing it.

This alarm triggers a stress response, sometimes making your heart beat faster, your breathing quicken, and your muscles tighten. Preparing you to either run away or defend yourself, it's meant to help you in dangerous situations, but when you feel this way without a clear reason, it can be confusing and overwhelming. This state of high alert can make it hard to focus, relax, or enjoy things you normally would.

In short, anxiety is your body's way of responding to stress, but it's kicking in too often and too strongly, turning everyday situations into more stressful experiences than they need to be. Needless to say, this takes a huge toll on your overall health and well-being.

As we dive into this section, let's attempt to understand anxiety not just as a psychological phenomenon, but as a deeply embodied experience that impacts us at our very core. Throughout this exploration, we'll look at anxiety through the innovative realm of somatic healing. We'll look at the intricate ways in which our bodies communicate emotional distress, which will allow us to recognize, acknowledge, and transform anxiety through practices rooted in bodily awareness. The aim is to integrate our body's sensations, movements, and intuitive wisdom to uncover triggers and begin healing the physical and psychological damage that results from this common form of ongoing stress.

Let's learn to engage with anxiety in a compassionate, embodied way, healing shadows on the way and renewing a deep sense of emotional liberation.

Exercises for Anxiety

Quite honestly, I used to catch myself regularly constricting my breath in moments of busyness or stress. Breathing is our most fundamental connection to life, yet in times of anxiety, our breath often becomes shallow, rapid, and constricted. By consciously changing our breathing patterns, we can signal the brain to activate the body's natural relaxation response.

Diaphragmatic Breathing

This involves deep breathing through the diaphragm rather than shallow breathing from the chest. To practice, place one hand on your chest and the other on your belly. Breathe in deeply through your nose, ensuring that the hand on your belly rises higher than the one on your chest. Exhale slowly through pursed lips.

4-7-8 Breathing Technique

Yes, this again! I need to emphasize just how powerful this technique is, especially once fully integrated as an automatic calming mechanism. If you haven't included this in your regular practice yet, it's time to give it a try.

Breathe in through your nose for a count of four, hold your breath for seven counts, and then exhale completely through your mouth for a count of eight. Repeat at least three consecutive times. This method helps reduce anxiety by increasing the amount of oxygen in your bloodstream and promoting a state of balance within the nervous system.

Add to breathwork other practices we've already explored, such as grounding techniques and mindful movement. These will be highly effective and help redirect your focus from the anxiety-inducing thoughts to the present moment, anchoring you in the here and now. They will also allow for the expression and release of pent-up energy and emotions that result from your body's physiological stress response.

Establishing a Safe Space

Creating a physical and mental space where you feel secure and at ease is crucial for managing anxiety. This space serves as a sanctuary where the practices of somatic therapy can unfold.

Your physical environment is often a reflection of your inner world and, in turn, influences the state of your mental well-being. Choose or create a quiet, comfortable spot where you won't be disturbed. Personalize it with items that evoke a sense of calm, such as soft blankets, soothing scents, or calming colors.

As you step into your safe space, take a moment to mentally affirm your commitment to nurturing your well-being. Choose a statement of gratitude to remind yourself of how fortunate you are to have access to this calm and safe place. Acknowledge that this time is a gift to yourself, a step towards reclaiming your inner peace.

It's important to see anxiety not as an invader to be battled, but as a signal to be understood and harmonized with. These practices—breathing exercises, grounding techniques, mindful movement, and the creation of a safe space—invite us to tune back into our body's natural rhythms, transforming the discord of anxiety into a symphony of calmness.

Addressing Depression Through Somatic Methods

In a world that can often feel drenched in shadow, somatic practices emerge as pathways out of the darkness of depression. The essence of these methods lie not in escaping our feelings but in meeting them with awareness, movement, and connection. It's through these channels we find routes to lift the fog of disconnection and numbness, making space for vibrancy and vitality to flow back into our lives.

Body Awareness and Depression

Depression can create a chasm between mind and body, enveloping us in a numbness that detaches us from the richness of living. Cultivating body awareness acts as a bridge across this divide, gently reintroducing us to the sensations, emotions, and experiences we've been missing. Techniques like mindful meditation focus attention on bodily sensations, teaching us to observe without judgment. This heightened awareness can slowly peel away layers of numbness, allowing us to reconnect with the subtle yet profound joys of sensory experience—like the warmth of sunlight on skin or the comforting weight of a blanket.

Energizing Movement Practices

Movement possesses a dual power to ground us in the present and elevate our spirits. For those weighed down by depression, energizing movement practices can act as a gentle but effective catalyst for emotional uplift. Consider incorporating:

- Dynamic Yoga Flows: Unlike more meditative forms, dynamic yoga introduces a series of flowing postures that build heat and energy within the body, sparking a lightness in spirit.
- Aerobic Exercise: Activities like brisk walking, jogging, or cycling increase heart rate and circulation, promoting the release of endorphins—nature's mood lifters.
- Dance: Freeform dance, in particular, invites spontaneity and joy. It encourages an exploration of movement that doesn't just move the body but also moves emotions, allowing for an expressive release.

These practices don't necessitate intensity or long durations; even short, regular sessions can significantly impact mood and energy levels.

Nature Therapy

Depression often isolates us, not just from others but from the world itself. Integrating nature into somatic practices is a powerful antidote to this isolation, rekindling our bond with the environment and, by extension, with life. Nature therapy involves activities such as:

- Forest Bathing: Simply being in the presence of trees and greenery can lower stress hormone levels, improve mood, and enhance cognitive function.
- Gardening: Engaging in gardening connects us to the cycles of growth and renewal, mirroring our healing process.
- Outdoor Yoga or Tai Chi: Practicing these disciplines outdoors combines the benefits of movement with the restorative effects of being in nature, offering a double dose of healing.

My personal go-to nature therapy activity is a daily sunrise beach walk and ocean swim - however, keep in mind that there are many different and unique ways in which to engage in this. The key here is simply the sensory immersion in nature—feeling the breeze, hearing birdsong, and seeing the myriad shades of green that signal growth and life.

Rituals for Reconnection

Creating rituals around somatic practices can deepen their impact, turning them into sacred acts of reconnection with oneself, others, and the world. These rituals can take many forms, such as:

- Morning Rituals: Start the day with a simple routine that incorporates a somatic practice, setting a positive and connected tone for the day ahead.
- Gratitude Practices: End each day by reflecting on moments of connection or joy, however small. This can reframe perspectives, highlighting the threads of positivity that weave through even the toughest days.
- Community Connection: Engage in group somatic practices, whether it's a yoga class, dance group, or hiking club. The shared experience can diminish feelings of isolation, reminding us of our place within a larger community.

These methods are points of stability within the chaos of life. They provide focus in the turbulence of depression, guiding us back to a sense of connection and belonging.

In exploring these somatic methods—body awareness, energizing movement, nature therapy, and rituals of reconnection—we find strategies for coping with depression that become pathways to a richer, more connected way of living. Each step taken, each breath drawn, and each moment spent in nature or movement creates a stronger, more vibrant thread into the fabric of our lives. This gradually dispels the darkness of depression with the light of awareness, movement, and connection.

———

Physical trauma, whether from an injury, accident, or surgery, leaves imprints not just on the body but also on the emotional landscape of an individual. The aftermath often carries a dual burden: the physical pain and limitations, coupled with emotional responses such as fear, frustration, and a sense of vulnerability. Recognizing the intertwined nature of these responses opens up pathways for healing that go beyond conventional medical treatments, truly delving into the realm of somatic therapy.

Somatic therapy, with its holistic focus on the relationship between body and mind, provides tools and techniques that can be particularly beneficial for those recovering from physical trauma. It acknowledges the body's remarkable capacity for healing and aims to support this process by addressing both the physical and emotional aspects of recovery.

Somatic Experiencing for Physical Trauma

One of the key techniques in somatic therapy tailored to physical trauma recovery is Somatic Experiencing (SE). Developed by Dr. Peter Levine, SE is based on the observation that animals in the wild do not suffer from trauma despite regularly facing life-threatening situations. They manage to "shake off" the energy from such experiences, something humans have lost touch with due to our complex brains and societal norms.

SE introduces this concept to trauma recovery, guiding us through exercises that help release the 'stuck' energy and stress responses trapped in our bodies since the trauma. For someone recovering from a physical injury, this might involve:

- Tracking Sensations: Gently becoming aware of bodily sensations, differentiating between those associated with trauma and those signaling recovery.
- Titration and Pendulation: Gradually revisiting the traumatic experience in small doses (titration) and oscillating between the trauma and resources that offer relief

(pendulation), facilitating a controlled release of pent-up stress.

- Discharge: Engaging in exercises that allow the body to physically release trapped energy, which might manifest as trembling, heat, or spontaneous movement.

Rebuilding Trust in the Body

Physical trauma can severely disrupt one's relationship with their body, leading to distrust and disconnection. Rebuilding this trust is a critical step in the healing process. Some strategies include mindful movement, visualization, and therapeutic touch. Engaging in gentle, mindful exercises can help reestablish a sense of control and agency over one's body. Focusing on movements that feel safe and restorative encourages a positive reconnection with the body. Imagining the body healing, envisioning wounds knitting together and strength returning, can foster a supportive mental environment that complements physical recovery. As for therapeutic touch, whether through professional massage or self-administered techniques like gentle rubbing or patting areas of tension, reinforces the body's capacity for pleasure and relaxation, countering the memories of pain.

Integrative Practices

For those on the path to recovery from physical trauma, integrating somatic therapy with conventional medical treatment offers a holistic approach to healing.

This integration might look like:

- Physical Therapy with a Somatic Lens: Working with physical therapists who are open to incorporating somatic elements into rehabilitation exercises can enhance the healing process. This could involve focusing on bodily sensations during physical therapy sessions or incorporating breathing exercises to manage pain.
- Collaborative Care Teams: Assembling a care team that includes medical professionals, somatic therapists, and mental health practitioners ensures that all aspects of

recovery are addressed. Open communication and collaboration among team members facilitate a unified approach to healing.

- Personalized Healing Plans: Recognizing the uniqueness of each person's experience with trauma, integrative practices emphasize creating personalized healing plans. This might involve adjusting the balance between different therapies based on progress and evolving needs.

Through somatic experiencing, mindful movement, and the integration of conventional and holistic therapies, a path toward wholeness and well-being is not just imagined but actively forged.

Overcoming Emotional Blockages with Body Work

Within us, emotions flow like rivers, sometimes meandering gently, at other times rushing fiercely. Yet, when obstacles interrupt this flow, our emotional currents can stagnate, leading to blockages that impact our physical and mental well-being. Understanding how to recognize, release, and maintain the fluidity of these emotional currents is crucial for holistic health. This section guides you through navigating the landscape of emotional blockages with the aid of somatic therapy.

Identifying Emotional Blockages

Our bodies can serve as maps to our inner emotional states, with certain areas acting as repositories for unexpressed emotions. Recognizing these blockages requires attunement to the subtle cues our bodies provide. At times, these blockages can look and feel like:

- Tension: Persistent tension in areas like the shoulders, neck, or jaw can indicate harbored stress or unexpressed anger.
- Discomfort: Recurring discomfort or pain in specific body parts, without a clear physical cause, might signal underlying emotional distress.
- Breathing Patterns: Shallow, restricted breathing can be a response to anxiety or fear, suggesting an emotional blockage that limits full respiratory expansion.

Tuning into these bodily sensations with curiosity rather than judgment allows for the first step in acknowledging and addressing emotional blockages.

Releasing Techniques

Once blockages are identified, somatic therapy offers a variety of techniques to facilitate their release, encouraging the resumption of emotional flow. Some effective methods include:

- Expressive Movement: This practice invites spontaneous, uninhibited movement, allowing the body to move as it wishes without choreography or structure. It can unlock and express emotions that have been stifled or unacknowledged, serving as a powerful outlet for release.
- Breathwork: Specific breathing techniques, such as deep diaphragmatic breathing or rhythmic breath cycles, can directly impact our emotional state. By consciously altering our breathing patterns, we can release emotional tension and foster a sense of calm.
- Vocalization: Using the voice through humming, chanting, or singing can help release blockages related to communication and self-expression. The vibration of vocalization can be particularly effective in loosening the tightness in the throat and chest areas.

Incorporating these practices into a regular self-care routine will promote release and recovery, whilst paving the way for the continuous flow of emotions, preventing the formation of new blockages.

Fostering Emotional Fluidity

To maintain an open and fluid emotional state, it's essential to cultivate practices that encourage regular emotional expression and processing. Consider the following:

- Daily Check-ins: Dedicate a few moments each day to check in with your body and emotions. This can be a quiet time of reflection or a brief journaling session where you note any areas of tension and the emotions they might be harboring.

- Creative Expression: Engage in creative activities such as painting, writing, or playing music. These outlets offer alternative ways to process and express emotions, contributing to emotional fluidity.
- Mindfulness Meditation: Regular mindfulness practice can heighten body awareness and sensitivity to emotional states, allowing for earlier recognition of emotional blockages and facilitating their release.

These practices assist in releasing current blockages, also playing a preventive role by ensuring emotions continue to flow freely and healthily.

Support Systems and Resources

While self-help practices are invaluable, navigating deep-seated emotional blockages often requires the guidance of professionals. Here are some avenues to consider:

- Somatic Therapy Professionals: Seek out therapists who specialize in somatic practices. Their expertise in the connection between body and emotion can provide tailored guidance for identifying and releasing blockages.
- Workshops and Groups: Participating in workshops or group sessions focused on somatic practices can offer both professional guidance and the support of a community with similar experiences.
- Online Resources: Numerous online platforms offer resources ranging from instructional videos on somatic techniques to forums for sharing experiences and advice. These can be valuable supplements to personal and professional support.

Exploring emotional blockages through somatics is a delicate balance of recognizing when to move and when to pause, when to push forward and when to yield. This dance is not always straightforward,

but it is deeply rewarding. Through the practices of identifying blockages, releasing them, fostering emotional fluidity, and leaning on support
systems, we equip ourselves with the tools to ensure our emotions flow
unimpeded, enriching every aspect of our lives with their vitality and
depth.

Enhancing Self-Esteem and Body Image

In a world that often bombards us with unrealistic standards of beauty
and success, it's no surprise that many struggle with self-esteem and
body image. However, turning inward and connecting with our bodies
through somatic practices can open doors to greater self-acceptance and
appreciation. These methods help us to recognize our worth, as well as
to celebrate the unique journey of our bodies through life.

Body Neutrality and Acceptance

Moving towards a stance of body neutrality and acceptance is the
first step in reshaping how we view ourselves. This approach encourages
us to view our bodies through a lens of functionality and gratitude,
rather than solely appearance. Practices such as mindful meditation
focused on gratitude for the body's capabilities can be transformative.
For instance, dedicating moments to thank our legs for carrying us
through the day or our hands for their ability to create and connect can
shift the narrative from criticism to appreciation.

Another effective practice involves body mapping, where one
creates a visual representation of their body, marking areas of strength,
resilience, and even pain with symbols or colors. This exercise not only
fosters an intimate understanding of one's physical self but also highlights the body's journey and inherent worth beyond aesthetic standards.

Empowerment Through Movement

Movement practices offer a dynamic pathway to feeling empowered
in our own skin. Engaging in activities that emphasize the body's
strength, flexibility, and presence can dramatically improve self-esteem.
For example, martial arts or strength training can be particularly empow-

ering, as they focus on what the body can achieve and endure, rather than how it looks.

Similarly, dance provides a powerful medium to explore and express our identity freely. It teaches us to take up space confidently and to value our bodies for their expressive potential rather than their conformity to societal norms.

Mirror Work and Self-Compassion

Mirror work involves standing in front of a mirror and engaging in positive self-talk, affirmations, or even simply observing oneself with kindness and compassion. While this practice may initially feel uncomfortable for some, it gradually helps in breaking down the barriers of self-criticism and fosters a more compassionate relationship with oneself.

Coupled with self-compassion exercises—such as writing letters to yourself with words of understanding, acceptance, and love—mirror work can significantly impact how we perceive and value ourselves.

Celebrating the Body

Recognizing and celebrating the body's capabilities and uniqueness can significantly shift the focus from appearance to appreciation. Practices that encourage this shift include:

- Creating a Joy List: Compile activities that make your body feel good, like stretching, walking in nature, or swimming. Regularly engaging in these activities reinforces the body's role in providing joy and satisfaction.
- Body Positive Yoga: Participate in yoga classes that emphasize body positivity, focusing on how poses feel rather than how they look, and adapting practices to suit all body types and abilities.
- Sharing Stories: Participate in groups or forums where people share their journeys of body acceptance and self-love. Hearing others' experiences can be affirming and inspiring, reminding us that we are not alone in our struggles with self-esteem and body image.

Embracing body neutrality, finding empowerment in movement, practicing self-compassion, and celebrating our bodies lays the foundation for lasting self-esteem and a positive body image.

As we conclude this exploration of enhancing self-esteem and body image through somatic practices, we're undoubtedly reminded of the transformative power of connecting with our bodies. These practices lead to an unconditional acceptance and appreciation of our physical selves while contributing to a broader sense of well-being and fulfillment.

Our bodies are not adversaries to be critiqued, but companions on our life's journey, deserving of care, respect, and celebration.

EIGHT
DEEP DIVES AND NEW HORIZONS

PICTURE YOURSELF STANDING, nervously swaying at the edge of a diving board for the first time.

Below you, the water promises refreshing new insights but also hints at the challenge of the plunge.

This moment, right here, encapsulates the essence of exploring Somatic Experiencing beyond the basics. This work is about taking that leap, armed with trust in the resilience of your own body and spirit, to uncover deeper layers of healing.

Now, let's move from the edge and take that dive into the depths of advanced somatic practices, where the true transformation unfolds.

Foundations of Somatic Experiencing

Somatic Experiencing stands as a safe and supportive pathway for those navigating trauma. Rooted in the observation that animals in the wild naturally discharge stress without lingering effects, this therapy offers guidelines for humans to release and resolve the physical manifestations of trauma.

At its core, SE shifts the focus from recounting traumatic events to tuning into the body's subtle cues, leading to a profound release and rebalancing of the nervous system.

Consider a moment when your heart raced at the memory of a

stressful event. SE teaches techniques to ground yourself in such moments, using the body's wisdom to transform panic into peace.

Advanced Exercises

Beyond the foundational practices, SE offers a variety of advanced exercises tailored for deep trauma work. These exercises invite a nuanced exploration of bodily sensations, encouraging the nervous system to reset its response to past traumas.

TERMS TO FAMILIARIZE YOURSELF WITH:

- Resourcing: Identifying and tapping into internal and external resources that provide a sense of safety and stability.
- Pendulation: Gently oscillating between sensations associated with trauma and those linked to resources, facilitating a natural rhythm of activation and settling in the nervous system.
- Coupling Dynamics: Observing how contrasting sensations interact within the body, such as warmth and coolness or tension and relaxation, to foster integration and healing.

The power of SE is utterly transformative. One compelling case (similar to so many others) involved a firefighter struggling with PTSD after a particularly harrowing rescue operation. Through progressive SE, he was able to reconnect with his body's innate resilience, gradually finding peace in moments that once triggered intense flashbacks.

Remember, SE has the capacity to mend the fractures trauma leaves in its wake, guiding us back to a sense of wholeness and balance.

The SE Process

To help you familiarize yourself with the Somatic Experiencing process, I have created a representation of the sequence and key elements of the therapy, from the initial steps to final stages.

Here's your structured breakdown of how the SE process can be depicted:

1. Introduction to SE and Building Resources

OBJECTIVE: Prepare ourselves by building a sense of safety and resilience.

Key Concepts:

- Grounding techniques
- Establishing a safe environment
- Identifying internal resources

2. Titration and Pendulation

OBJECTIVE: Gently approach traumatic memories without becoming overwhelmed.

Key Concepts:

- Titration: Introducing small amounts of traumatic material
- Pendulation: Moving back and forth between regulation and dysregulation

3. Identifying and Releasing Trauma

OBJECTIVE: Identify, process, and release trauma stored in the body.

Key Concepts:

- Tracking bodily sensations
- Releasing stored trauma through physical responses

4. Integration

OBJECTIVE: Integrate the processed experiences into a coherent sense of self.

Key Concepts:

- Reflecting on changes in perception and self-awareness
- Stabilizing the new state of balance

5. Expansion and Growth

OBJECTIVE: Practice ongoing self-awareness and resilience after therapy.

Key Concepts:

- Developing new coping strategies
- Encouraging emotional and physiological resilience

Reflection Questions

IN THE JOURNEY of healing and self-discovery through Somatic Experiencing, reflection plays a crucial role. This section of the book provides a series of questions designed to deepen your understanding of SE principles and enhance your application of its techniques. As you explore these questions, consider adding to your journal to document your thoughts and experiences. This practice can be instrumental in facilitating personal growth and healing.

Once completed, remember that these reflection questions are meant to be revisited periodically throughout your therapy journey. Each time you return to them, you might discover new insights or observe changes in your responses. I promise you that engaging deeply and regularly with these questions will enhance your understanding of somatic healing principles and improve your therapeutic outcomes.

1. Reflecting on Body Sensations and Stress

What sensations do I notice in my body when recalling a stressful event, and how can I ground myself in the present?

Identify specific physical sensations (tightness, heat, shivering, etc.) associated with stress. Reflect on various grounding techniques, such as deep breathing, feeling your feet on the ground, or focusing on sensory experiences (sight, sound, touch), and consider which methods most effectively bring you back to the present moment.

_____

_____

_____

_____

_____

_____

_____

_____

_____

_____

_____

_____

2. Accessing Internal Resources

How do my internal resources feel in my body, and how can I access these sensations in moments of distress?

Focus on recognizing feelings of strength, calm, or resilience within your body. These might manifest as a warm feeling in your chest or a sense of solidity in your feet. Consider how you can intentionally connect with these sensations during challenging times to cultivate a sense of stability and safety.

_____

_____

_____

_____

_____

_____

_____

_____

_____

_____

_____

_____

3. Understanding Pendulation

In what ways have I observed pendulation in my own healing process, and how can I consciously engage with this rhythm?

Reflect on moments when you've naturally oscillated between feeling emotionally or physically overwhelmed and a state of relaxation or neutrality. Identify triggers and calming factors, and think about how you can actively use this understanding to help manage your reactions in a healing context.

_____

_____

_____

_____

_____

_____

_____

_____

_____

_____

_____

_____

The Role of Polyvagal Theory in Somatic Therapy

In the fascinating realm of somatic therapy, the polyvagal theory stands out as a pivotal framework that reshapes our understanding of the body's response to stress and trauma. This theory, introduced by Dr. Stephen Porges, reveals the ways in which our nervous system mediates our interactions with the world, influencing our capacity for safety, connection, and healing. At its heart, polyvagal theory elucidates how different states of our autonomic nervous system dictate our experiences of safety and danger, fundamentally altering our approach to therapy and self-regulation.

Understanding polyvagal theory begins with recognizing the three primary states of the autonomic nervous system: the ventral vagal state, associated with feelings of safety and social connection; the sympathetic state, linked to the fight or flight response; and the dorsal vagal state, related to shutdown and disconnection. Grasping this triad is crucial for interpreting our bodily sensations and emotional responses as signals of these underlying physiological states, rather than isolated experiences.

With this understanding, somatic therapy integrates polyvagal principles to foster a sense of safety and connection, foundational elements for healing. The aim is for us to identify which state we are operating from and employ techniques designed to shift towards a more regulated, ventral vagal state. This process involves cultivating an environment of safety, both internally and externally, where the nervous system can relax and open up to connection and healing.

Specific exercises based on polyvagal theory are instrumental in this shift. These practices might include:

- Deep, slow breathing: This can signal the body to shift from a sympathetic state to a ventral vagal state, promoting calm and a sense of safety.
- Social engagement: Simple acts of connection, like making eye contact or engaging in gentle conversation, can activate the ventral vagal system, reinforcing feelings of safety and trust.
- Muscle relaxation techniques: Consciously relaxing the muscles, especially around the neck and face, can encourage

a shift away from fight or flight responses, inviting a sense of calm and groundedness.

- Grounding exercises: Practices that enhance bodily awareness and present-moment experience can help pull individuals out of the dorsal vagal state of shutdown, reconnecting them with their surroundings and themselves.

Being aware of polyvagal states in daily life transforms how we experience our world and interact with others. Simple shifts in our routines can reinforce a ventral vagal state, enhancing our sense of connection and well-being. Here are a few simple tips for tapping into this awareness.

1. Routine mindfulness: Taking moments throughout the day to check in with ourselves, noting our current state and using grounding or breathing exercises as needed.
2. Cultivating connection: Prioritizing genuine social interactions that foster a sense of belonging and safety, from sharing a meal with loved ones to engaging in community activities.
3. Physical touch: Engaging in safe, consensual physical touch, such as hugs or hand-holding, which can significantly bolster the ventral vagal system and reinforce feelings of connection and security.
4. Laughter and play: Activities that evoke joy and laughter naturally stimulate the ventral vagal system, promoting relaxation and a sense of communal bonding.

This polyvagal approach does not merely address symptoms, but targets the underlying physiological states that shape our experiences of safety, connection, and ultimately, healing. It allows us to go through the emotional recovery process with a deeper sense of agency and compassion for our body's innate wisdom and resilience.

Titration: A Technique for Managing Intense Emotions

In the realm of somatic therapy, titration is a method that stands out for its gentle approach to processing and releasing intense emotions. This technique, akin to adding a drop of dye to water and watching it slowly disperse, involves experiencing emotions in small, manageable doses. This careful, measured approach ensures that we are not overwhelmed by our feelings, making the process of emotional healing more accessible and less daunting.

Titration in somatic therapy is inspired by the chemical process of the same name, where substances are combined in a controlled manner to prevent adverse reactions. Similarly, this technique acknowledges the potency of our emotions and the impact they can have on our psychological and physiological state. By breaking down the experience of intense emotions into smaller, digestible pieces, titration allows individuals to engage with their feelings without the risk of re-traumatization or overwhelm.

The practice of titration is particularly effective for those who have faced trauma. For these individuals, emotions linked to past events can often feel too intense or frightening to confront all at once. Titration offers a pathway to healing that respects the body's and the mind's limits, encouraging a slow and steady engagement with difficult emotions.

Guided Titration Exercises

Implementing titration into somatic therapy involves a series of guided exercises that facilitate a gradual emotional release. The following are simplified steps to illustrate the process.

1. Finding a Safe Starting Point: Begin by identifying a neutral or positive memory, sensation, or thought to serve as a grounding point. This will be your safe harbor to return to if the emotional waters get too rough.
2. Introducing the Emotional Stimulus: Gently bring to mind a challenging emotion or memory, but only to the extent that you can handle without feeling overwhelmed. This might mean only thinking about the event in the broadest terms or focusing on a single aspect of it.
3. Monitoring the Response: Pay close attention to how your body reacts to this stimulus. Notice any changes in breathing, muscle tension, or heart rate, and observe any emotions that surface.

4. Returning to Safety: Before the emotional response becomes too intense, shift your focus back to your safe point, allowing your body and mind to calm.
5. Repeating the Process: Gradually, and over time, you can return to the emotional stimulus, each time venturing a little further into the emotion as your capacity to process it increases.

Benefits of Titration

The titration method offers several benefits that make it a valuable tool in the healing process:

- Prevents Overwhelm: By breaking down the experience of intense emotions into manageable pieces, titration ensures that individuals do not become overwhelmed, making the therapy process safer and more approachable.
- Cultivates Emotional Resilience: Each successful engagement with challenging emotions strengthens the individual's confidence and ability to cope, building resilience over time.
- Encourages Deep Healing: Titration allows for a thorough and deep processing of emotions, as it enables individuals to engage with the full spectrum of their feelings at a pace that they can handle.
- Supports Self-regulation: Through the practice of shifting focus between emotional stimuli and safety, individuals learn valuable self-regulation skills that are beneficial beyond the therapy session.

Incorporating Titration into Practice

Incorporating titration into one's somatic practice, whether independently or with a therapist, involves a few key considerations:

- With a Therapist: Working with a therapist skilled in somatic techniques can provide the necessary guidance and support to navigate titration effectively. A therapist can help identify appropriate starting points, monitor the process, and provide immediate support if the emotional intensity becomes too great.

- Independently: For those practicing titration on their own, it's crucial to have a clear understanding of the technique and to approach the process with patience and self-compassion. Keeping a journal to document the experience can offer insights into patterns and progress.
- Creating a Supportive Environment: Whether practicing titration solo or with professional guidance, ensuring that the environment is conducive to relaxation and safety is vital. This might include a quiet space, comfortable seating, and the absence of distractions.
- Combining with Other Techniques: Titration can be effectively combined with other somatic practices, such as grounding exercises or mindful breathing, to enhance the process of emotional release and regulation.

By thoughtfully integrating titration into somatic therapy, we are offered a compassionate pathway to confront and heal from intense emotions. This technique respects the natural capacity for emotional processing, providing a structured yet flexible approach to navigate the complex terrain of healing. Through titration, the daunting task of facing our deepest fears and pains becomes a journey marked by gradual discovery, resilience, and deep transformation.

Integrating Somatic Therapy with Other Healing Modalities

Uniting somatic therapy with other healing approaches creates a network of wellness strategies that address the multifaceted nature of individual healing needs. This synergy allows for a more rounded approach, addressing not just the symptoms but the root causes of emotional and physical discomfort. Here, we delve into how blending somatic therapy with psychotherapy, art therapy, mindfulness practices, and shadow work can offer a holistic path to well-being.

Blending Somatic Therapy and Psychotherapy

While somatic therapy focuses on bodily sensations and the non-verbal cues related to trauma and stress, psychotherapy often centers on verbal expression, exploring thoughts, beliefs, and personal history. When these two modalities converge, they offer a dual pathway to healing. Somatic therapy can unlock and release trapped emotional energy in the body, which might be too difficult to access through words alone. Psychotherapy provides a space to process these releases cognitively, allowing for insight and understanding, which can be critical for long-term emotional health.

This integrated approach can be particularly effective for those of us who feel stuck in their healing process, as it engages both the mind and body in the journey towards recovery.

Art Therapy and Somatic Practices: A Creative Union

Art therapy, with its emphasis on expression through creativity, naturally complements somatic therapy's focus on bodily awareness. This combination allows individuals to explore their internal landscape not just through physical sensations but through visual and tactile forms.

Drawing, painting, or sculpting physical sensations or emotions that arise during somatic exercises can provide a tangible form to abstract experiences, making them easier to understand and process. Moreover, engaging in art immediately after somatic practices can capture the raw, unfiltered essence of the emotional and physical release, providing deep insights into personal healing symbols and themes.

For many, this creative process becomes a powerful tool for non-verbal communication, offering a different lens through which to view and understand their healing journey.

The Symbiosis of Mindfulness Practices and Somatic Healing

Mindfulness practices, with their emphasis on present-moment awareness, naturally enhance the benefits of somatic therapy. By fostering an acute awareness of bodily sensations and thoughts, mindfulness practices can amplify the effectiveness of somatic work. For instance, mindfulness meditation before somatic exercises can deepen the state of bodily awareness, making it easier to connect with and release trapped emotions. Mindful walking or yoga can be seen as somatic exercises in themselves, promoting a harmonious blend of physical movement and conscious awareness.

For individuals seeking to deepen their connection with their bodies and emotions, incorporating mindfulness into their somatic therapy regimen offers a path that enriches both practices.

Shadow work, a concept in psychology introduced by Carl Jung, involves exploring the darker, unconscious parts of our personality that we often deny or suppress. When paired with somatic healing, these two practices can offer profound mental, emotional, and physical benefits. Here's how integrating shadow work with somatic healing can be utterly transformative.

Mental Benefits

Shadow work encourages self-awareness and insight, helping us recognize and understand hidden emotions and motivations that influence our behavior. By incorporating somatic practices, we can physically experience where these suppressed emotions manifest in the body, such as tension or discomfort in specific areas. This awareness can lead to a clearer and more cohesive mental state, reducing anxiety and creating a greater sense of peace and mental clarity.

Emotional Benefits

Engaging in shadow work helps bring repressed feelings to the surface. It can be an intense process, as facing one's inner darkness is not easy. Somatic healing supports this by helping the body process and release these emotions. Techniques like deep breathing, mindfulness, and physical movement allow us to experience our emotions in real-time and let them go more effectively. This process can lead to improved emotional resilience and healthier coping mechanisms.

Physical Benefits

Somatic practices emphasize the connection between emotional health and physical health, and working through our psychological shadows often leads to experiencing physical relief related to decreased emotional burden. Chronic pains, aches, and tensions that are manifestations of emotional distress can be alleviated as the body releases the underlying emotional blockages.

HERE ARE some practical tips to combine shadow work and somatic healing:

- **Start with Awareness:** Begin by becoming aware of your physical sensations and emotional states. Regularly check in with your body through the various somatic practices we have discussed, and learn to understand where you might be holding emotional tension.
- **Journaling and Reflection:** Use journaling to explore thoughts and feelings that arise during or after somatic exercises. This can help link physical sensations with emotional experiences, a key aspect of shadow work.
- **Guided Imagery:** Employ guided imagery during somatic exercises to confront and communicate with shadow aspects. For example, while in a relaxed state induced by deep breathing, visualize meeting a part of yourself that you dislike or fear and engage in a mental dialogue with this aspect. This will also be highly beneficial to support inner child work.
- **Integrate Regular Practice:** Make both practices a regular part of your routine. Consistency is key in achieving deep and lasting transformation. Allow your experiences in shadow work to inform your somatic practices and vice versa.

Approaching somatic therapy within a broader spectrum of healing modalities offers a holistic approach that honors the complexity of the human experience. By acknowledging and nurturing the interconnectedness of mind, body, and spirit, we can explore a more comprehensive path to personal growth.

The Future of Somatic Therapy: Trends and Innovations

In recent times, the field of somatic therapy has begun to glitter with new research findings and innovative practices, signaling a promising horizon for this healing modality. The landscape is evolving, shaped by advancements that bring fresh perspectives and expand the toolkit available to practitioners like yourself. This section explores the dynamic shifts and possibilities that are charting the future of somatic therapies.

Emerging Research

A wave of recent studies has started to solidify the scientific foundation of somatic therapy, offering compelling evidence of its efficacy. Researchers are exploring the intricate ways bodily sensations and movements influence psychological well-being, with findings that underscore the therapy's potential in treating a wide range of conditions, from PTSD to chronic pain. Notably, neuroscientific investigations into the body-mind connection are revealing how somatic practices can rewire neural pathways, offering a biological explanation for the profound changes practitioners experience. This burgeoning body of research validates the experiences of those who have found healing through somatic therapy and paves the way for its broader acceptance in the therapeutic community.

Innovative Practices

The horizon of somatic therapy is expanding with the introduction of innovative practices that blend traditional techniques with cutting-edge technologies. Virtual reality (VR), for instance, is being explored as a tool to create immersive environments that facilitate somatic exploration and healing. By simulating scenarios that evoke bodily responses, VR offers a unique platform for clients to safely engage with and process traumatic memories or phobias. Additionally, wearable tech that monitors physiological responses in real-time is enhancing the way therapists and clients understand the body's signals, offering immediate feedback that can guide therapeutic interventions. These innovations are not only broadening the scope of somatic therapy but also making it more accessible and tailored to individual needs.

The Role of Community

The power of community in the healing process cannot be overstated, and somatic therapy is increasingly recognizing and leveraging this force. Group-based somatic practices are gaining traction, providing spaces where individuals can explore their bodily experiences within a supportive community setting. These groups offer the dual benefits of personal exploration and collective healing, creating a shared energy that amplifies the therapeutic impact. Moreover, the rise of online platforms has fostered global communities where practitioners and clients can connect, share experiences, and learn from each other. This collective engagement is enriching the practice with a diversity of perspectives and experiences.

Looking Ahead

As we peer into the future of somatic therapy, several trajectories suggest exciting developments and challenges. On one hand, the integration of somatic practices into mainstream healthcare offers the potential for wider recognition and application, promising to bring these transformative techniques to a broader audience. On the other hand, this growth necessitates rigorous training and certification processes to ensure the fidelity and quality of somatic practices as they become more widely adopted. Moreover, the ongoing exploration of somatic therapy's applications, from enhancing athletic performance to supporting aging populations, hints at the vast potential of this modality to contribute to various aspects of human well-being.

The field of somatic therapy stands on the cusp of significant evolution, buoyed by emerging research, innovative practices, and the strengthening role of community. These developments are exciting as they promise to deepen our understanding of the body-mind connection, as well as expand the reach and efficacy of somatic healing.

NINE

JOURNALING AS A SOMATIC COMPANION

IF YOU COULD HOLD a mirror to your soul, one that reflects not just thoughts and visages but the very vibrations of your being, what would it show?

Well, dear reader, your journal is your mirror. It listens, absorbs, and speaks back in whispers of insight and bursts of revelation. Journaling in the context of somatic therapy and shadow healing is a dialogue with the deepest parts of yourself, a practice as simple as it is profound, mystically turning the intangible into something concrete.

In a world where we're constantly bombarded with stimuli, journaling offers a pause, a moment to breathe and connect deeply with ourselves. It's akin to sitting down with an old friend in a cozy cafe, where the hustle of the world fades into the background, leaving space for honest conversations. Here, in the quiet, we find clarity.

Enhancing Self-Awareness

Journaling acts like a personal archaeologist, gently excavating the layers of our experiences to reveal the artifacts of our inner world. It encourages a heightened awareness of the body's whispers and screams, often ignored in the rush of daily life. By documenting physical sensations, we begin to notice patterns and triggers that were previously shrouded in the subconscious. For example, after a long day, sitting down to write about a persistent tension in your shoulders might reveal its connection to an overlooked emotional stressor, offering a chance for recognition and release.

Processing Emotions

Writing provides a safe haven for emotions, a place where they can be expressed without judgment or immediate consequences. It allows for the distillation of feelings, transforming nebulous emotions into clear, manageable entities.

Strengthening the Mind-Body Connection

In somatic therapy, the interplay between mind and body is central. Journaling about bodily experiences brings this connection to the forefront, creating a tangible record of the body's language. This practice honors your body's role in your emotional life and strengthens your relationship with it.

Supporting Memory and Reflection

Journaling serves as a chronicle of our healing process, each entry a snapshot in time. This archive becomes a resource for reflection, allowing us to track our progress, celebrate victories, and learn from challenges. On days filled with doubt, looking back at earlier entries can provide tangible proof of how far you've come, reigniting hope and determination.

Mapping Your Somatic Journey

Embarking on a somatic healing journey through journaling can be a transformative process. This section provides a comprehensive guide to help you tune into your body's sensations and emotions, and capture them effectively in your journal. By using the provided flowchart, templates, and tips, you'll create a personal space to explore and enhance your somatic awareness.

Tips for Creating a Conducive Journaling Atmosphere

Setting: Choose a quiet, comfortable spot with minimal distractions. You might prefer a nature setting, a designated corner of your home, or anywhere that feels safe and calming.

Mood: Enhance the atmosphere with elements that help you relax and focus. This might include soft lighting, soothing music, or a few drops of lavender oil.

Timing: While you can journal at any time, many find early morning or late evening to be ideal for reflective practice. Choose a time when you are least likely to be interrupted.

Materials: Use a journal that feels personal and inviting. Whether it's a simple notebook or a beautifully bound journal, choose one that inspires you to write. Keep a favorite pen handy—one that flows easily across the page.

Routine: Try to establish a regular journaling routine. Consistency helps deepen your somatic awareness and enriches your healing journey.

By integrating these tools and tips into your practice, you'll enhance your capacity for self-awareness and nurture your path towards healing. Remember that each entry and reflection is a step forward, helping to map out the intricacies of your mind-body connection.

Flowchart for Tuning into Bodily Sensations and Emotions

1. **Settle Into a Comfortable Space:** Begin by finding a quiet and comfortable place where you won't be disturbed. Sit or lie down in a relaxed posture.
2. **Close Your Eyes and Breathe:** Take a few deep breaths to center yourself. Focus on the rhythm of your breathing and allow your mind to quiet.

3. **Scan Your Body:** Slowly scan your body from head to toe. Notice any areas of tension, discomfort, or ease without trying to change anything.
4. **Acknowledge Emotions:** As you scan, pay attention to any emotions that arise. Are they linked to specific physical sensations or memories?
5. **Deepen Your Focus:** Choose one physical sensation or emotion to focus on more deeply. Observe its qualities—is it sharp, dull, moving, or constant?
6. **Reflect on Context:** Think about any events or circumstances that might be influencing these sensations and emotions.
7. **Prepare to Journal:** Open your eyes and prepare your journaling materials. Keep your focus on the sensation or emotion as you transition to writing.
8. **Journal:** Write freely about what you observed. Don't worry about grammar or style; let your experiences flow onto the page.
9. **Reflect and Relax:** After journaling, spend a few minutes reflecting on the experience. Close the session with a few deep breaths, acknowledging your work and healing.

Tip: To break the ice, try writing a letter to your body, thanking it for its resilience and expressing your intentions to listen more attentively to its needs.

My Somatic Journal

This section is dedicated to providing you with thought-provoking journaling prompts that will help you explore the deep connections between your body and emotions. These are designed to encourage you to tap into bodily sensations and emotions, observing and developing a profound understanding of the interplay between the two. Use these prompts as starting points to ignite introspection and discovery in your writing sessions.

Guided Journal Prompts for Emotional Release

In the quiet moments of reflection, journaling bridges the unspoken truths of our bodies with the stories we tell ourselves.

Journaling, in the context of somatic therapy, is an important practice of turning inward, of listening deeply, and of speaking truths. It also happens to be a bridge between the seen and the unseen, the conscious and the subconscious, the body and the mind. Regularly engaging with these prompts can dramatically increase your somatic awareness and emotional understanding. By reflecting deeply through journaling and exploring the answers that come forth, you build a richer connection to your internal world.

This section presents a series of prompts designed to facilitate a deeper conversation with oneself, a dialogue with our being, touching on sensations, emotions, healing, and gratitude. These questions are your allies, guiding you to explore your inner world with an open mind.

Prompts for Exploring Bodily Sensations

- On waking, take a moment to scan your body from head to toe. What are the first sensations that greet you? Describe them without judgment, as if you're a curious observer discovering a new landscape.
- Consider a recent moment of stress or discomfort. Can you recall where in your body you felt it the most? Write about that sensation as if it were a character in a story. What does it want to say?
- Reflect on a time when you felt completely at ease. What physical sensations accompanied this state? Describe these feelings with as much detail as possible, noting any changes in your breath, muscle tension, or posture.

Prompts for Identifying and Processing Emotions

- Think of an emotion that's been prominent for you lately. Where do you feel it in your body? Describe this emotion's texture, weight, and temperature as if you're explaining it to someone from another planet.

- Recall an encounter or event that triggered a strong emotional response. Write about the experience focusing on the physical sensations that arose with the emotion. How did your body react in the moment, and what did it communicate to you?
- Imagine your emotions as weather patterns in the landscape of your body. What kind of weather have you been experiencing lately? Write a weather report detailing the emotional climate, including any storms, calm periods, or unexpected changes.

Prompts for Envisioning Healing

- Visualize yourself in a state of complete healing and balance. What does this version of you look, feel, and act like? Describe your day from start to finish, focusing on the sensations and emotions that accompany this healed state.
- Write a letter to yourself from a future where you have healed from your current challenges. What words of wisdom or encouragement does your future self-have for you? What steps did they take to achieve this state of well-being?
- Reflect on a fear or barrier that feels like it's hindering your healing process. Now, imagine overcoming it. Write about this victory, focusing on how your body feels before, during, and after this breakthrough.

Prompts for Gratitude and Positive Experiences

- Start your day by listing three bodily sensations you're grateful for. These could be as simple as the warmth of your bed or the feeling of your feet on the ground. How do these sensations contribute to your sense of well-being?
- Think of a time when your body surprised you with its strength, resilience, or intuition. Write a thank-you note to your body for that moment, acknowledging its role in your life.

- Reflect on the positive experiences that your body has made possible for you. Choose one memory and dive deep into the sensations associated with it. What role did touch, taste, sight, smell, or hearing play in this positive experience?

In using these prompts, the aim is to uncover the layers of experience that reside within, to listen deeply to the whispers and shouts of your body and emotions, and to document this journey with honesty and openness.

Remember, there is no right or wrong way to respond to these prompts—the goal is to explore and discover what is true for you in your somatic journey. As you hold your pen and face the blank page, remember that this is not just about filling lines but about opening a dialogue with yourself, one that holds the potential to reveal, heal, and transform.

Body-Mind Dialogues: Writing as Conversation

In the quiet spaces where thoughts meander and emotions oscillate, there exists a potent form of communication waiting to be tapped into: the dialogue between body and mind. This conversation, often drowned out by the raucousness of daily life, holds keys to unlocking inner conflicts and maintaining a harmonious relationship between our physical and mental selves. Through the practice of writing dialogues, we can create a bridge for these two aspects of our being to converse, negotiate, and integrate.

Introducing Dialogues

If you've previously explored the practices of shadow work and inner child healing, you have most likely already tapped into the framework of this exploratory activity.

Imagine sitting at a table where both your body and mind are invited to speak, each granted the freedom to express their truths without interruption. This is the essence of body-mind dialogues. It's a method that transcends simple reflection, moving into the realm of active engagement with the various facets of our self. Here, the body might voice its exhaustion or tension, while the mind might articulate worries or dreams. The act of writing becomes the medium through which this conversation unfolds, offering new insights into our inner workings.

Guidance for Conducting Dialogues

To embark on this journey of dialogue, consider the following steps, designed to ensure authenticity and openness.

1. Set the Stage: Find a quiet spot where you feel at ease. Have your journal and pen ready, creating a space that feels inviting for this intimate conversation.
2. Invite Both Parties: Mentally extend an invitation to both your body and mind to participate in this dialogue. Acknowledge their presence and express your intention for open communication.
3. Begin the Conversation: Start with a greeting or a question. For example, you might write, "Body, how are you feeling today?" Allow the response to flow naturally onto the page, without censorship.
4. Alternate Voices: Switch between speaking as your body and as your mind. This might feel odd at first, but soon you'll find a rhythm to the exchange. Remember, this isn't about grammatical perfection but about genuine expression.
5. Explore Deeper: Don't shy away from tough topics. Use this dialogue to probe into areas of tension, discomfort, or curiosity. Ask your body why it holds stress in certain areas or inquire about the emotions lurking beneath physical sensations.

Examples of Dialogues

To illustrate, here are snippets from hypothetical dialogues that reveal the potential depth of these conversations.

Body: "My shoulders are tight with the weight of carrying burdens not mine to bear." Mind: "I recognize this. It's time we set boundaries to protect our peace."

Mind: "I'm swirling in a storm of anxiety about the future." Body: "Let's find our anchor in the breath, grounding ourselves in the now."

The goal here is to allow the mind to speak freely, without the habitual conscious "ego" chatter. With practice, the answers you seek will seem to appear instantaneously, as though spoken by your higher self or in the form of intuitive messages. This is often the result of subconscious communication. These dialogues are powerful and can illuminate the interconnectedness of physical sensations and mental states, guiding us toward understanding and action.

Reflecting on Dialogues

After engaging in a dialogue, reflection is key. This isn't about analyzing each word but rather sitting with the emotions and revelations the conversation has stirred. Consider:

- Noticing Shifts: Has the dialogue brought a sense of relief, clarity, or further questions? Sometimes, simply giving voice to our body and mind can shift our inner landscape.
- Identifying Patterns: Look for recurring themes or concerns. These patterns can signal areas in need of attention or healing.
- Planning Action: If insights call for change, sketch out gentle steps forward. Perhaps the body requests more rest, or the mind seeks creative outlets for anxiety.
- Gratitude: Finally, extend gratitude to yourself for engaging in this dialogue. Acknowledge the courage it takes to listen and the wisdom found in the conversation.

The act of keeping a written record of these dialogues is another powerful tool for self-discovery. As we continue to engage in these conversations, we cultivate a relationship with ourselves that is rooted in compassion, understanding, and unity.

Tracking Your Somatic Journey: Reflecting on Progress

On the path to healing, journaling emerges as a faithful partner. It holds the space for every nuance of progress, from the subtle shifts in bodily awareness to the profound leaps in emotional healing. This section invites you to explore journaling as a ritual of tracking and celebrating your growth, a way to map the terrain you've navigated and to illuminate the path ahead.

Journaling as a Tracking Tool

Here are a few tips to harness journaling as a tool for tracking mental, emotional and physical changes:

1. Daily Check-ins: Make it a habit to jot down how you feel each day, noting any bodily sensations or emotions that arise. Pay attention to the rhythm of your breath, the tension in your muscles, or the flutter of excitement in your belly. These daily notes become breadcrumbs, leading you through the forest of your healing process.
2. Emotional Landscapes: Whenever you find yourself riding the waves of intense emotions, turn to your journal. Document these moments with as much detail as possible, describing what triggered the emotion, how it felt in your body, and how you navigated through it.
3. Bodily Maps: Occasionally, draw a silhouette of your body in your journal and mark areas where you frequently experience sensations, be it tension, warmth, or tingling. Over time, these maps reveal patterns, showing you where emotions tend to lodge in your body and how they shift as you heal.

Identifying Patterns and Milestones

As your journal fills with entries, it will begin to reflect some patterns of your healing journey. Here's how to spot them:

• Recurring Themes: Look for emotions or sensations that appear frequently in your journal. Do certain situations or thoughts consistently trigger a knot in your stomach or a tightness in your chest? Recognizing these themes can help you identify the core issues that need attention.

• Healing Milestones: Celebrate moments when you notice a shift in your patterns. Perhaps you handled a situation that would have previously sent you into a tailspin with grace and calm. Such milestones are beacons of progress, illuminating how far you've come.

- Triggers and Responses: By tracking your triggers and how you respond to them, you can gain insights into your coping mechanisms. Over time, you'll notice shifts in your reactions, marking significant progress in your healing journey.

Reflective Questions for Journaling

To deepen your engagement with the healing process, pepper your journaling practice with reflective questions. These inquiries invite introspection, challenging you to look beyond the surface and shedding some light on your experiences. Here are a few questions to get you started:

- What sensation in my body caught my attention today, and what might it be telling me?
- When did I feel most connected to myself this week, and what was happening at that moment?
- How has my response to a familiar trigger changed over time, and what does that say about my healing process?
- In what ways have I shown kindness and patience to myself today?

Celebrating Growth

Throughout all these practices, it is vital to pause and honor your growth. These moments of celebration, whether for monumental break-throughs or the quiet victories, are the heartbeat of your journey. They will remind you that every step forward, no matter how small, is a triumph.

Gratitude Entries: Dedicate journal entries to acknowledge and express gratitude for your progress. This could be as simple as thanking yourself for taking the time to sit and breathe or for the courage to face a difficult emotion head-on.

Victory Jar: Alongside your journal, keep a victory jar. Each time you recognize a moment of growth, write it down on a piece of paper and add it to the jar. Watching it fill up over time is a powerful visual reminder of your journey.

Letters to Future Self: Write letters to your future self, celebrating the milestones you've achieved. These letters, filled with hope and pride, become time capsules of your resilience, ready to be revisited in moments of doubt.

Creative Expression: Drawing and Writing Beyond Words

Within the scope of self-discovery and healing, the act of journaling evolves into an art form when infused with creative expression. This fusion of drawing and writing opens new doors to understanding your inner world, making the intangible, tangible. Colors, shapes, and textures can intertwine with words to narrate the stories of your body and mind in a language that's uniquely yours.

Incorporating Drawing into Journaling

Drawing, sketching, or doodling in your journal serves as a powerful conduit for emotions and sensations that words can't fully capture. This visual vocabulary adds depth to your somatic explorations, offering a different dimension to your reflections. Here are ways to include this practice into your journaling:

- Start with a symbol or shape that resonates with your current physical or emotional state. It doesn't require artistic skill; it's about capturing the essence of your feelings.
- Use colors to express emotions. Warm colors might represent energy or agitation, while cool colors could signify calm or detachment. Notice how color choice reflects your inner landscape.
- Sketch the sensations in your body. A tight knot in your stomach, the flutter of anxiety in your chest, or the warmth of happiness might translate into specific images or abstract forms on the page.

These visual elements are important as they reflect a dialogue with yourself, revealing layers of your experience that might remain hidden under the surface of words alone.

Expressive Writing Techniques

Moving beyond traditional journaling, expressive or intuitive writing taps into the subconscious, allowing for a raw and unfiltered exploration of thoughts and feelings. Techniques such as stream of consciousness and poetic forms enrich this practice.

Stream of consciousness writing bypasses the analytical mind, letting thoughts and emotions flow onto the page without censorship or judgment. One way to do it involves setting a timer and writing non-stop, capturing whatever comes to mind.

You may also feel drawn to experiment with poetic forms to distill emotions and experiences into concentrated expressions. Haikus, free verse, or rhymed couplets can all convey the intensity or subtlety of your feelings in unique ways.

Combining Words and Visuals

The combination of words and visuals in your journal creates even more valuable insight into your inner space. This combination allows for a multi-layered exploration of the somatic journey, where each element enhances the other.

You can choose to annotate your drawings with words, adding context or insights that the images evoke. This could be a single word, a question, or a longer reflection. Moreover, surrounding your written entries with doodles or sketches that emerge as you write can highlight emotions or themes in your text, providing another layer of understanding. Creating pages that alternate between written entries and visual expressions is also a good idea, allowing you to notice how each mode of expression influences the other.

Encouraging Experimentation

Our path through somatic therapy is deeply personal, and the way we express and integrate this experience is equally individual. I encourage you to experiment in your journaling practice to invite a sense of play and discovery.

Try different mediums such as watercolors, ink, or collage to express various states or shifts in your somatic experience. Each medium can evoke different emotions and insights.

Rotate your journaling practice through different settings — outdoors, in a quiet room, or in a café. Notice how the change in environment influences your creative expression.

Share your journaling journey with a trusted friend or therapist. Discussing your drawings and writings can offer new perspectives and deepen your understanding of your somatic experience.

Creative journaling is a central aspect of navigating the complexities of our somatic journeys. In this practice, we find a space to honor our experiences, to see them laid out in color and form, in words that dance across the page.

TEN

TOOLS FOR TRANSFORMATION

As you step into the world of somatic therapy, you will continue to discover a variety of techniques and exercises that await, ready to cater to your personal healing needs. Your willingness to explore and experiment is the only prerequisite.

Now, let's roll up our sleeves and dive into the first tool in your kit: grounding technique cards.

Grounding Technique Cards: A DIY Toolkit

When our world feels like it's spinning too quickly, finding moments of stillness and connection can seem like a rare treasure. Grounding techniques pull us back from the tumult of our thoughts and emotions to the solid earth beneath our feet. Imagine creating a personalized toolkit, one that fits neatly in the palm of your hand, ready to offer support and steadiness whenever needed. This section guides you on crafting your own set of grounding technique cards, turning abstract concepts into tangible allies in your quest for balance and calm.

Creating Grounding Cards

The process of making these cards is as therapeutic as their use. Begin with gathering your materials - cardstock or thick paper, colored pens or markers, and any other decorations that speak to you. Each card will represent a different grounding technique, a visual and textual reminder of the tools at your disposal. Here are a few steps to get you started:

1. Decide on the Size: A deck that's easy to carry allows for spontaneous use. Consider sizing your cards to fit in a standard card holder or a small pouch.
2. Outline Your Techniques: Before you start decorating, list the grounding techniques you want to include in your deck. Aim for a variety that addresses both physical and emotional needs.
3. Design Your Cards: On one side of the card, write the name of the grounding technique. On the other, describe the practice briefly and add any visual cues or symbols that resonate with the method. This could be as simple as a calming color for a breathing exercise or a drawing of roots for a visualization technique.

Suggestions for Grounding Techniques

Your deck should reflect practices that you find personally effective. Here are some techniques you may want to include, each with its unique way of bringing you back to the present:

- Five Senses Exercise: A method that involves naming something you can see, touch, hear, smell, and taste, engaging all your senses to ground you in the now.
- Focused Breathing: Breathing deeply and slowly, with attention on the breath's path in and out of your body, can serve as a powerful anchor.
- Nature Connection: Techniques that encourage a tactile connection with the natural world, like holding a stone or visualizing roots growing from your feet into the earth.
- Muscle Relaxation: Progressive muscle relaxation, where you tense and then slowly release different muscle groups, can release physical tension and mental stress.

Using the Cards

With your deck at the ready, incorporate these cards into your daily routine or turn to them in moments of distress. They can be used in various ways:

- Daily Draw: Start or end your day by drawing a card at random, using the chosen technique as a focus for grounding.
- Situation-Specific Selection: In moments of anxiety or overwhelm, sift through your deck and choose a technique that feels most suited to your current needs.
- Shared Practice: Use the cards as a way to introduce grounding techniques to friends or family members, encouraging collective moments of calm and connection.

Personalization and Creativity

The beauty of this toolkit lies in its capacity for personalization. As you become more familiar with grounding practices, you might discover new techniques that resonate with you. Update your deck to reflect these discoveries, keeping it dynamic and aligned with your evolving needs.

Here are some ideas to infuse your cards with creativity and personal significance:

- Artistic Flair: Use colors, drawings, or symbols that hold personal meaning or simply bring you joy. The process of decorating your cards can itself be a meditative and grounding practice.
- Inspirational Quotes: If certain words or quotes inspire calm and presence for you, consider including these on your cards as additional support.
- Texture and Sensation: Incorporating textures, such as fabric swatches or embossed patterns, can add a tactile element to the cards, enhancing the grounding experience.

The creation and use of grounding technique cards embody the principle that small acts, performed with intention, can have profound impacts on our well-being. They also remind us that we already possess the tools necessary to anchor ourselves, to find moments of peace amidst the chaos. As you craft, personalize, and utilize your deck, let each card be a stepping stone back to yourself, a tangible reminder of your capacity for calm and resilience.

Movement Exploration Log: Documenting Your Dance with Trauma

In the realm of healing through somatic therapy, we know that movement holds a key role, acting as both a mirror and a map. It reflects our inner states, translating emotions and traumas into physical expressions, and guides us toward understanding and integration. The Movement Exploration Log serves as a companion in this process, offering a structured way to document your engagement with various forms of movement. This methodical approach aids in recognizing the impact of movement on your journey through trauma, enabling you to tailor your practices to your unique path toward healing.

Guidance for Movement Documentation

The log is designed to be user-friendly, encouraging regular entries without feeling like an added burden. Here's how it's structured:

- Type of Movement: Whether it's yoga, dance, walking, or another form, specify the activity. This helps in identifying which practices resonate most with you.
- Duration: Note how long you engaged in the movement. This isn't about aiming for a certain time but observing how different durations affect you.
- Emotional and Physical Responses: After each session, record any emotions that surfaced, along with physical sensations. Was there a sense of relief, joy, or perhaps discomfort? How did your body feel during and after the movement?
- Contextual Factors: Were there external factors that influenced your experience? Perhaps the time of day, your environment, or your energy level played a role.

This systematic approach helps track what you do, whilst painting a picture of how movement supports your healing.

Prompts for Reflection

To deepen your engagement with the log, reflection prompts guide you beyond mere observation, encouraging a dialogue with yourself about the nuances of each experience. Some prompts include:

- How did this movement practice shift your energy or mood?
- Did any specific memories or insights arise during or after the movement?
- How does engaging in this type of movement align with your current needs or healing goals?
- Can you identify any resistance or hesitation toward certain movements? What might this indicate?

These questions are not meant to elicit right or wrong answers but to foster a deeper understanding of your relationship with movement and its role in your healing journey.

Patterns and Preferences

Over time, the log becomes a rich source of data, revealing patterns and preferences that can inform your healing process. You may discover that certain movements consistently evoke joy and energy, while others might bring up discomfort or resistance. Recognizing these patterns is invaluable, as it guides you to practices that nourish and support you while also challenging you to confront and work through more difficult emotions or memories.

To identify these patterns, look for:

- Repetitive emotional or physical responses to specific types of movement.
- Times of day or contexts in which movement feels most beneficial.
- Any correlation between the duration of movement and its impact on your mood or energy levels.

This awareness allows you to make informed choices about which practices to incorporate more regularly into your routine and which ones to approach with caution or additional support.

Encouraging Variety

While identifying what works best for you is essential, there's also immense value in variety. Different movements can stimulate the body and mind in unique ways, offering a broader spectrum of healing opportunities.

Try experimenting with new forms of movement that you haven't tried before. If you typically engage in slow, meditative practices like yoga, try something more dynamic, like dance or martial arts.

Changing your environment is another way to embrace variety. If possible, practice movement both indoors and outdoors, noting how the change in setting influences your experience.

You could also choose to attend classes or workshops. This can introduce you to new types of movement and offer the added benefit of community support.

Whichever you choose, the goal here is to expand your expressive range, exploring various avenues of movement to uncover what facilitates the deepest healing.

Maintaining Your Somatics Routine

Creating a rhythm in life that includes somatic self-care practices can sometimes feel like trying to maintain a delicate balance. The somatic self-care checklist provides a stable center from which to balance our daily and weekly commitments with the nurturing practices our bodies and minds need.

Comprehensive Self-Care Checklist

To ensure a holistic approach, this checklist encompasses a range of practices from body scanning and grounding to movement and breathwork. It's designed to be a living document, one that evolves along with you, adaptable to your changing needs and circumstances.

My Self-Care Checklist

Morning Rituals:

1. Grounding Technique:

- Start your day by connecting with the present moment and grounding yourself. This could involve:
- Standing barefoot on the ground and feeling the support of the earth beneath you.
- Visualizing roots extending from your feet into the ground, anchoring you in stability and strength.
- Practicing grounding affirmations or mantras to affirm your presence and resilience.

2. Mindful Breathing:

- Begin your day with a few minutes of mindful breathing to cultivate inner calm and centeredness:
- Practice deep breathing exercises, such as the 4-7-8 technique or box breathing, to regulate your nervous system and reduce stress.
- Use a mindfulness app or guided meditation to guide your breathing practice and bring focus to the present moment.

Midday Moments:

1. Short Mindful Movements:

- Incorporate brief moments of mindful movement throughout your day to rejuvenate your body and mind:

- Take short breaks to stretch your body and release tension, focusing on areas of tightness or discomfort.
- Practice simple yoga poses or qigong exercises to promote flexibility and energy flow.
- Perform a quick body scan to check in with your physical sensations and address any areas of discomfort or imbalance.

2. Mindful Awareness Breaks:

- Integrate mindful awareness breaks into your daily routine to pause and reconnect with yourself amidst busy tasks:
- Take a few deep breaths and observe your surroundings without judgment, using your senses to anchor yourself in the present moment.
- Practice mindful eating by savoring each bite of your meals, paying attention to flavors, textures, and sensations.
- Engage in a brief mindfulness practice, such as a 3-minute breathing space or body scan, to reset your focus and calm your mind.

Evening Wind-Down:

1. Longer Session of Movement Practice:

- Wind down your day with a longer session of movement practice to release accumulated tension and promote relaxation:
- Engage in a gentle yoga flow or restorative yoga sequence to soothe your body and quiet your mind.
- Incorporate self-massage techniques, such as foam rolling or trigger point therapy, to release muscular tension and promote relaxation.
- Go for a leisurely walk in nature to unwind.
- Dance freely to your favorite music, allowing movement to be a form of self-expression and emotional release.

2. Dedicated Breathwork Exercise:

- End your day with a dedicated breathwork exercise to release stress and prepare for restful sleep.
- Practice abdominal breathing to activate the body's relaxation response and promote deep relaxation.
- Experiment with alternate nostril breathing to balance the left and right hemispheres of the brain and calm the nervous system.
- Use a guided breathwork meditation specifically designed for relaxation and inner peace.

Other Holistic Self-Care Practices:

1. Shadow Work:

- Dedicate time for shadow work, the process of exploring and integrating the unconscious aspects of the self:
- Journaling prompts: Reflect on your fears, insecurities, and unresolved emotions to bring them into conscious awareness and explore their underlying roots.
- Creative expression: Use art, writing, or other forms of creative expression to explore and express aspects of yourself that may have been suppressed or ignored.
- Inner dialogue: Engage in compassionate self-talk and inner dialogue to nurture acceptance and integration of all parts of yourself, including the shadow aspects.

2. Nature Connection:

- Connect with nature as a source of healing and rejuvenation:
- Spend time outdoors, whether it's a walk in the park, gardening, or simply sitting under a tree.

- Practice grounding exercises in nature, such as walking barefoot on the grass or lying down and feeling the support of the earth beneath you.
- Cultivate a sense of awe and gratitude for the natural world, observing the beauty and interconnectedness of all living beings.

3. Community and Support:

- Prioritize building and nurturing supportive relationships with others:
- Reach out to friends, family members, or support groups for emotional support and connection.
- Participate in group activities or classes that align with your interests and values, fostering a sense of belonging and community.
- Seek professional support from therapists, counselors, or coaches who can provide guidance and assistance on your self-care journey.
- Remember, it's important to listen to your body and intuition to determine which practices resonate most with you at any given time. Allow this checklist to evolve and adapt as you grow and change, continually exploring new avenues to support your overall well-being.

Customization Tips

To MAKE this checklist truly yours, consider these personalization strategies:

- Adjust the timing and duration of practices based on your schedule and energy levels. Some days might allow for a longer morning ritual, while others might require shorter, more focused exercises.
- Experiment with different techniques to discover what resonates most with you. This might mean trying various grounding methods or exploring new movement activities.

- Listen to your body and mind. They will guide you toward what practices are most needed at any given time. This intuitive approach ensures your self-care routine remains relevant and nurturing.

Reflection and Adjustment

Treating this checklist as a flexible guide rather than a rigid schedule allows for growth and adaptation. Reflection is key to this process. Weekly check-ins with yourself to assess what's working and what needs tweaking can be incredibly enlightening. Questions to consider might include:

- Which practices have become non-negotiable parts of your day or week?
- Have you noticed any shifts in your physical or emotional well-being since integrating certain practices?
- Are there techniques that no longer serve you or that you're curious to explore further?

Adjustments based on these reflections ensure your somatic self-care routine remains aligned with your evolving needs, providing a solid foundation from which to navigate life's fluctuations. With time and consistency, the act of maintaining this routine will become a meaningful ritual, a way to honor the connection between your body and mind, and to nurture the balance that sustains you.

As we wrap up this chapter, remember that the aim here is not to add more to your plate, but to slowly integrate practices that bring you back to a state of balance and harmony. Make room for moments that reconnect you with yourself, ensuring that amidst the busyness of life, you remain grounded, aware, and present.

ELEVEN
THE POWER OF COMMUNITY IN SOMATIC HEALING

As HUMAN BEINGS, we are deeply wired for connection. When we embark on a personal healing journey, opening up to others and creating connections can seem quite challenging. However, it is also a crucial time to push past this discomfort and forge meaningful connections.

Creating your own community by surrounding yourself with individuals drawn together by a commitment to self-awareness and personal development can be life changing. This becomes a space where shared experiences and collective wisdom light up the path to personal growth and recovery.

In our fast-paced world, where individual achievement often takes center stage, the power of community in the healing process can sometimes be overlooked. Yet, there's something profoundly transformative about coming together with others who understand the nuances of somatic experiences. A place of refuge, learning, and connection.

Shared Experiences Foster Healing

When someone else articulates what you've felt but haven't found the words for, it's like a light being turned on in a dark room. Suddenly, you see that you're not alone in your struggles. Group settings, whether in person or online, provide a platform for these moments of connection. They remind us that our personal battles are part of a larger narrative, one that connects the lives of many. In sharing our stories, we unburden ourselves and light the way for others.

Consider the simple act of breathing together in a guided somatic workshop. There's a rhythm, a collective pulse that synchronizes individual energies. This act, seemingly basic, can profoundly influence our sense of belonging and shared humanity. It reinforces the idea that healing isn't just an individual endeavor; it's a communal voyage.

Community as a Resource

Learning from others who've navigated similar paths can offer invaluable insights and shortcuts to our own healing. Community acts as a living library, rich with resources, strategies, and support systems. From practical advice on integrating somatic practices into daily routines to recommendations for professional help, the collective knowledge within a community is a goldmine waiting to be tapped.

For instance, within a community meeting where members share their favorite grounding techniques, one person may mention how walking barefoot on grass helps them feel present, while another talks about the calming effect of mindful baking. Each suggestion adds to a collective repository of strategies, offering new tools for managing stress and anxiety.

Likewise, a discussion group focused on polyvagal theory can uncover a multitude of ways to engage the vagus nerve for relaxation—from singing and humming to cold water face immersion. Hearing how others apply these concepts in real life can spark creativity in our healing practices, encouraging us to experiment and find what resonates with our unique needs.

There's so much wisdom in numbers. When individuals from diverse backgrounds come together, they bring unique perspectives and experiences that enrich the collective understanding of healing. This mosaic of insights can challenge our assumptions, open our minds to new possibilities, and inspire innovative approaches to somatic therapy.

Overcoming Isolation

One of the greatest challenges on the healing path is the feeling of isolation that often accompanies deep personal work. Finding a community breaks through this isolation, offering a sense of companionship and mutual support. It's comforting to know there are others who not only understand what you're going through but are also rooting for your success.

Support groups, whether focused on specific techniques like TRE (Trauma Release Exercises) or broader topics like trauma recovery, can significantly reduce feelings of loneliness. They provide a safe space to express vulnerabilities, celebrate progress, and offer encouragement during setbacks.

Community Connection Exercise

Welcome to the Community Connection Exercise, an interactive activity designed to help you reflect on your current support system, identify any gaps, and set intentions for enhancing your community connections. Grab a pen and some paper, and let's get started.

Step 1: Listing Existing Support

TAKE a few moments to jot down the names of people and groups who currently provide support in your life. This could include:

- Friends
- Family members
- Therapists or counselors
- Support groups (e.g., recovery groups, hobby clubs)
- Online communities

Write down as many as you can think of, no matter how big or small their role may seem.

_____

_____

_____

_____

_____

_____

_____

_____

_____

_____

_____

_____

Step 2: Identifying Gaps

Now, consider areas where you feel there might be a lack of support or connection in your life. Reflect on aspects like:

- Emotional support
- Practical assistance (e.g., help with tasks or responsibilities)
- Intellectual stimulation
- Spiritual guidance
- Social interaction

Write down any areas where you feel you could benefit from additional support or connection.

_____

_____

_____

_____

_____

_____

_____

_____

_____

_____

_____

Step 3: Setting Intentions

BASED ON YOUR REFLECTIONS, set some actionable intentions for enhancing your community connections. Consider steps like:

- Reaching out to someone new for support or companionship
- Joining a local club or group related to your interests or hobbies
- Seeking out a mentor or counselor who aligns with your goals and values
- Volunteering in your community to connect with others and contribute to a cause you believe in

Write down at least one intention that feels achievable and meaningful to you. Feel free to brainstorm additional ideas as well.

_____

_____

_____

_____

_____

_____

_____

_____

_____

_____

_____

_____

Take a moment to review what you've written and to acknowledge the support that already exists in your life. Try to recognize any areas where you'd like to cultivate more connections. Remember, building community is an ongoing process, and it's okay to start small. By taking intentional steps to enhance your community connections, you're investing in your own well-being and creating a stronger support network for yourself.

Feel free to revisit this exercise whenever you feel the need to reassess your community connections and set new intentions for growth. Your support system is a valuable resource on your healing journey.

Online Forums and Groups: Connecting Virtually

In a world where digital landscapes stretch far and wide, online forums and groups present a unique opportunity. Spanning across geographical divides, they bring together individuals passionate about somatic therapy from all corners of the globe. The virtual world holds space for experiences, thoughts, and support, available at the click of a button.

Accessing Global Support

Imagine tapping into a wellspring of collective knowledge and empathy that spans continents. Online forums and groups dedicated to somatic therapy provide this exact opportunity. Here, you can find others who share your interests, challenges, and aspirations. Whether you're seeking advice, looking to share your own journey, or simply wanting to feel understood, these virtual communities can be a rich resource. They offer a sense of belonging that transcends physical boundaries, creating a global support network that's accessible anytime, from anywhere.

Finding the Right Fit

With the vast array of online communities available, finding one that resonates with your specific needs and values is crucial. Here are some tips to guide your search:

- Research: Start by exploring various platforms known for hosting supportive communities, such as Reddit, Facebook, or specialized forums. Look for groups that focus on somatic therapy, trauma recovery, or holistic healing.
- Read the Room: Spend some time lurking in potential groups. Observe the interactions, the types of posts, and the overall tone. Does it feel welcoming? Is there a sense of mutual respect and understanding?

- Privacy Matters: Consider the privacy policies of the forum or group. Some might be open, while others may require approval to join. Decide what level of privacy you're comfortable with, especially when it comes to sharing personal experiences.
- Trial and Error: Don't hesitate to join a few groups to get a feel for them. You can always leave if they don't meet your expectations. Finding your virtual tribe might take some time, but it's worth the effort.

Engaging Safely

While online forums and groups offer invaluable support, navigating them safely is paramount. Here are guidelines to ensure your virtual interactions remain positive and secure:

- Protect Your Information: Be mindful of the personal details you share. Use discretion when discussing sensitive aspects of your healing journey, and consider the potential implications of sharing identifiable information.
- Respect Boundaries: Just as in face-to-face interactions, respecting others' boundaries online is essential. Engage with empathy and kindness, and avoid offering unsolicited advice.
- Digital Etiquette: Remember the human behind the screen. The anonymity of the internet can sometimes lead to misunderstandings. Strive for clear communication and assume positive intent whenever possible.
- Seek Credible Sources: When exchanging resources or advice, prioritize information from reputable sources. This ensures the guidance you receive and offer is based on sound principles and practices.

Maximizing Virtual Connections

To transform your online interactions into meaningful connections, consider these strategies:

- Active Participation: Contribute to discussions, ask questions, and share insights. Active engagement helps build rapport with other members, making the experience more fulfilling.
- Virtual Meetups: Some groups organize virtual meetups or workshops. Participating in these events can deepen your connection with the community and provide opportunities for real-time interaction.
- Peer Support: Look for opportunities to offer or receive one-on-one support. Many forums have mechanisms for connecting members seeking individualized advice or companionship on their healing journey.
- Celebrate Milestones: Share your progress and celebrate the achievements of others. Recognizing growth and milestones fosters a positive environment and encourages continued engagement.

In the digital age, the quest for connection and understanding in the realm of somatic healing need not be a solitary one. Online forums and groups offer a platform for collective wisdom, empathy, and support that can significantly enrich your healing process. By approaching these virtual communities with mindfulness, respect, and a willingness to engage, you open the door to a world of connections.

Local Somatic Therapy Groups: Finding Your Tribe

The warmth of real-life connections, the energy of shared physical space, and the tangible support from local communities hold a unique charm in the healing process. When you step into a room with others who are on similar paths, the air fills with an unspoken understanding and empathy that digital platforms can struggle to replicate. This section sheds light on the significance of local somatic therapy groups, offering insights into discovering these communities and making the most of the invaluable support they provide.

The Advantages of Local Groups

Local somatic therapy groups offer a sanctuary where healing practices are discussed and experienced collectively. The live interaction and immediate feedback elevate the learning process, allowing for a deeper immersion in somatic practices. Here, the nuanced guidance from facilitators and the spontaneous sharing of insights add layers to your understanding that solo practice or virtual groups might miss. Being physically present with others also fosters a stronger bond, making every session an opportunity to build lasting support networks that extend beyond therapy sessions.

Resources for Finding Local Somatic Therapy Groups

Discovering a local group that feels right can be like finding a hidden gem. It requires some searching, but the rewards are well worth the effort. Start with:

- Community Centers and Wellness Clinics: Often, these local hubs host or can connect you to ongoing somatic therapy groups. They might also offer workshops or introductory sessions to give you a taste of different practices.
- Online Directories and Websites: Many professional somatic therapists and facilitators advertise their groups on dedicated websites or through therapy directories. A quick search can reveal options in your vicinity, complete with reviews and ratings to help you make an informed choice.
- Social Media and Local Forums: Local community boards on platforms like Facebook or Nextdoor can be surprisingly resourceful. Members often share information on upcoming group sessions or can direct you to known facilitators in the area.

Tips for Active Participation

Once you've found a group that resonates with you, diving in with an open heart can significantly amplify your experience. Consider:

- Volunteering: Offer to help with organizing sessions or events. It's a great way to deepen your engagement with the group and show your commitment.
- Sharing Your Journey: When comfortable, share your experiences and insights. Your story could be the encouragement or breakthrough moment for someone else.
- Practicing Regularly: Consistency strengthens your connection to the group and enhances the benefits of somatic practices. Try to attend sessions regularly, making them a priority in your schedule.

Local somatic therapy groups offer a unique blend of personal growth, shared healing, and community building. By actively participating in these groups, you can tap into a collective strength. Whether through community centers, online platforms, or social media, finding your tribe is a step towards not just individual healing but also towards contributing to a larger ecosystem of support and understanding. Make your journey less solitary and more interconnected.

Creating Your Own Support Group

So, you've decided to take the lead and start your group.

Now what?

Before you call the first meeting or send out an invitation, take a moment to reflect on the group's purpose. What do you hope to achieve? Is it to explore specific somatic practices, offer support for personal healing, or share knowledge and experiences? Writing down these intentions can guide the group's direction and ensure that activities align with these foundational goals.

- Define the group's focus: Be clear whether the group will concentrate on general somatic therapy practices or if it will cater to specific interests or needs, such as stress reduction or trauma recovery.
- Establish core values: What principles will your group embody? Consider inclusivity, confidentiality, respect, and mutual support as potential cornerstones.

- Set realistic expectations: Understand that the group will evolve over time. Flexibility and openness to change can help manage expectations for yourself and future members.

Finding Members and Creating a Safe Space

With your intentions set, the next step is to invite others to join your garden of growth. Finding members who share your interest in somatic therapy can begin within your existing networks or by reaching out to broader communities.

- Reach out to your network: Start with friends, family, or acquaintances who have expressed interest in somatic therapy or personal growth. Personal invitations can make individuals feel valued and welcomed.
- Utilize social media and community boards: Post in relevant online forums, community boards, or social media groups. Be clear about the group's intentions and whom it's for.
- Choose a conducive meeting space: Whether it's a quiet room in a community center, a private home, or a tranquil outdoor space, ensure the environment feels safe, welcoming, and suitable for group activities.

A crucial aspect of creating a conducive environment is establishing ground rules that prioritize safety and confidentiality. These rules should be discussed and agreed upon by all members from the outset.

Facilitating Group Dynamics

Dynamics within a support group require much care and attention. Facilitating a group where every member feels heard, valued, and connected involves several key practices:

- Foster open communication: Encourage members to share their thoughts, feelings, and experiences. Active listening and empathy should be promoted as fundamental group behaviors.

- Manage conflicts with care: Disagreements or misunderstandings may arise. Address these openly and constructively, aiming to strengthen the group rather than divide it.
- Celebrate diversity: Acknowledge and embrace the varied backgrounds, experiences, and perspectives within the group. This diversity can enrich the learning and healing process for everyone.

Organizing Group Activities

Activities are the heart of the support group, providing shared experiences that can deepen connections and facilitate healing. When planning activities, consider the group's intentions and the interests of its members.

Shared practices: Regularly include somatic exercises, such as guided body scans, mindful movement, or breathing techniques that members can experience together.

Guest speakers: Invite somatic therapists, experienced practitioners, or experts in related fields to share their knowledge and insights with the group.

Group discussions: Allocate time for members to discuss topics related to somatic therapy, personal growth, or healing. These discussions can foster a sense of community and collective wisdom.

Sustaining the Group Over Time

For a support group to thrive, it requires ongoing care and attention. Here are strategies to ensure its longevity and vitality:

- Leadership rotation: Consider rotating the facilitator role among members. This can distribute responsibility, offer varied perspectives, and keep the group dynamic fresh.
- Member engagement: Regularly check in with members about their needs, interests, and suggestions for the group. This feedback can guide adjustments and improvements.

- Scheduled check-ins: Establish periodic meetings to reflect on the group's progress, revisit intentions, and make any necessary changes to its direction or structure.

Creating your own somatic therapy support group is an opportunity to bring individuals together in pursuit of healing, growth, and connection. By setting clear intentions, fostering a supportive environment, and nurturing the group's development, you can cultivate a space where members feel empowered to explore somatic practices and share their journeys.

CONCLUSION

As WE PREPARE to close this chapter—not just of the book but of our initial foray together into the transformative world of somatic therapy—I find myself reflecting on the beauty and complexity of this journey. Somatic therapy, with its profound capacity to heal and integrate the mind, body, and spirit, reflects the deeply personal yet universally relevant path toward holistic healing. It is a journey as unique as each leaf on a tree, yet as connected as the forest they form.

Throughout these pages, we've navigated the core principles of somatic therapy, emphasizing the importance of body awareness, the grounding influence of mindfulness, the liberating power of movement, the nurturing practice of developing a somatic self-care routine, and the unparalleled support found within a community.

The key takeaways, I hope, are as vivid in your mind as they are in mine: the inextricable link between mind, body, and spirit; the profound wisdom our bodies hold; and the empowerment that blossoms from engaging with somatic practices. Together, we've unveiled the transformative potential of somatic therapy to not only release trauma and alleviate anxiety but to guide us toward a profound sense of inner peace.

I urge you, dear reader, to continue this exploration beyond the confines of this book. The journey to healing and self-discovery is not a destination but a continuous path, enriched with new practices, insights, and the ever-present potential for growth and change. Dive deeper, experiment with courage, and embrace the evolution of your healing practice with an open heart.

Remember, the significance of community and support in our healing journey cannot be overstated. Whether through virtual connections, local gatherings, or the shared space of professional therapy, finding your tribe offers a wellspring of understanding and encouragement. Healing, in many ways, is a shared journey, illuminated by the collective wisdom and compassion of those we walk with.

And so, I call upon you to take charge of your healing journey. Let the tools, insights, and practices shared in these pages guide you toward empowerment. Somatic therapy is not merely a method for healing; it is a call to live more fully, more authentically, embracing the full spectrum of human experience.

I acknowledge that this path is not without its challenges. There will be moments of doubt, of regression, of feeling lost in the wilderness of our own healing. Yet, it is in these moments that our resilience shines brightest. Your courage to embark on this journey, to face the shadows and seek the light, is a testament to the strength of the human spirit.

Thank you for your trust, your openness, and your willingness to explore the realms of somatic therapy. I am most grateful for your companionship on this journey. Remember, you are never alone. There is a world of support, understanding, and love waiting to embrace you.

As we part ways, I invite you to view somatic therapy not just as a series of practices but as a holistic approach to life. Integrate its principles into your daily existence to form a continuous, sacred connection between your mind, body, and soul. Let this book be a starting point, a springboard into a life lived with depth, awareness, and an unshakeable connection to the essence of who you are.

MAY your journey be filled with discovery, healing, and an abundance of peace.

BONUS 1: SOMATIC HEALING JOURNAL PROMPTS

———

Exploring Physical Anchors of Emotion

Choose an emotion you've felt recently. Where in your body do you feel this emotion most intensely? Describe the physical sensations associated with this emotion in as much detail as possible.

_____

_____

_____

_____

_____

_____

_____

_____

_____

_____

_____

_____

Mapping Emotional Triggers

Think about a recent situation that triggered a strong emotional response. What physical reactions accompanied these emotions? How did your body posture or sensations change with your feelings?

_____

_____

_____

_____

_____

_____

_____

_____

_____

_____

_____

_____

The Dialogue Between Body and Mind

Reflect on a day this past week. Write a conversation between your body and your mind about how they experienced the day differently. What might each say about the other's response to stress or joy?

_____

_____

_____

_____

_____

_____

_____

_____

_____

_____

_____

_____

Revisiting a Past Experience

Think of a significant event from your past and focus on remembering how your body felt during this event. What do those sensations tell you about your emotional state at that time?

_____

_____

_____

_____

_____

_____

_____

_____

_____

_____

_____

_____

Sensory Walk

Take a short walk and focus solely on your bodily sensations with each step. After your walk, journal about the experience. What did you notice that you normally overlook?

_____

_____

_____

_____

_____

_____

_____

_____

_____

_____

_____

Breath as a Pathway

Sit quietly and focus on your breathing for a few minutes. How does the rhythm of your breath change with different thoughts or emotions? Write about the connection you observe between your breathing patterns and your current state of mind.

_____

_____

_____

_____

_____

_____

_____

_____

_____

_____

_____

_____

Physical Manifestations of Joy and Pain

Identify one moment of joy and one of pain from your life. Describe how each was manifested physically in your body. How did your environment, thoughts, or actions influence these sensations?

_____

_____

_____

_____

_____

_____

_____

_____

_____

_____

_____

_____

The Story of a Scar

If you have a physical scar, write about the incident that caused it, focusing on the bodily sensations before, during, and after the event. How does this physical scar connect to your emotional ones?

_____

_____

_____

_____

_____

_____

_____

_____

_____

_____

_____

_____

Chronic Tensions and Their Tales

Consider any chronic tension or pain in your body. What emotions might be linked to these persistent sensations? Explore possible events or unresolved feelings contributing to this state.

_____

_____

_____

_____

_____

_____

_____

_____

_____

_____

_____

_____

Healing Through Movement

Engage in a gentle form of movement that you enjoy (e.g., yoga, stretching, dancing). Reflect on how your emotional and physical states shift with movement. What does this tell you about your body's needs and your emotional wellbeing?

_____

_____

_____

_____

_____

_____

_____

_____

_____

_____

_____

_____

_____

BONUS 2: BODY SCAN REFLECTION TEMPLATE

Date/Time: _____

Current Mood: _____

Physical Manifestation of Emotion:

- Head: _____
- Shoulders: _____
- Chest: _____
- Arms: _____
- Stomach: _____
- Legs: _____

Emotional State: _____

Associated Thoughts/Memories:

_____

Overall Reflection:

_____
_____
_____
_____
_____
_____
_____
_____
_____
_____
_____
_____
_____

VOLUME TWO

LEAVE A REVIEW

Don't forget to share the love and **leave your Amazon review** for:

The Polyvagal Theory Handbook

Nervous system regulation is health in motion.

Your nervous system fuels your immune system, hormonal system, and digestive system.

DR. LINNEA PASSALER

PREFACE

I SAT ON MY PORCH, the evening sun casting a warm, golden glow over my garden. Birds chirped softly, and a gentle breeze rustled the leaves of the old oak tree nearby. As I sipped my herbal tea, the warm liquid calming my mind and body, I reflected on my day, feeling a deep sense of peace and contentment that had eluded me for years.

For as long as I could remember, I had battled with anxiety. The ever-increasing demands of my high-pressure job, combined with the complex responsibilities of adulthood, often left me feeling overwhelmed. Despite trying various methods to manage my stress—meditation, yoga, even medication—nothing seemed to offer lasting relief.

One particularly stressful afternoon, I found myself – once again - in the throes of a panic attack. My heart raced, my breathing became shallow, and my mind spun with worry. I knew all the habitual steps to calm down, however, this time, nothing was working. That's when, desperate for comfort, I instinctively placed my hand on my chest and began to hum softly. To my surprise, I felt a wave of calm wash over me.

Curious about this unexpected relief, I started to pay closer attention to the small, seemingly insignificant actions I took when I felt anxious. I noticed that I often hummed to myself while cooking dinner, sang in the shower, or massaged the sides of my neck when I felt tense. These habits, though subconscious, seemed to have an immediate impact on my well-being.

Intrigued, I delved into research about the body's stress response and stumbled upon the concept of the vagus nerve—a critical component of the parasympathetic nervous system that helps regulate the body's response to stress. The more I read, the more I realized that my intuitive actions aligned with techniques known to stimulate the vagus nerve and promote relaxation.

I learned that humming and singing create vibrations that stimulate the vagus nerve, promoting a deep sense of calm. Similarly, gentle neck massages can activate pressure points that help soothe the nervous system. I discovered that these practices, in conjunction with somatic therapy, were powerful tools for regulating my nervous system and effectively managing stress.

With this newfound knowledge, I began to incorporate these techniques more intentionally into my daily routine. I started my mornings with deep breathing exercises and stretches, took mindful walks in my garden during lunch breaks, and ended my days with soothing neck massages and gentle meditative humming before bed.

As weeks turned into months, a remarkable transformation began to take place. My anxiety levels decreased, and I felt more grounded and resilient. I handled the challenges of my job with greater ease and found joy in my daily interactions with my colleagues, family, and friends. The sense of peace and contentment that had once been fleeting now felt like a constant companion.

One evening, as I shared my journey with a close friend, I grasped the extent of the infinite wisdom in listening to my body's intuitive signals. "It's as if my body knew what I needed all along," I said with a smile. "I just had to pay attention and trust myself." My friend, moved by my story, decided to explore these techniques for herself. As I watched her embark on a similar path of self-discovery and healing, I felt a deep sense of gratitude. I had not only found a way to soothe and comfort myself but had also inspired others to do the same.

This part of my journey was one step – albeit a crucial one - in my understanding of intuition and the body's innate ability to heal. By tuning into my natural instincts and embracing the wisdom of the vagus nerve, I had unlocked a pathway to lasting peace and well-being—one gentle hum at a time.

I hope that within these pages, you'll find comfort and peace in discovering a deeply soothing practice that reinvigorates your mind &

body every single day. I also hope that you will come to release your hold on every fleeting worry, tapping into the power of your body's innate ability to heal and restore.

INTRODUCTION

A FEW YEARS AGO, I met a woman named Emily at a workshop on trauma recovery. She had endured years of chronic anxiety and debilitating panic attacks. Her body was tense, her eyes constantly darted around the room, and she struggled to find a sense of safety. Emily had tried countless therapies, but nothing seemed to provide lasting relief. Through support-group connections, she discovered the power of Polyvagal Theory and vagus nerve exercises. This took some time, knowledge, and practice; however, slowly, she began to feel shifts in her body and mind. Her nervous system, once trapped in a state of constant alarm, started to find moments of calm.

It was, in large part, Emily's journey that inspired me to dive into the world of PVT, reinforcing my then developing belief in the transformative potential of this approach.

This book aims to provide you with a comprehensive, user-friendly guide to understanding and applying Polyvagal Theory principles. The tools presented in the following chapters are evidence-based practices that have been proven to aid in trauma recovery, reduce anxiety, decrease inflammation and psychosomatic ailments, promote nervous system regulation and support overall health. Whether you are new to these concepts or have some familiarity, the pages in this handbook are sure to unveil a new layer of valuable insights and practical methods to support your holistic healing journey.

What makes this tool unique is its dual nature as both a guide and a workbook. It not only explains the foundational concepts of Polyvagal Theory, but also offers actionable exercises that you can integrate into your daily life. Starting with the basics of Polyvagal Theory, we will dive into the mechanics of the vagus nerve and its role in the body, exploring a variety of techniques for self-regulation and nervous system reset.

Each chapter will offer a combination of informative content, practical exercises, and reflection prompts. This is my preferred approach as it ensures that you can actively engage with the material and apply what you learn in a meaningful way. I encourage you to dive in fully, completing the exercises at your own pace, with positive intent and an open mind. Take your time with each section. Reflect on what you learn and how it applies to your life. The more you put into this process, the more you will get out of it.

Organized to guide you through a progressive journey, each chapter will build upon the previous one, allowing you to deepen your understanding and skills over time. Don't be surprised to find a certain amount of repetition, particularly when it comes to PVT technical concepts. This is a very intentional aspect of this work, as our brain requires repeated exposure to information in order to strengthen neural pathways. Each time you revisit a concept, you will reinforce the connections between neurons, making it easier to recall and apply that knowledge when needed. Repetition will help deepen your understanding and establish new habits, whether it's practicing mindfulness, setting boundaries, or engaging in self-compassion. Over time, unfamiliar Polyvagal concepts and practices will become second nature. Moreover, this structure ensures that you will not feel overwhelmed and can take steady steps toward your healing goals.

Now, I truly do understand the complexity and uniqueness of the experiences and challenges many of us face with trauma, anxiety, and stress. I have dedicated much of my life to understanding, studying and practicing trauma-informed therapies. My background in education, psychology, as well as work in the health & fitness industry have given me a deeper understanding of how the mind and body are interconnected. This continues to drive my commitment to trauma-informed practices, as I have seen firsthand the incredible impact they can have on our lives. My hope is that this book will open your eyes to the power of sensory experiences and empower you with the knowledge and tools for self-regulation. You are certainly not alone on your quest to mind and body health, and this handbook can be an important resource to add to your arsenal and support you every step of the way.

At the end of this book, you will find a glossary, which I recommend reading at least once before you begin, especially if you are unfamiliar with the jargon surrounding Polyvagal Theory. This will allow you to integrate some of the vocabulary while having a simple reference guide to understand and apply the many PVT techniques presented in this work. By the end of this book, you should possess a well-founded toolkit of strategies and exercises that you can use to navigate life's challenges with greater ease and resilience.

So, dear reader, I invite you to take this step on your healing journey with confidence and hope. The path to trauma recovery and harmonious allostasis is not always easy, but it is one worth taking. Together, we are about to explore the incredible power of healing with the vagus nerve, unlocking the potential for a healthier, more balanced life.

The adventure awaits, and I am honored to be your guide.

ONE
UNDERSTANDING POLYVAGAL THEORY

Emily's story isn't unique.

Many women live with unrelenting anxiety, feeling as if their bodies are constantly on high alert. However, what is often underplayed is how this heightened state goes beyond the mental experience, manifesting in physical symptoms—racing heart, tense muscles, and a sense of impending doom. Understanding why this happens and how to change it can transform your life. This chapter is an introduction to Polyvagal Theory, the groundbreaking framework that explains how our nervous system responds to safety and threat, offering hope and practical solutions for those living with trauma, anxiety, and chronic stress.

The Basics of Polyvagal Theory

Dr. Stephen Porges, a distinguished neuroscientist, developed Polyvagal Theory after decades of research into how the autonomic nervous system (ANS) regulates psychological and physiological states. His groundbreaking work has provided the scientific community with significant revelations about the connection between the mind and body. Dr. Porges' journey began with a curiosity about how the nervous system influences behavior, particularly in social contexts and trauma recovery. His research revealed that the vagus nerve, the tenth cranial nerve, plays a pivotal role in regulating our responses to stress and safety.

Historically, the study of the nervous system focused primarily on the sympathetic (fight or flight) and parasympathetic (rest and digest) branches. While these models offered some understanding, they lacked the depth needed to explain the complex responses observed in trauma survivors. Polyvagal Theory introduced a new perspective by highlighting the vagus nerve's role in these responses. The theory was first published in scientific literature in the mid-1990s and has since revolutionized our understanding of trauma, stress, and emotional regulation.

Polyvagal Theory's significance in modern trauma therapy cannot be overstated. It provides a model for understanding how our body's physiological state affects our behavior and emotions, and has been instrumental in developing therapeutic approaches that address not only the mind but also the body, offering a more holistic path to healing. At its core, Polyvagal Theory explains that the vagus nerve is a key player in how we respond to our environment. Also known as the "wandering nerve," the vagus runs from the brainstem through the neck and thorax to the abdomen, influencing various organs along the way.

For self-help and personal growth, PVT offers practical tools to manage stress and improve emotional health. By learning to recognize and influence your ANS states, you will become much more self-aware and develop personalised methods to deal with negative triggers, intentionally and progressively easily regulating your nervous system.

In therapeutic settings, the knowledge of Polyvagal Theory helps clinicians create environments that promote safety and trust. Furthermore, as we will also explore in depth, techniques such as vagal nerve exercises, mindfulness practices, and body-based therapies can help clients shift from states of anxiety or shutdown to a more regulated state.

The Role of the Vagus Nerve in Emotional Regulation

The vagus nerve, also known as cranial nerve X, is the longest nerve in the body. Its journey starts in the brainstem, specifically the medulla oblongata, and extends down through the neck, chest, and abdomen. Along its path, it connects with major organs, including the heart, lungs, and digestive tract, playing a central role in various bodily functions. In fact, the incredible wandering nerve is like a superhighway of communication between the brain and the body, transmitting signals that regulate heart rate, breathing, digestion, and even immune responses, all of which are linked to our emotional states. Therefore, its role extends far beyond mere physiological control; it plays a pivotal part in how we experience, process, and regulate emotions. When we encounter stress, the sympathetic nervous system triggers an immediate response: the heart rate increases, breathing becomes shallow, and muscles tense up, preparing the body to react. In contrast, activation of the vagus nerve engages the parasympathetic nervous system, which slows the heart rate, deepens breathing, and induces a sense of calm, effectively counterbalancing stress responses. This vagal activity allows the maintenance of emotional stability, enabling us to recover quickly from stressors and return to a state of equilibrium.

Its dual branches, the ventral and dorsal vagal pathways, serve different functions. The ventral vagal branch is associated with social engagement and relaxation, while the dorsal vagal branch is linked to immobilization and shutdown during extreme stress. Together, these help maintain balance in the body's autonomic nervous system, particularly within the parasympathetic nervous system, which is responsible for rest and digest functions.

Considering that its main job is to help maintain balance between the body and mind during stimulating experiences, the vagus nerve has a significant influence on our well-being. Vagal tone, which refers to the activity of the vagus nerve, is a critical factor in how our bodies respond to stress and relaxation. The vagus nerve connects to the brain's emotional centers, including the amygdala and prefrontal cortex, which play key roles in processing emotions and stress responses. When vagal tone is high, the body can easily switch from a state of stress to a state of relaxation, promoting calm and reducing anxiety. We will look at this in further detail, but for the time being, keep in mind that high vagal tone is associated with a greater ability to regulate emotions and lower levels of stress.

Case Study: Vagus Nerve in Action

Meet Sarah, a 35-year-old woman who has always struggled with anxiety, particularly in social situations. Like many of us, she often finds herself overwhelmed by sudden waves of panic—her heart races, her breathing quickens, and a sense of dread washes over her, leaving her feeling trapped and powerless. After years of trying to manage her anxiety with limited success, Sarah was introduced to deep diaphragmatic breathing.

During one particularly challenging day, Sarah felt the familiar grip of anxiety as she prepared to speak at a work presentation. Her palms began to sweat, her mind raced, her entire being teetered on the brink of panic. However, this time, she paused and inhaled for an initial deep, slow breath, allowing the air to settle deeply into her diaphragm. Exhaling slowly with a gentle hum, she repeated this technique several times.

It wasn't long before she felt her heart rate slow, the tension in her muscles ease, and her mind become clearer. A switch had been flipped—her body shifted from a state of high alert to one of calm attentiveness. Sarah's body was no longer solely reacting to external stressors; instead, she actively engaged her vagus nerve to shift her physiological state, influencing her emotional response. The intense anxiety that initially controlled her now felt manageable, and she completed her presentation with newfound confidence and poise.

Through this vagal stimulation technique also known as belly breathing, Sarah was able to activate her parasympathetic nervous system by intentionally stimulating her vagus nerve. The simple act of focusing on our breath's rhythm can appease the mind; however, deep breath work, with the unique addition of humming, is a very powerful method of hacking our ANS. Humming is highly effective as it causes gentle vibrations in the vocal cords, which are connected to branches of the vagus nerve, therefore driving the activation of the parasympathetic nervous system. Humming is a simple, soothing action that provides almost immediate results; there is no doubt that it is a powerful technique when it comes to regulating emotional responses with the vagus.

Polyvagal Theory and the Autonomic Nervous System

To fully appreciate Polyvagal Theory, it helps to understand the structure of the autonomic nervous system (ANS). The ANS is like the body's autopilot, managing functions we rarely think about such as heart rate, digestion, and respiratory rate. It consists of two main branches: the sympathetic and the parasympathetic nervous systems. The sympathetic nervous system is often described as the "fight or flight" system. Imagine being startled by a loud noise; your heart races, your muscles tense, and you become hyper-alert. This is your sympathetic nervous system kicking into gear, preparing you to either confront the threat or escape it. On the other hand, the parasympathetic nervous system is responsible for "rest and digest" activities. This system helps your body relax after stress, slowing your heart rate and promoting digestion and other restorative processes. The enteric nervous system, often called the "second brain," is another crucial part of the ANS. It is a complex network of neurons that that governs the gastrointestinal tract, therefore operating independently to regulate digestion. The ENS operates independently from the central nervous system, although it communicates closely with the brain via the vagus nerve. Furthermore, it plays a significant role in modulating mood and emotional states, as it produces neurotransmitters like serotonin and dopamine, which affect overall mental health.

Polyvagal Theory redefines our understanding of the ANS by introducing a hierarchical organization. At the top of this hierarchy is the ventral vagal complex, which fosters feelings of safety and social engagement; when we feel safe and connected, the ventral vagal state is at work. Below this is the sympathetic nervous system, which mobilizes the body for fight or flight responses. And, at the bottom, we find the dorsal vagal complex, responsible for immobilization or shutdown in extreme stress situations. One fascinating aspect of this hierarchy is that it reflects how our nervous system has evolved over time.

It was Dr. Porges, through his development of PVT, who significantly expanded our understanding of the dorsal vagal state by highlighting its role in the hierarchical organization of the autonomic nervous system. He identified the dorsal vagal complex as the most primitive branch of the vagus nerve, emphasizing its function as part of a three-tiered response system that includes the sympathetic nervous system (fight or flight) and the ventral vagal complex (social engagement and calm states). Early vertebrates relied primarily on the dorsal vagal system for survival, but as mammals evolved, the ventral vagal system developed to support social bonds and more complex social structures. When activated, the dorsal vagal complex triggers a shutdown or "freeze" response, characterized by reduced heart rate, slowed metabolism, and decreased energy levels, which can manifest as feelings of numbness, dissociation, or immobilization. This state is thought to be an ancient defense mechanism, similar to playing dead, helping the body conserve energy and protect itself when fight or flight responses are not viable options. While it can be protective in life-threatening situations, we know that prolonged activation of the dorsal vagal state can lead to maladaptive responses, contributing to conditions like depression, chronic fatigue, and feelings of emotional disconnection.

The interplay between these three states is a dynamic process that our bodies navigate constantly. Imagine you're in a calm state, feeling safe and connected. Suddenly, a loud noise – perhaps ambulance sirens - triggers your sympathetic nervous system, shifting you into a state of alertness. If a threat persists, escalates, or becomes overwhelming (often when perceived as life-threatening) your body might transition into the dorsal vagal state, leading to feelings of numbness or disconnection. Neuroception plays a central role in these transitions; like an internal radar, it is continuously scanning our environment for cues of safety or danger. Chronic stress can severely impact these transitions, often keeping us trapped in a heightened state of alertness or a prolonged state of shutdown. This can make it challenging to return to a state of calm, even when the immediate threat has passed.

Understanding the ANS and its hierarchical organization has practical implications for managing emotional and physiological responses. Recognizing the signs of state shifts will help you check-in and intervene before becoming overwhelmed. For example, noticing an increased heart rate or shallow breathing can be a cue to engage in practices to transition into a ventral vagal state.

Stress Response Mechanisms

Our various stress response mechanisms showcase the diverse ways our body and mind adapt to perceived danger, illustrating both the complexity of human survival strategies and the deep impact of trauma on behavior and emotional regulation. Here is a rundown of some of the ways in which our bodies respond to varying degrees of stress and perceived threat, as well as how they reflect the workings of the ANS and vagus nerve.

FIGHT-OR-FLIGHT

The fight-or-flight response is primarily related to the sympathetic nervous system (SNS), not directly the vagus nerve. However, within the context of vagal pathways, the vagus plays a key role in balancing the fight-or-flight response through its parasympathetic functions. In fact, this instinctive reaction to perceived danger is central to the traditional stress response model, in which the sympathetic nervous system is activated to prepare for immediate action. When faced with a threat, the body releases adrenaline and cortisol, increasing heart rate, blood pressure, and blood flow to the muscles while shutting down non-essential functions like digestion. The goal is to either confront the threat (fight) or escape from it (flight). This response is characterized by heightened alertness, quickened breathing, muscle tension, and a surge of energy, allowing us to respond swiftly and decisively to danger.

The fight-or-flight response is largely governed by the SNS, which means that the vagus nerve's role is primarily in regulating and bringing the body back to a state of calm and balance through its parasympathetic actions, particularly after the immediate stressor is no longer present.

FREEZE

The "shutdown" or immobilization response is associated with the dorsal vagal complex, the more primitive, unmyelinated branch of the vagus nerve. This response is deeply rooted in our evolutionary past, serving as a survival strategy seen in many animals when escaping or fighting is not an option. The instinctive freeze reaction occurs when our nervous system becomes overwhelmed while faced with an extreme (potentially perceived) threat, making our body enter a state of immobility. Unlike fight or flight, where our body is pushed to take action, the freeze response leads to physical stillness, a decrease in heart rate, and a numbing or dissociative feeling. This response can be adaptive in situations where remaining motionless reduces visibility to predators or threats. As the dorsal vagal complex suppresses sensory and emotional experiences to protect us from pain or psychological overwhelm, common signs include feeling stuck, dissociative experiences, emotional numbness, feeling disconnected from our environment, a sense of time slowing down, and an inability to move or speak. Basically, the freeze response is our body's ancient, automatic strategy for dealing with extreme stress, prioritizing survival by shutting down non-essential functions, often leaving us feeling helpless or paralyzed, both physically and mentally.

. . .

Fawn

The fawn response is primarily related to the ventral vagal complex of the vagus nerve. The ventral vagal pathway (*ventral* meaning *front*) is responsible for social engagement, connection, and safety, and it is the part of the nervous system that manages adaptive social behaviors in response to perceived threats. When faced with a threat, especially interpersonal, the fawn response activates behaviors that aim to appease, comply with or please others to prevent conflict and maintain safety. This is often developed in situations where resistance or escape seems impossible, such as in abusive relationships. The individual will seek to reduce danger by being overly accommodating, submissive, or people-pleasing, often at the expense of their own needs. The fawn response acts as a way to reduce perceived danger by aligning with others' expectations or demands; it is a ventral vagal reaction that aims to de-escalate threats through connection rather than direct confrontation (fight), escape (flight), or immobilization (freeze).

The fawn response can also be a learned survival strategy that prioritizes maintaining peace over confronting conflict, deeply rooted in seeking safety through relational harmony and the avoidance of perceived threats. While it uses the ventral vagal pathways to promote social harmony and reduce conflict, it often comes at the cost of our boundaries and authentic needs. This response can lead to chronic stress, anxiety, and a sense of disconnection from ourselves because it relies on external validation and avoidance of perceived rejection or conflict.

TEND-AND-BEFRIEND

The tend-and-befriend response is related to the ventral vagal complex (VVC) of the vagus nerve and is characterized by seeking social support, nurturing others, and forming alliances to reduce threat levels. The VVC is the most evolved branch of the vagus nerve, specifically linked to facial muscles, heart rate regulation, and the ability to connect socially. It facilitates behaviors that promote safety, social bonding, and nurturing—key elements of the Tend-and-Befriend response. Unlike fight or flight, the tend-and-befriend response emphasizes connection and cooperation, often driven by the release of oxytocin, which promotes bonding. It is more commonly observed in women, reflecting evolutionary strategies of protecting offspring and forming supportive social networks. This response is thought to be an adaptive strategy that is driven by the desire to enhance safety and reduce stress through social bonding and caregiving behaviors, for example through reaching out to friends, forming new alliances, or relying on community support. Physiologically, it calms us by enhancing feelings of safety and trust, counterbalancing the effects of cortisol and adrenaline.

FLOP

Similar to the freeze response but with a more pronounced collapse, the flop response is characterized by a sudden loss of muscle tone or the body going limp. It is related to the dorsal vagal complex and associated with a primitive, involuntary survival mechanism that triggers immobilization or shutdown in the face of extreme or inescapable threats.

This response can occur in extreme stress or shock, particularly when fight, flight, or social engagement responses are not viable. The dorsal vagal complex triggers a "flop" response, characterized by a state of collapse, freezing, or complete shutdown. This response involves a drastic reduction in heart rate, blood pressure, and overall physiological activity, making the body appear passive or even lifeless. It is a form of surrender where the body essentially "plays dead" as a last resort survival tactic. The flop response involves an overwhelming sense of helplessness and is often seen in severe traumatic situations, such as during extreme fear or physical assault. In essence, it represents the nervous system's most extreme protective mode, driven by the dorsal vagal complex's shutdown mechanisms, helping the body conserve energy and protect itself in life-threatening situations.

SUBMIT

The submit response, associated with the dorsal vagal complex, involves yielding or surrendering to a threat as a means of survival. As another primitive survival strategy, it is often observed in situations where resistance would be futile or dangerous. It's a passive acceptance of one's circumstances, often with the hope of reducing the intensity of the threat by not resisting. Physiologically, it is characterized by a reduced heart rate, immobilization, lowered energy, and resignation or surrender in the face of a threat. This response, often reflected by passivity, disengagement, hopelessness and compliance, can protect us from further harm by minimizing confrontation. Unfortunately, it also often leaves lasting emotional impacts, such as feelings of powerlessness or shame.

CRY FOR HELP

This response involves actively seeking assistance or protection during times of stress or danger. Through vocalized distress, we are able to reach out or signal for help, aiming to draw attention to our plight and gain support. It is a survival strategy often seen in social species, including humans, where communal protection is possible. This response engages both the sympathetic nervous system (as our alert state signals urgency) and the parasympathetic nervous system when help arrives, providing a sense of relief and safety.

DISSOCIATION

Dissociation is a psychological defense mechanism where we detach from reality as a way to escape unbearable stress or trauma. This response is primarily linked to the dorsal vagal complex which, when faced with extreme stress or life-threatening situations where fight or flight is not possible, activates a freeze or shutdown response.

Dissociation manifests as feeling disconnected from our body, surroundings, or emotions, often described as "checking out" mentally. Physiologically, it involves slowing of the heart rate, reduced blood pressure, and diminished respiration, conserving energy as a protective mechanism. It also provokes alterations in brain activity, particularly in areas involved in emotional processing and memory, as the brain attempts to shield itself from overwhelming sensations. Dissociation can range from mild daydreaming to severe disconnection, such as depersonalization or derealization, providing temporary emotional relief but often complicating the ability to process and heal from trauma.

Remember that the ventral vagal pathways, associated with social engagement and connection, are inhibited during a dorsal vagal response. This inhibition contributes to the sense of isolation and disconnection characteristic of dissociation, as the nervous system shifts away from states that promote social bonding and safety.

CONSERVATION-WITHDRAWAL RESPONSE

The conservation-withdrawal response is a coping mechanism where we retreat and conserve energy in response to prolonged or unmanageable stress. This response can lead to behaviors like social withdrawal, fatigue, and reduced motivation, as the body shifts into a low-energy state to protect itself from further stress, as well as emotional and psychological overwhelm. Conservation-withdrawal can also involve changes in neurotransmitter levels and hormonal shifts, contributing to a sense of lethargy or depression. It is a way in which our body signals we need to rest and recuperate, though it can sometimes contribute to longer-term disengagement from life.

HYPERVIGILANCE RESPONSE

Hypervigilance, characterized by an excessive state of alertness and a constant scanning of the environment for potential threats, is related to the sympathetic nervous system and the ventral vagal complex pathways. While hypervigilance itself is not directly controlled by the vagus, it is influenced by the balance between the SNS and the vagal pathways that regulate calming and social engagement responses. When functioning optimally, the ventral vagal helps inhibit hypervigilance by downregulating the body's stress response and creating a sense of safety. However, when the VVC is underactive or overwhelmed—often seen in trauma survivors—it can fail to counteract the heightened sympathetic arousal, allowing hypervigilance to dominate. Hypervigilance is actually primarily driven by the sympathetic nervous system. It often develops in response to trauma, especially in those of us with PTSD. When this stress response is activated, our sympathetic nervous system remains in a heightened state, leading to increased heart rate, rapid breathing, muscle tension, and difficulty concentrating or relaxing.

Hypervigilance is adaptive in dangerous environments, keeping us prepared and perpetuating a state of constant vigilance. However, when chronic, it leads to anxiety, insomnia, and difficulty feeling safe, even when threats are no longer present. This reaction to perceived danger reflects a nervous system stuck in a cycle of threat detection due to an overactive sympathetic response and inadequate parasympathetic regulation. The vagus nerve, particularly the ventral vagal complex, will ideally help counterbalance this by calming the body. However, in trauma-affected individuals, the regulatory capacity of the vagal pathways can be compromised, allowing hypervigilance to persist as a protective but maladaptive response.

Neuroception: The Subconscious Evaluation of Safety

Understanding neuroception is key in grasping Polyvagal Theory's depth and its real-life applications. Unlike perception, which involves conscious awareness and thought, neuroception operates below the level of conscious awareness. It is an automatic and instinctual process, constantly analyzing our environment for cues that signal safety, danger, or life threat, feeding us intuitive hunches and forms of inner knowing.

Neuroception significantly affects our behavior by directly influencing the autonomic nervous system. When neuroception detects safety, it engages the ventral vagal system, allowing us to feel calm, connected, and socially engaged. Conversely, when neuroception senses danger, the sympathetic nervous system kicks in, preparing the body for fight or flight. In extreme cases, when the body perceives a life threat, the dorsal vagal system may activate, leading to immobilization or shutdown. These responses are not within our conscious control but are automatic reactions driven by our nervous system's assessment of our environment.

It is important to note that trauma can significantly alter neuroceptive processes, leading to heightened sensitivity to threats even in relatively safe situations. For example, a person who has survived a car accident might experience heightened anxiety when hearing the sound of screeching tires, even if they are in a safe environment. This altered neuroception contributes to symptoms of PTSD, such as hypervigilance and exaggerated startle responses. In these cases, the nervous system becomes stuck in a state of high alert, making it difficult to feel safe and calm. There are some practical strategies for recalibrating neuroception, including mindfulness practices which help increase awareness of the present moment and reduce automatic responses to perceived threats.

Body awareness exercises, such as scanning the body for tension or discomfort, can also help recalibrate neuroception by bringing attention to physical sensations and promoting relaxation.

MINDFUL MEDITATION

One effective exercise to improve neuroceptive awareness is mindfulness meditation. It does so by training your brain and nervous system to become more attuned to internal signals of safety and danger, allowing for a more accurate and balanced perception of your body's state. Mindful meditation works wonders in enhancing interoception, which is your ability to sense internal body signals such as heartbeat, breath, and muscle tension. By focusing attention on the breath, bodily sensations, or emotional states, meditation strengthens the connection between your brain and body, making you more aware of subtle changes that indicate stress or calm. Focusing on sensory experiences such as feeling the ground beneath you or noticing the sensation of breathing allows us to pay attention to signals from our body, increasing overall bodily awareness. This heightened interoception makes it easier for our nervous system to differentiate between real and perceived threats, reducing false alarms of danger that can lead to anxiety or hyper-vigilance.

Meditation is also helpful in lowering cortisol levels, decreasing amygdala reactivity (the brain's fear center), and increasing activity in the prefrontal cortex, which is responsible for executive function and emotional regulation. It promotes a non-judgmental awareness of thoughts and emotions, teaching the brain to observe rather than react impulsively. This practice enhances the brain's ability to regulate emotional responses, particularly in the context of perceived threats. Often involving elements such as self-compassion and loving-kindness, which create a sense of internal safety and acceptance, mindfulness practices reduce the perception of threats and foster a feeling of security within ourselves.

Moreover, by focusing on the breath and observing thoughts and sensations without judgment, mindfulness engages the parasympathetic nervous system, particularly through the activation of the vagus, promoting a state of calm and relaxation. This activation counterbalances the sympathetic nervous system, helping to recalibrate the nervous system's response to stress. By regularly engaging in meditation, your nervous system will learn to shift more easily from states of heightened alertness to calmness, improving your ability to accurately perceive safety and reduce maladaptive responses to non-threatening stimuli.

SAFE SPACE VISUALIZATION

Another helpful technique to enhance neuroceptive awareness is known as safe space visualization. It is done by intentionally creating vivid mental images of a calming, safe environment. Neuroceptive recalibration refers to the process of retraining the brain and body's perception of safety and threat, particularly in those of us whose nervous system is hypervigilant due to trauma, anxiety, or chronic stress. This calming and soothing exercise is helpful as it provides sensory experiences that activate the ventral vagal system, promoting feelings of safety and relaxation.

HOW TO PRACTICE Safe Place Visualization

Before we jump into a safe place visualization practice, below is an overview of the main components of this method. This might come in handy as you familiarize yourself with this practice and feel the need to tweak sections to make it your own. As you now know, this is a powerful tool to support neuroceptive recalibration, which will help retrain your nervous system's perception of safety, promoting a more resilient and regulated state. This guided practice sequence will no doubt help you access a state of calm and reduced anxiety. Please note that that the more frequently the visualization is practiced, the more effective it becomes in creating an accessible mental refuge during stressful moments.

The practice often begins with a guided imagery session, where a therapist or self-guided script encourages us to close our eyes, breathe deeply, and imagine a place where we feel completely safe, calm, and at peace. This could be a real location (like a favorite beach) or a completely imagined setting.

Then, to enhance neuroceptive recalibration, the visualization focuses on engaging all the senses:

1. **Sight**: What do you see in your safe place? The color of the sky, the trees, or familiar objects?
2. **Sound**: Are there soothing sounds like waves crashing, birds singing, or a gentle breeze?
3. **Touch**: What textures do you feel—sand under your feet, a soft blanket, or warm sunshine on your skin?
4. **Smell**: Can you smell the ocean air, fresh flowers, or something comforting like a favorite candle?
5. **Taste**: Is there a taste that brings comfort, like hot tea or sweet fruit?

The visualization aims to anchor emotions of safety, comfort, and peace. These positive sensory experiences signal to the nervous system that it's safe, counteracting the body's habitual stress response.

Safe Space Visualization: Practice Sequence

Preparation and Grounding

Begin by finding a comfortable, quiet place where you won't be disturbed. Sit or lie down in a relaxed position, with your eyes closed if that feels comfortable. Start by taking a few deep breaths, inhaling slowly through your nose, and exhaling gently through your mouth.

LET'S start by bringing your attention to your breath. Inhale slowly and deeply through your nose, feeling your chest and belly expand. Exhale gently through your mouth, releasing any tension with each breath. Notice how your body feels supported by the chair or floor. Let your muscles relax and allow yourself to feel grounded and present in this moment.

Body Scan to Ease into Relaxation

Perform a brief body scan to tune into your senses, releasing any lingering tension and further deepening relaxation while preparing your mind for visualization.

Now, bring your attention to your body, starting at your toes. Notice any sensations there, and if you feel any tension, imagine it melting away as you breathe out. Slowly move your attention up through your legs, hips, and lower back, releasing any tightness. Continue scanning upwards, letting your shoulders drop and your face soften. With each breath, feel your body becoming lighter and more at ease.

Introduction to the Safe Place

Introduce the idea of creating a safe, comforting space in the mind's eye, setting the tone for a serene and supportive environment.

Imagine that you are about to enter a place where you feel completely safe, calm, and at peace. This is your safe place. It can be somewhere you've been before, like a quiet beach, a cozy room, or a beautiful forest. Or it can be an entirely imagined space, filled with everything that brings you comfort. There are no rules—just allow your mind to create a space that feels just right for you.

Visualize the Safe Place in Detail

Take a deeper dive, leaning into a most detailed visualization of your safe place, engaging all the senses to deepen the experience and enhance the calming signals to your nervous system.

Take a moment to look around your safe place. What do you see? Notice the colors, the textures, the light around you. Is the sky a clear blue? Are there trees, flowers, or water nearby? Now, listen closely. What sounds are present in your safe place? Maybe you hear the soft rustling of leaves, the gentle lapping of waves, or birds singing in the distance. Notice how these sounds bring a sense of calm and safety.

As you stand or sit in this space, feel the sensations around you. Perhaps you feel the warm sun on your skin, a gentle breeze brushing past, or the soft ground beneath your feet. Breathe in deeply. What can you smell? The fresh scent of pine, salt in the air, or perhaps the aroma of flowers? Each breath brings you deeper into relaxation. If there's a comforting taste, like sweet fruit or a warm drink, allow yourself to savor it.

Anchor Emotions of Safety and Peace

Allow yourself to connect emotionally with your safe place, anchoring the feelings of safety, comfort, and relaxation to your senses.

Now, take a moment to really soak in the feeling of being in this space. Notice how your body feels lighter, your heart calm, and your mind at ease. You are safe here. There is nothing you need to do except be present. Let these feelings of comfort and safety fill you up, knowing that you can always return to this place whenever you need.

Create a Personal Symbol or Anchor

Tap into your intuition to help create a personal symbol, gesture, or word that can serve as a quick mental anchor to recall the safe place whenever needed.

To help bring this feeling of safety with you, imagine creating a small symbol or gesture that represents your safe place. It could be a simple word, like 'peace' or 'calm,' or a gesture, like placing your hand over your heart. This symbol is a reminder that your safe place is always within reach, ready to bring you comfort and calm whenever you need it.

Gradual Transition Back to the Present

Gently transition back to the present moment, while maintaining a sense of calm and safety.

When you're ready, slowly begin to bring your awareness back to the room you're in. Wiggle your fingers and toes, feeling the surface beneath you. Take a deep breath in, and as you exhale, know that you carry the peace of your safe place with you. Open your eyes gently, and take a moment to notice how you feel—calm, centered, and safe.

Reflect and Reaffirm the Practice

Take a moment to reflect on how the visualization felt and reaffirm the accessibility of the safe place in daily life. This is also a beautiful opportunity for mindful journaling.

Take a moment to reflect on how it felt to be in your safe place. Remember, this space is always available to you. Whenever you feel over-

whelmed, anxious, or need a moment of calm, you can close your eyes and
return to this place. It is your personal sanctuary, and it's always here to
support you.

The Three States of the Nervous System

The human nervous system is a dynamic and adaptive network that governs our responses to the world around us, constantly adjusting to maintain balance, safety, and well-being. Central to this process are three distinct states of the autonomic nervous system: the sympathetic state, the ventral vagal state, and the dorsal vagal state. As we've seen, these states, which form the core of Polyvagal Theory, represent a hierarchy of responses that range from social engagement and calmness to fight-or-flight reactions, and, in extreme cases, to a shutdown mode. Each state plays a central role in how we perceive, interact with, and respond to our environment, reflecting the many ways in which our bodies and minds manage stress, safety, and connection. Understanding these three states illuminates the complexities of our physiological responses and provides further insights into how we can better regulate our emotions and enhance our overall mental and physical health.

First, we have the ventral vagal state, which is our body's way of telling us that we are safe and can connect with others. In this state, we feel a sense of calm and well-being. Our heart rate is steady, our breathing is slow and deep, and we can engage in social interactions without feeling threatened. This allows us to build relationships and develop a sense of community. When in the ventral vagal state, our bodies are in a mode that supports healing and restoration. We can think clearly, make decisions, and manage our emotions effectively. This state not only benefits our mental health but also our physical health. It promotes better digestion, reduces inflammation, and boosts our immune system.

In contrast, the sympathetic state is what we experience when our bodies perceive a threat. This is the fight or flight response. Our heart rate accelerates, our muscles tense, and we become hyper-alert. This state is designed to prepare us for immediate action. In the short term, it can be beneficial, helping us respond quickly to danger. However, if we remain in this state for too long, it can have detrimental effects on our health. Chronic activation of the sympathetic state can lead to anxiety, high blood pressure, and a weakened immune system. It can also impair our ability to think clearly and make rational decisions. Recognizing the signs of sympathetic activation, such as rapid heartbeat and shallow breathing, can help us take steps to calm our nervous system.

The dorsal vagal state, on the other hand, is associated with immobilization and shutdown. This occurs when our bodies perceive an overwhelming threat that we cannot escape or fight. In this state, our heart rate slows, our energy levels drop, and we may feel numb or disconnected. This response can be a protective mechanism in life-threatening situations. However, chronic activation of the dorsal vagal state can lead to feelings of helplessness and depression. It is often linked to trauma and chronic stress, where the body remains in a state of shutdown even when the immediate threat has passed. Learning to recognize indicators of dorsal vagal activation, such as extreme fatigue and emotional numbness, is helpful for taking steps to re-engage with life.

Dorsal Vagal Responses

Now that we have explored some of the theory behind this nervous system state, let's look at six common dorsal vagal responses to perceived threats. Typically characterized by a shutdown or immobilization reaction as part of the body's survival strategy, these responses are usually involuntary. Derived from ancient survival mechanisms, they help the body endure situations where active defense is not possible.

1. **Freezing or Immobilization**: The body becomes still, muscles lose tone, and movement ceases, as if the person is "playing dead" to avoid detection by a threat.
2. **Fainting or Near-Fainting**: Blood pressure drops significantly, potentially leading to dizziness, lightheadedness, or fainting as the body reduces energy output.
3. **Disconnection or Dissociation**: A person may feel emotionally numb, disconnected from their surroundings, or as if they are observing events from a distance, often as a way to protect the psyche from overwhelming stress.

4. **Reduced Heart Rate and Breathing**: The body slows heart rate and respiration, conserving energy in response to extreme stress or perceived danger.
5. **Lethargy or Exhaustion**: An overwhelming sense of fatigue, where the body feels heavy and unmotivated, can be a response aimed at minimizing further physical or mental stress.
6. **Nausea or Digestive Shutdown**: The digestive system slows or halts, leading to symptoms like nausea or a lack of appetite, as the body prioritizes survival over non-essential functions.

MANAGING transitions between these three states is key to maintaining emotional and physical health. As we discovered with Sarah's story, techniques such as deep, diaphragmatic breathing help shift the nervous system into a ventral vagal state. You'll also find that engaging in social activities, practicing mindfulness, and spending time in nature often promote feelings of safety and well-being. To calm sympathetic arousal, grounding exercises such as placing your feet firmly on the ground and focusing on the sensations can be effective. Progressive muscle relaxation, where you tense and then release each muscle group, can also help reduce sympathetic activation.

Note: As we continue to discuss and explore various techniques, feel free to create your own list of preferences, or a "wish list" of practices to try for yourself.

Emerging from dorsal vagal shutdown requires gentle re-engagement with life. This usually takes form through gently and gradually guiding the body and mind back to a state of safety and engagement. As we reconnect with the present moment, we reactivate the ventral vagal system (responsible for social engagement and calm), which enables a sense of safety and connection. To begin this process, you'll want to start with small, manageable activities that bring a sense of accomplishment. Of course, these will need to suit your needs, personality, and abilities; however, the ones to prioritise are gentle physical activities such as yoga or walking, as they help re-activate the nervous system. Surrounding yourself with calm, supportive people and engaging in activities that bring joy also aid in moving out of a shutdown state. It's important to approach this process with patience and self-compassion, acknowledging that it may take time to fully re-engage.

Vagal Tone: The Indicator of Nervous System Health

As your body's secret superpower that keeps you calm, balanced, and resilient, vagal tone is an important indicator of our overall health. This term refers to the activity level of the vagus nerve, which can provide valuable insights into how well your vagus is functioning. This will reflect your body's ability to manage stress and maintain homeostasis. Measuring vagal tone is a way to assess the activity and health of the vagus nerve, which – as we know - plays a central role in regulating various bodily functions.

High vagal tone means that the vagus nerve is functioning well, providing a calming influence on the heart and other organs. It is closely associated with heart rate variability (HRV), which measures the variation in time between each heartbeat. A high HRV reflects a healthy, responsive vagus nerve, capable of quickly adapting to stress and returning to a state of calm. Conversely, low vagal tone and low HRV indicate a less adaptable nervous system, often linked to chronic stress and poor health outcomes.

WHAT DOES vagal tone look like?

Vagal tone, often referred to as the health or flexibility of the vagus nerve, is not unlike the subtle strength of a well-trained muscle—it can be cultivated and enhanced, but left unexercised, it can weaken, leaving the nervous system vulnerable to dysregulation. In our PVT context, vagal tone represents the dynamic interplay between the ventral vagal complex and the sympathetic and dorsal vagal states.

Picture a moment when your body is gripped by tension after a demanding, chaotic day. Your sympathetic nervous system, in an evolutionary bid for survival, quickens your heart rate, flooding your bloodstream with cortisol and other stress hormones, heightening your alertness. In a nervous system with strong vagal tone, the ventral vagal pathway swiftly re-engages as soon as the immediate threat subsides, modulating the heart rate, lowering blood pressure, and inhibiting excessive cortisol release. This instantaneous recalibration supports emotional and physiological recovery, enabling your body to return to a state of homeostasis.

Essentially, high vagal tone reflects an enhanced capacity for autonomic flexibility—the ability to oscillate between states of activation and relaxation without getting stuck in hyperarousal or hypoarousal. This flexibility underpins emotional resilience: rather than being overwhelmed by stress or remaining trapped in shutdown, your nervous system can fluidly respond to and recover from environmental cues, returning to a state of safety and connection. This dance of vagal activity —balancing engagement and restoration—forms the bedrock of nervous system healing, allowing not only recovery from acute stress but also the gradual restoration of the system's capacity to handle future challenges with greater ease.

A common experience where vagal tone comes into play is during an argument. Conflict can cause us to feel chest tightness and a racing mind, or perhaps even transition into a freeze or fawn response, depending on your prior experiences. Again, this is your body's fight-or-flight system getting triggered, causing rapid heartbeats, shallow breathing, and muscle tension. A high vagal tone will allow your vagus nerve to quickly engage, stepping in to effectively increase heart rate variability (HRV) and sending calming signals that slow breathing and reduce tension. This response will help regulate your emotions, allowing you to stay calm, think clearly, and respond rather than react impulsively.

Exercise is another common activity that creates complex physiological and nervous system responses. After an intense workout, your heart might be pounding, your breathing heavy. The body's sympathetic activity is high—a racing heart and elevated adrenaline levels are at play. In this case, strong vagal tone will enable quick activation of the parasympathetic system, which will lower your heart rate and stabilize your breathing. This rapid recovery helps our bodies to physically reset, while enhancing emotional resilience by training the body to quickly shift from high arousal states to calm. Exercise improves vagal tone and is an excellent preventive method to support ANS function and effective nervous system regulation. Physical activities stimulate the vagus nerve and the autonomic nervous system, therefore enhancing the body's ability to balance between sympathetic and parasympathetic responses.

Another scenario where vagal tone can be observed is during more focus-centered and calming physical activities. If you've ever done yoga or meditation, you've probably noticed how body tension eases and relaxation sets in as you breathe deeply and slowly. This is your vagus at work, stimulating your parasympathetic system to lower stress levels, reduce anxiety, and promote a sense of calm. Meditation and yoga stimulate the vagus nerve through deep, controlled breathing and conscious movement, which increase tone by enhancing HRV and lowering stress hormone levels. This activation of the parasympathetic nervous system helps calm the mind, reduce anxiety, and build emotional resilience by creating a state of inner peace and balance, even in the face of stress. This is another powerful illustration of vagal tone in action, turning your mindful movement practice into a powerful tool for emotional regulation.

Tools for Measuring Vagal Tone

To help you assess and track your vagal tone, several tools and methods are available. Self-assessment questionnaires can guide you in identifying signs of high or low vagal tone. These questionnaires typically include questions about your emotional responses, stress levels, and physical health indicators. Techniques for monitoring HRV, such as using wearable fitness devices, provide a more objective measure of vagal tone. These devices can track your heart rate variability throughout the day, offering insights into how your nervous system responds to various activities and stressors. Journaling and reflection practices are also valuable. By regularly noting your emotional and physical states, you can identify patterns and track improvements over time.

Heart Rate Variability (HRV)

What It Is: HRV is the variation in time between consecutive heartbeats. A higher HRV typically indicates a greater ability of the body to adapt to stress and return to a state of calm, which reflects good vagal tone.

How It's Measured: HRV can be measured using an electrocardiogram (ECG or EKG) or wearable devices like smartwatches and fitness trackers that have heart rate monitoring features. The data collected can be analyzed to determine the variability between heartbeats.

Significance: A higher HRV is generally associated with a stronger vagal tone, meaning the vagus nerve is effectively managing the body's stress responses and promoting relaxation.

Respiratory Sinus Arrhythmia (RSA)

What It Is: RSA refers to the natural increase in heart rate during inhalation and the decrease during exhalation. This phenomenon is largely mediated by the vagus nerve.

How It's Measured: RSA is usually measured using an ECG in a clinical setting. The difference in heart rate between breathing in and out is analyzed, with greater differences indicating higher vagal tone.

Significance: Higher RSA is associated with better vagal tone, as it reflects the vagus nerve's influence on the heart during breathing.

Pulse Rate Variability (PRV)

What It Is: Similar to HRV, PRV measures the variability in pulse rate, which can be an indirect indicator of vagal tone.

How It's Measured: PRV can be measured using photoplethysmography (PPG) sensors found in wearable devices like fitness trackers and smartwatches. These sensors use light to measure blood flow changes and thus the pulse rate.

Significance: While not as accurate as HRV, PRV can provide an accessible and non-invasive way to estimate vagal tone.

Electroencephalography (EEG)

What It Is: EEG measures brainwave activity and can be used to assess the vagal tone by analyzing the relationship between brain activity and heart rate.

How It's Measured: During an EEG, electrodes are placed on the scalp to detect electrical activity in the brain. Specific patterns in brainwaves, when correlated with heart rate data, can indicate vagal tone.

Significance: EEG provides a more complex and detailed understanding of vagal tone, particularly in research settings.

Vagal Reflexes

What It Is: Certain reflexes, such as the gag reflex or the diving reflex (slowing of the heart rate when the face is submerged in cold water), are mediated by the vagus nerve and can provide insights into vagal tone.

How It's Measured: These reflexes can be tested in a clinical setting, where the response intensity and timing are observed and analyzed.

Significance: Strong, appropriately responsive reflexes suggest a healthy vagus nerve and good vagal tone.

Baroreflex Sensitivity (BRS)

What It Is: The baroreflex is a feedback mechanism that helps maintain blood pressure stability. BRS refers to the sensitivity of this reflex, which is influenced by the vagus nerve.

How It's Measured: BRS can be measured by monitoring blood pressure and heart rate simultaneously while applying stimuli that cause blood pressure changes, such as breathing exercises or medication.

Significance: Higher BRS indicates better vagal tone, reflecting a more robust and responsive cardiovascular system.

Breath-Holding Test

What It Is: This test involves holding your breath for as long as possible, which stimulates the vagus nerve and can indicate vagal tone based on heart rate changes.

How It's Measured: During the breath-holding test, heart rate is monitored before, during, and after the breath is held. The recovery of heart rate after resuming breathing is analyzed.

Significance: A quicker and more pronounced heart rate recovery after breath-holding suggests better vagal tone.

Vagus Nerve Stimulation (VNS) Response

What It Is: In certain medical settings, direct stimulation of the vagus nerve using an implanted device or non-invasive methods can be used to assess its function.

How It's Measured: VNS involves applying electrical impulses to the vagus nerve and observing the body's response, particularly changes in heart rate and HRV.

Significance: The body's response to VNS provides direct information about the functioning and health of the vagus nerve.

Vagal Tone Takeaway

Vagal tone is essential for recognizing the health of your nervous system. High vagal tone signifies a strong, resilient nervous system and is an indicator of good emotional and physiological health, as it reflects your body's ability to return to a state of calm after stress. Low vagal tone, on the other hand, indicates vulnerability to stress and emotional dysregulation. It is linked to chronic stress and various health issues like inflammation and heart disease.

Improving your vagal tone *is* possible and, as we've seen, it can be achieved through various techniques and lifestyle changes. One of my favorite and most effective methods is humming or chanting, which stimulate the vagus nerve through vibrations. It can be practised any time when we notice our body or mind tipping into dysregulation. Cold exposure, such as splashing cold water on your face or taking a cold shower, is another method to activate the vagus nerve. Regular practice of vagus nerve exercises, such as deep controlled breathing and gentle yoga, will stimulate your vagus and enhance its function. Mindfulness and relaxation techniques, including independent or guided meditation and progressive muscle relaxation, also play a significant role in promoting high vagal tone. Another critical factor is maintaining strong social connections and supportive relationships – we will take a deeper dive into the workings of co-regulation later on. For now, keep in mind that positive social interactions also play a central role in activating the ventral vagal system, reinforcing feelings of safety and connection, which are vital to a healthy nervous system.

As you continue to explore and implement these techniques, you will likely notice improvements in your ability to manage stress by easily shifting from states of arousal to calm. This journey toward enhancing your vagal tone is a continuous process, one that requires patience and persistence – and a touch of intuitive self-care. However, the benefits are well worth the effort, offering a sure path to greater emotional resilience and stability.

TWO

TRAUMA, PTSD, AND YOUR NERVOUS SYSTEM

PICTURE THIS: You're sitting in traffic when you suddenly hear the screech of tires behind you. Your heart races, your muscles tense, and you feel a surge of adrenaline. This immediate reaction is your body's acute stress response, preparing you to either confront the threat or escape it. But what happens when the threat isn't a one-time occurence, but a chronic experience? How does our mind and body cope with living through an ongoing traumatic event or enduring a prolonged period of stress? This chapter aims to explore how trauma, with its varying complexities, disrupts the autonomic nervous system, leading to lasting changes that affect both your physical and emotional well-being.

Trauma and the Autonomic Nervous System

Trauma can manifest in various forms, each affecting us differently depending on the nature of the event, its duration, and our individual response. Nonetheless, its complexity and profound impact on the autonomic nervous system, which is responsible for regulating involuntary bodily functions like heart rate, digestion, and respiratory rate, is notable. When you experience a traumatic event, your ANS enters an acute stress response. As we've look at in the previous chapter, these responses are immediate and intense, designed to protect you from harm. As a basic mechanism, your body might react with adrenaline flooding your system, increasing your heart rate and blood pressure, while your breathing becomes rapid and shallow. These physiological changes prepare your body to either confront the danger or flee from it.

However, the aftermath of a traumatic event is where the real disruption begins. The initial acute stress response may subside, but for many, the ANS remains dysregulated, unable to return to a state of equilibrium. This long-term dysregulation manifests in two primary ways: chronic activation of the sympathetic nervous system and persistent dorsal vagal shutdown. Chronic activation of the sympathetic nervous system keeps your body in a constant state of readiness, as if danger lurks around every corner. This prolonged state of alertness can lead to a host of physical and emotional issues, including chronic anxiety, insomnia, and high blood pressure.

On the other hand, persistent dorsal vagal shutdown is the body's way of dealing with overwhelming stress or life-threatening situations by essentially "playing dead." This response is characterized by a significant decrease in heart rate, energy levels, and a sense of numbness or emotional disconnection. While this might be adaptive in the short term, long-term activation of this state can lead to severe issues like depression and emotional numbness.

Physiological changes associated with trauma are extensive and far-reaching. One of the most immediate changes is an increase in heart rate and blood pressure, which can become chronic if the sympathetic nervous system remains activated. This state of hyperarousal also affects breathing patterns, leading to shallow and rapid breaths, which can exacerbate feelings of anxiety and panic. Additionally, trauma impacts digestion, often leading to gastrointestinal issues like irritable bowel syndrome, bloating, and constipation. It causes a disruption to the normal regulation of the gut-brain axis, primarily via the vagus nerve, which is responsible for stimulating digestive functions such as the secretion of digestive enzymes, gut motility, and the regulation of the gut's immune response. This disrupted vagal functioning not only affects the physical process of digestion but also contributes to the gut-brain feedback loop, worsening anxiety and emotional dysregulation, creating a vicious cycle of stress and poor digestive health. Naturally, this will also impact your immune function, making you more susceptible to illnesses and infections.

The psychological impacts of ANS dysregulation are equally significant. Chronic activation of the sympathetic nervous system often results in anxiety and panic attacks. These episodes can be overwhelming and debilitating, making it difficult to function in daily life. Persistent dorsal vagal shutdown, on the other hand, leads to depression and emotional numbness. You might find it hard to feel any emotions, good or bad, leading to a sense of disconnection from yourself and others. This emotional numbness can make it challenging to engage in social activities or maintain relationships, further isolating you.

Take, for example, a lovely woman I met named Evie. Evie had always been confident and lively, but after the violent car crash, something within her shifted. The screech of tires, once background noise, now jolted her into a state of terror—her heart pounding, palms sweating, her body bracing for an impact that never came. Even the mere thought of stepping into a car made her chest tighten, her breath shallow. Her once open world had shrunk, and she moved through it in constant hypervigilance, trapped in a loop of sympathetic overdrive.

Then there was Laura. The trauma of her abusive childhood had left invisible scars, but they were deep. In her thirties, she moved through life as if underwater, everything muffled and distant. She felt emotionally numb, watching others connect and thrive, while she remained disengaged, indifferent. It was as though her body had learned long ago that safety meant withdrawal. Her nervous system, overwhelmed by the chronic stress of her past, had resorted to dorsal vagal shutdown—an adaptive survival response, but one that left her disconnected from the world, from her emotions, from herself. Laura's world was quiet, not from peace, but from profound detachment, a lingering aftereffect of her early trauma.

Understanding how trauma can disrupt our nervous system is the first step in addressing its long-term effects. Recognizing the physiological and psychological symptoms can help us take proactive steps toward healing. In the following sections, we will explore various techniques and exercises designed to help you regulate your ANS, bringing body and mind back into balance.

Types of Trauma

To better understand the complex repercussions of traumatic events, here is an overview of some common types of trauma. The purpose here is to illustrate just how diverse traumatic experiences can be, each affecting our nervous system, emotional regulation, and overall well-being in unique ways. Understanding these categories can also help in recognizing and addressing the numerous impacts on our lives.

Acute Trauma

Acute trauma results from a single, distressing event that overwhelms an individual's ability to cope, leading to immediate psychological and physical stress responses. This type of trauma is typically short-lived but can have lasting effects.

Examples:

- **Car Accident**: Imagine being involved in a severe car crash where your car is hit from behind, leaving you shaken and fearful of driving.
- **Natural Disaster**: Experiencing a tornado that destroys your home, leaving you in a state of shock and fear.
- **Witnessing Violence**: Seeing a violent altercation on the street or witnessing a robbery can cause acute trauma due to the sudden and intense nature of the event.

Chronic Trauma

Chronic trauma occurs from repeated or prolonged exposure to stressful events. Unlike acute trauma, chronic trauma involves ongoing or recurrent situations that can deeply affect emotional and physical well-being over time.

Examples:

- **Domestic Abuse**: Living in a household where physical or emotional abuse is a constant threat creates a persistent state of fear and anxiety.
- **Bullying**: Experiencing repeated bullying at school or work can erode self-esteem and create lasting psychological scars.

- **War and Conflict**: Living in a war-torn area with ongoing violence, bombings, and uncertainty creates continuous stress and hypervigilance.

Complex Trauma

Complex trauma results from exposure to multiple, varied traumatic events, often of an invasive, interpersonal nature, such as repeated abuse or neglect. This type of trauma is especially harmful because it disrupts emotional, psychological, and social development, particularly in childhood.

Examples:

- **Childhood Abuse and Neglect**: Growing up in an environment where neglect, physical, emotional, or sexual abuse is a regular occurrence deeply affects a child's sense of safety, trust, and self-worth.
- **Traumatic Relationships**: Being in a toxic relationship where manipulation, control, and emotional abuse are pervasive can create layers of trauma.
- **Repeated Loss**: Experiencing multiple losses in a short period, such as losing several family members, can create complex layers of grief and trauma.

Developmental Trauma

Developmental trauma refers to adverse experiences that occur during critical periods of a child's development, particularly in their early years. This type of trauma disrupts emotional and physical development, impacting attachment, self-regulation, and cognitive functioning.

Examples:

- **Emotional Neglect**: Growing up in a home where emotional needs are consistently unmet, leading to attachment issues and difficulties with self-worth.

- **Exposure to Parental Substance Abuse**: Living with a parent who struggles with addiction, leading to instability, fear, and a lack of safety.
- **Unpredictable Caregiving**: Experiencing inconsistent caregiving, where a parent's mood swings or mental health issues make the child feel unsafe and unsure of their environment.

Secondary or Vicarious Trauma

Secondary trauma occurs when an individual is indirectly exposed to the trauma of others, often through empathy or close association. This is common among caregivers, therapists, first responders, and those closely supporting trauma survivors.

Examples:

- **Therapists and Counselors**: Listening to traumatic stories from clients over time can lead to emotional exhaustion and vicarious trauma.
- **Emergency Responders**: Paramedics who frequently witness severe accidents or fatalities may develop trauma symptoms from their repeated exposure to distressing scenes.
- **Family Members**: Supporting a loved one with PTSD or severe trauma can cause secondary trauma due to the emotional burden of seeing someone close suffer.

Historical or Intergenerational Trauma

Historical trauma refers to the cumulative emotional and psychological wounds passed down through generations due to collective experiences of oppression, war, genocide, slavery, or cultural loss.

Examples:

- **Indigenous Communities**: The trauma from colonization, forced assimilation, and loss of culture continues to affect future generations emotionally and psychologically.

- **Holocaust Survivors' Descendants**: Children and grandchildren of Holocaust survivors may experience heightened anxiety, fear, or depression linked to the unresolved trauma of their ancestors.
- **African American Communities**: The legacy of slavery, systemic racism, and segregation can manifest as ongoing stress, mistrust, and trauma passed down through generations.

Medical Trauma

Medical trauma arises from distressing experiences related to illness, injury, or medical procedures that can cause fear, helplessness, and anxiety, particularly when an individual feels out of control or vulnerable.

Examples:

- **Intensive Care Stays**: Being in an ICU, hooked up to machines and surrounded by uncertainty, can leave patients feeling deeply traumatized.
- **Chronic Illness Diagnoses**: Receiving a diagnosis of a life-threatening or chronic illness can be overwhelming, leading to a sense of loss and ongoing fear.
- **Surgical Complications**: Experiencing complications during surgery, especially when unexpected, can lead to ongoing anxiety about medical procedures.

Environmental Trauma

Environmental trauma involves exposure to traumatic events related to natural or human-made disasters, often resulting in loss, displacement, or ongoing fear of recurrence.

Examples:

- **Earthquakes, Hurricanes, and Floods**: Surviving a natural disaster that destroys homes and disrupts lives creates ongoing fear and anxiety.
- **Industrial Accidents**: Experiencing a chemical spill, fire, or other industrial accidents can create trauma related to the environment.
- **Pandemics**: The COVID-19 pandemic, for example, caused global trauma through fear, isolation, loss of loved ones, and health-related anxieties.

The Dorsal Vagal Shutdown: A Response to Extreme Stress

Have you ever felt so overwhelmed by stress that you simply shut down, unable to move or respond? This is the dorsal vagal shutdown in action. It's the body's protective mechanism, designed to conserve energy and protect you in life-threatening situations. Imagine a deer caught in the headlights, freezing to avoid detection. This response is derived from our evolutionary history, helping us survive by playing dead in the face of predators. The dorsal vagal complex, part of the vagus nerve, is responsible for this reaction. When activated, it slows down your heart rate and breathing, reduces energy levels, and can even cause a sense of numbness or detachment.

The long-term implications of chronic dorsal vagal activation are far-reaching and can significantly impact your quality of life. Emotional numbness and dissociation are common, making it difficult to feel connected to yourself or others. You might find yourself going through the motions of daily life without truly engaging, feeling like a spectator rather than a participant. Physical symptoms often accompany this state, including chronic fatigue and unexplained pain. These symptoms can make even simple tasks feel overwhelming, further isolating you from social interactions and activities you once enjoyed. Over time, the constant state of shutdown can strain your relationships, as you may withdraw from loved ones, unable to connect emotionally or physically.

Recognizing dorsal vagal shutdown in yourself and others is an important first step toward recovery. Lack of energy and motivation are significant indicators. You might find it challenging to get out of bed, complete everyday tasks, or engage in activities you once found enjoyable. Withdrawal from social activities is another common sign. You may avoid gatherings, cancel plans, or isolate yourself from friends and family. Reduced emotional responsiveness often accompanies these behaviors. You might feel emotionally flat, unable to experience joy, sadness, or excitement. This numbness can extend to physical sensations as well, making it difficult to feel pain or pleasure. If you recognize these symptoms in yourself, there are preliminary strategies you can take to begin emerging from dorsal vagal shutdown. Gentle physical activity is a good starting point. Activities like slow walking, gentle yoga, or stretching can help re-engage your nervous system without overwhelming it. These activities promote blood flow, increase energy levels, and can be done at your own pace. Safe and supportive social interactions are also essential. Surround yourself with people who make you feel safe and understood. Even brief, positive interactions can activate the ventral vagal system, promoting feelings of safety and connection.

As a method of healing from overwhelming stress or trauma, gradual exposure to stressors in a controlled manner is another effective strategy. There are ways to enable our nervous system to gently re-engage, without triggering re-traumatization or an overwhelming sympathetic response. Part of this process involves slowly reintroducing yourself to situations or activities that you have been avoiding, starting with those that are least triggering. For example, if social gatherings are overwhelming, start with a brief coffee date with a close friend. Titration is a technique used in somatic trauma therapy, where a person is gradually exposed to small doses of traumatic memories, emotions, or bodily sensations. Instead of diving into the full intensity of the trauma, we are guided to work with "tiny" amounts of stress or discomfort in a slow, controlled manner. Titration allows the nervous system to slowly process and integrate difficult emotions or sensations without becoming overwhelmed. A simple example of titration can be illustrated by a discussion around a minor aspect of the traumatic event, while simultaneously focusing on a comforting sensation, such as warmth in your hands. This creates a balance between feeling the stress and maintaining a sense of safety. This method is also linked to a process called pendulation, which refers to the natural rhythm of moving between states of activation (stress or discomfort) and relaxation (safety and calm). Often used in somatic therapy, pendulation involves consciously shifting between moments of engaging with a stressor (activation) and then retreating to a state of safety or calm (deactivation). This back-and-forth movement mimics the body's natural capacity to recover from stress. By intentionally moving between states of stress and calm, pendulation teaches our nervous system that it can tolerate activation without becoming stuck in a freeze or shutdown state. This rhythmic process helps rebuild emotional resilience and a sense of control over stressful experiences, allowing the us to "pendulate" back to a grounded, safe state.

Properly addressing dorsal vagal shutdown can be utterly transformative. By applying recovery practices and working in small, manageable steps, we can avoid the risk of triggering the full dorsal vagal shutdown again. Gradual re-engagement helps the body become more resilient, recalibrating the nervous system so it can tolerate stress without shutting down. As you build confidence and resilience, you can gradually increase the duration and complexity of these interactions. It is important to approach this process with patience and compassion, giving yourself permission to take small steps and celebrate every bit of progress.

Hypervigilance and the Sympathetic Nervous System

Imagine living in a constant state of alertness, always on the lookout for potential threats. This relentless heightened cautiousness is the essence of hypervigilance, a state often triggered by trauma. It keeps you perpetually ready to fight or flee, even when there's no immediate danger. Trauma rewires your nervous system, leading to the chronic activation of the sympathetic nervous system. This system, designed for short bursts of activity, becomes overactive, keeping your body in a heightened state of readiness long after the initial threat has passed. Hypervigilance is an enhanced state of alertness and constant scanning for potential threats in the environment. It keeps us on edge, hyper-aware of our surroundings, and may lead us to overreact to stimuli that others might perceive as non-threatening.

The symptoms of hypervigilance are both varied and pervasive. Startle responses become more pronounced; even minor, unexpected noises can make you jump or feel panicked. Irritability becomes a constant companion, making you more prone to snap at loved ones or colleagues. Concentration becomes a Herculean task. Your mind feels scattered, making it difficult to focus on work or simple daily tasks. Sleep, that elusive sanctuary, becomes nearly impossible to attain. You may find yourself lying awake, mind racing, unable to drift off, or waking frequently through the night. Overreacting to perceived threats is another hallmark. A benign comment might feel like a personal attack, or a crowded room might trigger a sense of panic.

Hypervigilance casts a long shadow over every aspect of life. Personal relationships often bear the brunt of it. The constant state of alertness can make you seem distant or irritable, creating a rift between you and those you care about. Loved ones may not understand why you're always on edge, leading to feelings of isolation. In professional settings, hypervigilance can be equally disruptive. Difficulty concentrating can affect your performance, and irritability can strain relationships with colleagues and supervisors. Mentally, the constant state of alertness exhausts you, leaving little room for joy or relaxation. Physically, the toll is significant. Chronic stress can lead to headaches, gastrointestinal issues, and a weakened immune system.

Undeniably, managing hypervigilance is essential to reclaiming a sense of normalcy. Grounding exercises can be incredibly effective. Simple techniques like feeling the ground beneath your feet, holding a comforting object, or focusing on your breath can anchor you in the present moment. Mindfulness and relaxation techniques also play a pivotal role. Practices like meditation, progressive muscle relaxation, and guided imagery can help calm the sympathetic nervous system and promote a sense of peace. Safe and controlled exposure to triggers can gradually reduce hypervigilance. This involves slowly and methodically confronting the situations or objects that trigger your hypervigilance, starting with those that cause the least anxiety and gradually working up to more challenging ones.

One classic grounding exercise you might find helpful is the "5-4-3-2-1" technique. Start by identifying five things you can see around you. Next, identify four things you can touch, followed by three things you can hear, two things you can smell, and finally, one thing you can taste. This exercise can help bring your focus to the present, diverting your mind from perceived threats and calming your nervous system. Another useful technique is progressive muscle relaxation. This involves tensing and then slowly releasing each muscle group in your body, starting from your toes and working your way up to your head. This can help release built-up tension and promote a sense of relaxation.

Once again, mindfulness meditation can also be a powerful tool for managing hypervigilance. Find a quiet space where you won't be disturbed. Close your eyes and take several deep, calming breaths. Focus your attention on your breath as it moves in and out of your body. When your mind wanders, gently bring your focus back to your breath. This practice can help train your mind to stay grounded in the present moment, reducing the constant state of alertness that characterizes hypervigilance.

The Vagal Brake and Emotional Regulation

We have previously discussed how vagal tone, which refers to the overall health and functioning of the vagus and its ability to downregulate physiological arousal after stress. Your vagal brake, on the other hand, reflects the dynamic and immediate control that the ventral vagal branch of the vagus nerve has over heart rate. It acts as a physiological "brake," slowing down heart rate to maintain calm and social engagement.

Picture your body as a car navigating the twists and turns of life. The vagal brake functions much like the brake in your car, regulating your speed and ensuring you don't spiral out of control. This mechanism is necessary for maintaining emotional balance, creating a calming effect that extends beyond the heart. It influences our entire autonomic nervous system and helps us stay grounded and responsive rather than reactive.

Having a strong vagal brake equips us with the ability to manage stress more effectively. When faced with a stressful situation, a well-functioning vagal brake allows us to pause, take a deep breath, and approach the situation with a calm mind. This enhanced emotional resilience means that we can recover more quickly from setbacks and maintain a more balanced emotional state. Additionally, a strong vagal brake improves social interactions. When we feel calm and safe, we are more likely to engage positively with others, cultivating deeper connections and a sense of belonging. This enhanced social engagement not only benefits our emotional health but also reinforces our support network, creating a positive feedback loop that further strengthens our vagus nerve.

Strengthening your vagal brake, just like vagal tone, will involve both exercises and lifestyle changes. Deep and slow breathing exercises are among the most effective methods. Practices like diaphragmatic breathing, where you focus on deep breaths that expand your diaphragm, can activate the vagus nerve and enhance its function. Engaging in social and community activities also plays a significant role. Positive social interactions, whether through volunteering, joining clubs, or simply spending time with loved ones, can activate the ventral vagal system, promoting feelings of safety and connection. You will also find that regular physical exercise is another powerful tool. Activities like yoga, walking, or swimming not only improve physical health but also enhance vagal tone, contributing to better emotional regulation.

The Role of Neuroception in Trauma Responses

Neuroception is the body's subconscious way of detecting safety or threat in the environment, and it is inevitably affected by trauma. When you experience a traumatic event, your neuroceptive processes can become altered, making you hypersensitive to perceived threats. This heightened sensitivity means that even neutral or non-threatening cues can trigger a stress response. For example, a loud noise or a sudden movement might instantly put you on high alert, as your body interprets these signals as potential dangers. Here, the difficulty lies in distinguishing between what is truly dangerous and what is not, causing your nervous system to remain on edge, always prepared for the worst.

The impacts of altered neuroception on behavior are significant and multifaceted. You might find yourself avoiding social interactions because your body perceives them as unsafe. Being in a constant state of hypervigilance certainly makes it challenging to relax and enjoy the company of others. Overreactivity tends to become a common occurrence; simple misunderstandings or minor inconveniences can lead to intense emotional reactions. These behaviors are not just inconveniences; they can severely impact your quality of life, making it difficult to maintain relationships, hold down a job, or simply enjoy everyday activities. The world becomes a minefield of potential threats, and you find yourself tiptoeing through life, constantly on guard.

In other words, when neuroception is miscalibrated, especially after trauma or chronic stress, the body may perceive danger in safe situations, leading to heightened anxiety, hypervigilance, or emotional dysregulation. In order to recalibrate neuroceptive processes, we must retrain our body's subconscious detection of safety and danger signals in our environment. To do this, we can use a variety of techniques that help our nervous system learn how to differentiate between actual and perceived threats, returning it to a state where it can accurately detect safety. This process involves both bottom-up (body-to-brain) and top-down (brain-to-body) approaches. Let's explore some methods, illustrated with examples to bring these concepts to life.

The following eight strategies, aimed at recalibrating neuroception, have already been explored to some extent. However, even as we move forward, these remain a foundational part of this healing work, which is why I think it wise to integrate them properly. They require consistent practice, but are highly effective in recalibrating neuroceptive processes, thus reducing the constant state of alertness (often characterised by worry and stress) and reclaiming a sense of safety and well-being.

1. Somatic Awareness and Body Scanning

One of the first steps in recalibrating neuroception is developing somatic awareness, which means becoming aware of physical sensations in the body. As we know, some types of trauma can cause us to become disconnected from our bodies, making it difficult to interpret signals of safety or danger accurately.

EXAMPLE: Imagine a person who feels anxious every time they enter a crowded room. Instead of simply avoiding crowds, they practice body scanning by sitting quietly, closing their eyes, and mentally moving through each part of their body, noticing any areas of tension, discomfort, or ease. They might recognize a tightness in their chest or rapid breathing. Over time, they learn that these sensations aren't necessarily signals of danger, but rather the body's habitual response to stress. By practicing slow, deep breathing during these moments, they teach their nervous system to associate calmness with previously stressful environments.

· · ·

2. Breathwork

Again, deep diaphragmatic breathing is one of the most direct ways to engage the vagus nerve, playing a crucial role in calming the nervous system and recalibrating neuroception. Slow, deep breathing sends signals to the brain that the body is safe, which can downregulate the fight-or-flight response.

EXAMPLE: Before entering a stressful work meeting, practice diaphragmatic breathing by inhaling slowly for a count of four, holding the breath for a count of four, and exhaling for a count of six. As you breathe, focus on the sensation of your belly expanding and contracting. This type of breathwork stimulates the parasympathetic nervous system, sending signals of safety to the brain, which helps reduce unnecessary anxiety in future high-stress situations.

3. Engaging in Positive Social Interactions

As we have previously discussed, the ventral vagal complex is associated with social engagement and feelings of safety. Positive social interactions are a powerful way of recalibrating neuroception by providing real-life experiences where safety is confirmed through body language, tone of voice, and eye contact.

EXAMPLE: Consider someone with social anxiety who perceives social situations as threatening. They begin by attending small gatherings with friends who make them feel comfortable. Over time, they focus on positive cues like warm smiles, kind words, and light touches on the shoulder. These experiences help their nervous system learn that social situations can be safe, gradually reducing the hypervigilance and threat perception in larger gatherings.

4. Sensory Regulation

Grounding techniques help us reconnect with the present moment, which can shift our nervous system from a state of hyperarousal or dissociation to one of safety. Most methods include focusing on sensory experiences like touch, sight, sound, or movement.

EXAMPLE: Whenever you are feeling overwhelmed, use the "5-4-3-2-1" grounding exercise. Sit quietly and identify five things you can see, four things you can touch, three things you can hear, two things you can smell, and one thing you can taste. This sensory engagement will bring your attention back to the present moment and signal to your nervous system that you are safe. With regular practice, our bodies learn to associate sensory grounding with safety, recalibrating neuroception to correctly detect non-threatening environments.

5. Gradual Exposure to Stressors

Titration (exposure to small amounts of stress) and pendulation (shifting between states of stress and calm) are techniques used to gradually reintroduce the nervous system to stressors in a way that doesn't overwhelm it.

EXAMPLE: In one instance, a person with a fear of heights might start by standing on a low balcony while focusing on their breathing and noticing sensations of safety in their body (like the feeling of the ground beneath their feet). Over time, they slowly increase the exposure by moving to slightly higher places, pendulating between moments of stress (being on the balcony) and calm (sitting safely on the ground afterward). Each experience helps recalibrate their neuroception, allowing their body to understand that these heights aren't dangerous, even if their initial perception said otherwise.

7. Movement and Somatic Practices

Gentle movement practices that involve slow, deliberate movement, such as yoga, tai chi, and mindful walking, help re-train our body to accurately perceive signals of safety rather than remaining in a hypervigilant or anxious state. This stimulates the ventral vagal complex to promote relaxation while gently engaging our nervous system in a way that reinforces sensations of safety and ease. This also encompasses interoceptive exercises, which focus on internal body sensations, a central aspect of PVT recovery. These exercises involve paying close attention to subtle bodily cues, like the sensation of your heartbeat, breathing cycle, muscle tension, hunger; basically, *feeling* any and all physiological shifts. As such, these practices teach us to focus on the physical sensations in the body, which enables us to strengthen the connection between body and mind, allowing us to better interpret internal cues. Over time, this improved interoceptive awareness recalibrates neuroception, helping our body more accurately assess its internal and external environment.

EXAMPLE: One interoceptive exercise involves focusing on the sensation of your heartbeat. Sitting quietly, close your eyes and place a hand on your chest, simply noticing your heart's rhythm without judgment. Another exercise might involve mindful eating, where you carefully notice each bite, the texture of the food, and the feeling of fullness. Over time, this helps reduce anxiety, as the body learns to recognize internal sensations as part of normal bodily functioning rather than threats.

The Window of Tolerance

The concept of the window of tolerance is essential for understanding how trauma affects emotional and physiological regulation. Imagine this metaphorical space as the optimal arousal zone where you can function effectively. Within this window, you can manage stress, stay emotionally balanced, and respond to life's challenges without feeling overwhelmed. It's the sweet spot where you feel neither too anxious nor too numb. Maintaining this balance is essential for both mental and physical health. When you are within your window of tolerance, your nervous system operates smoothly, allowing you to think clearly, make decisions, and engage socially.

Perhaps you've heard about homeostasis, a healing state and process by which living organisms maintain a stable internal environment despite external changes. This balance is essential for survival and optimal functioning, as various physiological systems (like temperature, blood pressure, and pH levels) need to remain within certain ranges for our body to operate efficiently. The body achieves homeostasis through a series of feedback loops that constantly monitor and adjust these systems. For instance, when you become too hot, your body sweats to cool down, and when you become too cold, you shiver to generate heat. Similarly, when blood sugar levels rise, the pancreas releases insulin to help cells absorb glucose, preventing excessive fluctuations that could be harmful.

So, when we remain within our window of tolerance, our autonomic nervous system is well-regulated, with a healthy balance between the sympathetic (fight-or-flight) and parasympathetic (rest-and-digest) branches. Our brain's neuroception is able to accurately interpret the environment, perceiving safety in non-threatening situations. This allows our body to maintain homeostasis, or internal balance, across physiological systems such as heart rate, digestion, hormone production, and immune function.

In the window of tolerance, our body can smoothly transition between sympathetic activation when needed (e.g., dealing with challenges) and parasympathetic recovery (e.g., rest, digestion). This balance helps keep heart rate, blood pressure, and other bodily functions within normal ranges. Staying within the window of tolerance prevents extreme stress responses, such as hyperarousal (anxiety, panic) or hypoarousal (numbness, shutdown). When in this zone, the vagus nerve and ventral vagal complex remain engaged, promoting calm, connection, and social engagement. This emotional stability supports homeostasis by preventing our body from overreacting to stress and shifting into survival mode.

Trauma, however, significantly narrows this window. When you've experienced trauma, your nervous system becomes more sensitive to stress. Small triggers that wouldn't have bothered you before can suddenly feel overwhelming. This increased susceptibility to stress makes it difficult to maintain emotional equilibrium. You might find yourself oscillating between states of hyperarousal, where you feel anxious and on edge, and hypoarousal, where you feel numb and disconnected. This constant fluctuation can be exhausting and debilitating, making it hard to engage in daily activities or maintain healthy relationships.

Of course, expanding your window of tolerance is possible through several strategies. Gradual exposure to stressors is one effective method, which involves slowly reintroducing yourself to situations that trigger anxiety, starting with the least stressful and gradually working your way up. This controlled exposure helps your nervous system adapt and expand its capacity to handle stress. Again, our foundational techniques such as mindfulness and grounding techniques are also invaluable. Simple practices like deep breathing, body scans, or focusing on your senses will help anchor you in the present moment, reducing the intensity of your emotional responses. Building resilience through consistent practice is another key strategy. Regularly engaging in activities that promote well-being, such as exercise, meditation, and social interaction, also strengthen your nervous system over time.

Take, for instance, the story of Emily, who struggled with severe anxiety. She found it hard to leave her house without feeling overwhelmed. By gradually facing her fears, starting with short walks around her neighborhood and slowly increasing the distance, she managed to expand her window of tolerance. Over time, she began to interact with others. This started with brief visual contact, which turned into a nonverbal acknowledgement of their presence, and, eventually, a verbal greeting. She could go to the grocery store and even attend social events without feeling paralyzed by anxiety.

The window of tolerance is not static; it can expand and contract based on your experiences and how you manage stress. Regularly practicing the techniques we've explored can help you maintain and even expand your window, allowing you to flow through life's challenges with greater ease. Understanding the window of tolerance and how trauma affects it provides a framework for managing stress and emotional dysregulation. By employing strategies to increase your tolerance, you will develop a capacity to handle stress and maintain emotional balance.

THREE

VAGUS NERVE EXERCISES FOR NERVOUS SYSTEM REGULATION

IMAGINE A MOMENT OF SERENITY, sitting by a tranquil lake, the gentle breeze caressing your face. This deep sense of calm and peace is both a mental state and a physiological response that can be summoned and cultivated through specific techniques. In this chapter, we will explore practical vagus nerve exercises designed to regulate your nervous system and promote relaxation. Although some have already been presented as foundational tools, we will explore them more in depth, as they are powerful ways to seamlessly integrate vagal tone fitness into our daily routines.

Breathing Techniques for Vagal Stimulation

Diaphragmatic breathing, also known as deep belly breathing, is a foundational technique for stimulating the vagus nerve. This form of breathing engages your diaphragm, a large muscle located at the base of your lungs. When you breathe deeply into your diaphragm, you activate the vagus nerve, triggering the relaxation response of the parasympathetic nervous system. This technique is not only effective for reducing stress and anxiety but also for improving heart rate variability (HRV), a key indicator of nervous system health.

To practice diaphragmatic breathing, find a comfortable, quiet place to sit or lie down. Place one hand on your chest and the other on your abdomen. Inhale deeply through your nose, allowing your abdomen to rise while keeping your chest relatively still. Exhale slowly through your mouth, feeling your abdomen fall. Repeat this process for several minutes, focusing on the rise and fall of your abdomen. Regular practice of diaphragmatic breathing is sure to enhance your vagal tone, promoting better emotional regulation and overall well-being.

The physiological sigh is another remarkably powerful tool for regulating the nervous system because it naturally engages the body's built-in mechanisms for calming and resetting, all through vagal activation. It virtually mimics a natural response the body uses to reset the respiratory system and reduce stress. This simple yet highly effective breathing technique is a double inhale followed by a slow, extended exhale. While we often sigh unconsciously -especially in moments of anxiety, fatigue, or even relief - the deliberate practice of the physiological sigh effectively taps into the body's parasympathetic nervous system to rapidly reduce stress and restore balance.

The power of the physiological sigh lies in its ability to recalibrate the levels of carbon dioxide (CO_2) and oxygen (O_2) in the body. During stress, shallow breathing can cause a buildup of CO_2, which leads to feelings of anxiety and discomfort. The physiological sigh helps to release this excess CO_2 while maximizing oxygen intake, immediately relieving tension and signaling safety to the nervous system.

This technique also stimulates the vagus, sending signals from the brain to the heart, lungs, and digestive system, helping to slow the heart rate, lower blood pressure, and promote relaxation. This vagal activation shifts the body from a state of sympathetic arousal to parasympathetic recovery, making the physiological sigh an ideal method for quickly calming the nervous system.

So, how does this breathing method actually work? As we said, the physiological sigh involves a two-step process of breathing:

1. **Double Inhale**: Begin by taking a deep breath in through your nose, followed by a second, smaller inhale. This second inhale fully inflates the tiny sacs in your lungs called alveoli, which maximizes oxygen intake and improves gas exchange.
2. **Slow Exhale**: After the double inhale, slowly and fully exhale through your mouth, allowing the breath to release gradually. This long exhale activates the vagus nerve,

slowing the heart rate and reducing the fight-or-flight response.

Don't hesitate to repeat this soothing exercise as often as necessary. As we said, a deep sigh is an instinctive way in which our bodies self-regulate; therefore, we can certainly learn to use it consciously to bring about a nervous system reset. It is a beautifully calming, simple, and effective way of immediately calming body and mind, making it a powerful technique to use during moments of stress, anxiety, or when you need to quickly restore balance in your nervous system.

To help you integrate these breathing exercises into your daily routine, set aside specific times each day for practice. You might start your morning with a few minutes of diaphragmatic breathing to set a calm tone for the day, or practise deep controlled sighs and humming while stuck in traffic. During breaks at work, you can practice alternate nostril breathing to enhance focus and reduce stress. In the evening, use your preferred and most calming breath work technique to unwind and prepare for restful sleep. You can also find audio or written guides for these exercises to support your practice. Consistency is key, and even a few minutes of daily practice can yield significant benefits for your nervous system and overall well-being.

Guided Diaphragmatic Breathing Sequence

Welcome to this calming diaphragmatic breathing exercise, designed to help you reconnect with your breath, calm your nervous system, and visualize the inner workings of your body as you move toward a state of relaxation and balance. This practice will stimulate your vagus nerve, helping your body shift from a state of stress or anxiety into one of rest and restoration.

Step 1: Find a Comfortable Position

Begin by finding a quiet space where you won't be disturbed for a few minutes. Sit in a comfortable chair with your feet flat on the ground, or lie down on your back with your arms resting gently at your sides. Allow your body to settle and relax into the surface beneath you.

If sitting, make sure your back is supported but your chest is open, allowing space for full, deep breaths.

Step 2: Become Aware of Your Breath

Close your eyes and bring your attention to your breath. Without trying to change anything just yet, notice how your body is breathing naturally. Is your breath shallow or deep? Fast or slow?

Place one hand on your chest and the other hand on your belly, just below your ribcage. This will help you tune into your breathing pattern and feel the difference between chest and diaphragmatic breathing.

Step 3: Begin Diaphragmatic Breathing

Inhale Slowly and Deeply: Begin by taking a slow, deep breath through your nose. As you do, imagine your breath traveling down into your diaphragm. Feel your belly gently rise under your lower hand, while the hand on your chest remains still. Picture your lungs expanding like balloons, filling up completely with fresh air. Visualize this air moving down into the depths of your lungs, stimulating your diaphragm.

Hold for a Moment: At the peak of your inhale, pause for a moment. Feel the fullness in your belly and notice the stretch across your diaphragm. This is where the vagus nerve, the key communicator between your brain and body, begins to activate. Imagine this gentle pause as a signal of calm, telling your nervous system that everything is safe.

Exhale Slowly and Completely: Now, exhale through your mouth, slowly and gently, allowing your belly to fall back toward your spine. Visualize the air leaving your body, carrying away tension, stress, and anxiety. As you exhale, imagine your nervous system receiving the message that it can relax and let go. Feel your heart rate begin to slow and your muscles soften.

Step 4: Lengthen Your Exhale

Continue this slow, deep breathing, but now focus on making your exhale longer than your inhale. For example, if you inhale for a count of four, try exhaling for a count of six. This extended exhale enhances the activation of your parasympathetic nervous system, which helps bring your body into a state of calm and restoration.

With each long exhale, imagine your vagus nerve gently sending calming signals throughout your body. Picture it as a soothing current, moving from your brain to your heart, slowing your heartbeat, and then to your digestive system, easing any tension or discomfort.

Step 5: Visualize What's Happening in Your Body

As you continue to breathe deeply and slowly, visualize the calming effects this breath is having on your body:

Diaphragm and Lungs: With each inhale, your diaphragm moves downward, creating more space for your lungs to expand fully. Picture the fresh oxygen filling your lungs and reaching every cell in your body, giving you a sense of vitality and clarity. As you exhale, feel the diaphragm gently lifting back up, assisting in expelling any stale air or built-up tension.

Heart Rate and Circulation: Imagine your heart, which may have been beating quickly before, starting to slow down with each exhale. Visualize your blood vessels widening slightly, allowing oxygen-rich blood to flow freely to your organs and muscles, promoting a sense of warmth and relaxation throughout your body.

Vagus Nerve: Picture your vagus nerve as a gentle messenger, running from your brainstem down through your chest and into your abdomen. As you breathe deeply, this nerve is stimulated, sending signals to your heart to slow down and to your digestive system to activate. You might even feel a softening in your stomach or a quiet grumble—these are signs that your body is returning to a state of rest-and-digest, signaling safety and relaxation.

Mind and Emotions: As your breath deepens, notice how your mind begins to quiet. Any racing thoughts start to slow down, and you may feel a sense of calm and clarity washing over you. Imagine each inhale bringing in peace and stillness, while each exhale releases any remaining worries or tension.

Step 6: Continue and Deepen Your Practice

Continue this deep, slow breathing for as long as you feel comfortable. Try to maintain your focus on your belly rising with each inhale and falling with each exhale.

As your nervous system begins to calm, notice how your body feels grounded and relaxed. You may feel your muscles loosening, your heart beating steadily, and your mind becoming more serene.

Step 7: Gently Transition Back

When you're ready to end the practice, take a few final deep breaths. Slowly bring your awareness back to the room around you.

Wiggle your fingers and toes, and gently roll your shoulders to wake up your body. If your eyes were closed, open them slowly, allowing your vision to adjust.

Notice how calm and centered you feel. Acknowledge the shift that has taken place in your nervous system, and know that you can return to this practice whenever you need to reset and bring yourself back to a state of peace.

Mindfulness Practices to Enhance Vagal Tone

Mindfulness meditation is a practice that involves focusing your attention on the present moment while calmly acknowledging and accepting your feelings, thoughts, and bodily sensations. It's a simple yet powerful technique for enhancing vagal tone and promoting emotional regulation. By bringing your awareness to the present moment, you activate the parasympathetic nervous system, which calms the body and mind. This practice helps improve heart rate variability (HRV), making it easier to manage stress and anxiety.

To begin, find a quiet space where you can sit comfortably. Close your eyes and take a few deep breaths. Focus on your breath as it flows in and out. If your mind wanders, gently bring your attention back to your breath. With regular practice, mindfulness meditation can become a valuable tool for maintaining emotional balance and resilience.

Loving-kindness meditation, also known as "Metta" meditation, is a specific form of mindfulness that focuses on cultivating compassion and love for yourself and others. This practice enhances vagal tone by promoting positive social engagement and emotional well-being. To practice loving-kindness meditation, start by finding a comfortable seated position. Close your eyes and take a few deep breaths. Begin by directing loving-kindness towards yourself. Silently repeat phrases such as "May I be happy, may I be healthy, may I be safe, may I live with ease." After a few minutes, extend these wishes to someone you care about, then to a neutral person, and finally to someone with whom you have difficulty. This practice can help foster a sense of interconnectedness and empathy, which are vital for emotional health and social relationships.

Mindful breathing exercises, a slight variation of the breath work techniques we have already explored, are another effective way to enhance vagal tone. These exercises involve focusing on your breath to calm the nervous system and promote relaxation. One technique is breath counting. Sit comfortably and close your eyes. Take a deep breath and count "one" as you exhale. On the next exhale, count "two," and continue this pattern up to a count of ten, then start again at one. If your mind wanders, gently bring your focus back to your breath and the count.

Another popular technique that I also adore is the "box breathing" method. Inhale for a count of four, hold your breath for a count of four, exhale for a count of four, and hold again for a count of four. Repeat this cycle for several minutes. This is so simple yet incredibly powerful. It provides instant relief, reducing stress and improve focus by activating the vagus nerve and promoting a state of calm.

Integrating mindfulness into your daily life doesn't require significant changes to your routine. It can be done systematically or practised as the need arises. Use mindfulness cues throughout the day to bring your attention back to the present moment. For example, you can take a few mindful breaths while waiting in line or during a work meeting. Combining mindfulness with other activities, such as mindful walking, can also be beneficial. As you walk, focus on the sensation of your feet touching the ground, the rhythm of your breath, and the sights and sounds around you. This can transform simple daily activities into a calming and restorative experience.

Reflecting on Breath & Presence

Take a moment to reflect on how you can incorporate mindfulness and breath work into your daily routine. Think about setting a specific time each day for meditation or choosing a mindfulness cue to bring your attention back to the present moment. Perhaps, for example, you will feel the need to create a grounding mantra to help reconnect with yourself and the present moment in any given situation. Whichever you choose, write down your thoughts and any challenges you anticipate, along with strategies for overcoming them. This reflection will help you create a personalized mindfulness practice that suits your lifestyle.

Body Scans: Connecting Mind and Body

Body scans offer a powerful way to connect with your physical sensations and enhance vagal tone. By systematically focusing on different parts of your body, you can develop a deeper awareness of physical sensations, tension, and areas of relaxation. This practice not only promotes self-awareness but also helps stimulate the vagus nerve, leading to a state of relaxation and calm. Body scans are particularly effective if you struggle with anxiety or stress, as they provide a structured method to tune into your body and anchor yourself in the present moment. The benefits extend beyond immediate relaxation; regular practice can improve emotional regulation, reduce chronic stress, and enhance overall well-being.

To perform a body scan, find a quiet, comfortable place where you can lie down or sit without distractions. Close your eyes and take a few deep breaths to settle into the practice. Start by directing your attention to your toes. Notice any sensations, whether it's warmth, coolness, tingling, or tension. Gradually move your focus upwards, to your feet, ankles, calves, and so on, until you reach the top of your head. As you focus on each body part, try to release any tension you might be holding and allow that area to relax. If your mind wanders, gently bring your attention back to the body part you're focusing on. This step-by-step approach helps you systematically relax your entire body, promoting a sense of calm and connection.

There are several variations of body scans that you can try, depending on your needs and the amount of time you have available. A short body scan, which takes about five to ten minutes, is great for quick relaxation. This version focuses on major body parts, such as the feet, legs, abdomen, chest, arms, and head. It's a useful practice for a mid-day break or when you need a quick reset. On the other hand, an extended body scan can last anywhere from twenty minutes to an hour, allowing for a deeper state of relaxation and self-awareness. This version involves a more detailed focus on smaller body parts and can be particularly beneficial before bed to promote restful sleep.

Body scans with guided visualization add another layer of relaxation and can be highly effective for those who find it difficult to focus solely on physical sensations. Guided visualizations involve imagining a peaceful scene or comforting imagery as you move through the body scan. For example, you might visualize a warm, soothing light moving through your body, melting away tension and stress as it goes. This combination of body awareness and visualization can enhance the calming effects of the practice, making it easier to relax and let go of stress.

To help you get started with body scans, you can find guided sessions in both audio and written formats. You can find a beautiful guided body scan meditation sequence in *The Somatic Therapy Handbook: A Transformative Guide to Trauma Recovery, Anxiety Relief, Nervous System Regulation and Releasing Emotional Blockages by Connecting Mind, Body & Soul* (Y.D. Gardens, 2024). Audio guides such as the above-mentioned one can be particularly helpful, as they provide a soothing voice to lead you through the practice, allowing you to fully immerse yourself in the experience. Written tools, on the other hand, offer the flexibility to adapt the practice to your own pace. Whichever format you choose (perhaps both), remember the importance of creating a peaceful environment for your practice. Find a quiet space where you won't be disturbed, and consider using calming elements such as soft lighting, comfortable cushions, or soothing music to enhance your relaxation.

Movement-Based Activities: Yoga and Tai Chi

Yoga offers a profound way to enhance vagal tone and promote nervous system regulation. The practice of yoga involves a series of physical postures, breathing exercises, and meditation techniques that work together to balance the autonomic nervous system. Yoga's impact on the nervous system is multifaceted. It stimulates the vagus nerve through deep, mindful breathing and specific physical postures that encourage relaxation and stress relief. As you move through different poses, you're not only stretching and strengthening your muscles but also activating the parasympathetic nervous system, which helps to calm the body and mind. By incorporating yoga into your routine, you can create a sense of inner peace and stability, even amidst the chaos of daily life.

Certain yoga poses are particularly effective for stimulating the vagus and enhancing vagal tone. Child's Pose (Balasana) is a gentle resting pose that promotes relaxation and helps to calm the nervous system. To practice Child's Pose, kneel on the floor with your big toes touching and knees spread apart. Sit back on your heels and stretch your arms forward, resting your forehead on the mat. This pose encourages deep, diaphragmatic breathing, which activates the vagus nerve and promotes a state of calm. Another beneficial pose is Cat-Cow Pose (Marjaryasana-Bitilasana), which involves moving the spine through a series of flexion and extension movements. Start on your hands and knees, with your wrists aligned under your shoulders and your knees under your hips. Inhale as you arch your back and lift your head (Cow Pose), then exhale as you round your spine and tuck your chin (Cat Pose). This gentle flow helps to release tension in the spine and stimulate the vagus nerve through rhythmic breathing.

Legs-Up-The-Wall Pose (Viparita Karani) is another powerful pose for enhancing vagal tone. This restorative pose involves lying on your back with your legs extended up the wall. Position your hips close to the wall and allow your arms to rest by your sides. This inversion helps to promote circulation, reduce stress, and stimulate the vagus nerve. Finally, Corpse Pose (Savasana) is a deeply relaxing pose that allows the body to fully rest and recover. Lie flat on your back with your legs extended and arms resting by your sides. Close your eyes and focus on your breath, allowing each exhale to release any remaining tension. This pose encourages a state of deep relaxation and helps to reset the nervous system.

Tai Chi, an ancient Chinese practice, offers another effective way to balance the autonomic nervous system and promote relaxation. Tai Chi involves a series of slow, flowing movements combined with deep breathing and mindfulness. The principles of Tai Chi emphasize soft-ness, balance, and the integration of mind and body. This practice stim-ulates the vagus nerve through gentle, rhythmic movements and focused breathing, helping to calm the nervous system and enhance vagal tone. Tai Chi's emphasis on smooth, continuous motion and mindful aware-ness makes it an ideal practice for reducing stress and promoting overall well-being.

A beginner-friendly Tai Chi routine can help you get started with this practice. Begin with warm-up exercises to prepare your body for movement. Stand with your feet shoulder-width apart and gently shake out your arms and legs. Take a few deep breaths to center yourself. The basic Tai Chi movements include "Wave Hands Like Clouds," where you shift your weight from one foot to the other while gently waving your hands in front of your body, and "Parting the Wild Horse's Mane," where you step forward and extend one arm forward while the other arm reaches back. Focus on smooth, controlled movements and deep, rhythmic breathing. Conclude your practice with cool-down techniques, such as gentle stretching and deep breathing, to help your body transition back to a state of rest.

Whether you choose to start your day with a gentle yoga flow or unwind with a Tai Chi session in the evening, these practices will help you cultivate a sense of calm, balance, and resilience.

Somatic Experiencing: Healing Through Body Awareness

Somatic Experiencing (SE™) is a body-oriented approach to healing trauma, developed by Dr. Peter Levine. The core principle of this method is that trauma is stored in the body, and by paying attention to physical sensations, you can release stored tension and trauma. Somatic Experiencing focuses on the body's natural ability to heal itself and emphasizes the importance of body awareness in this process. As per our exploration of Polyvagal Theory, the aim of somatic therapy is to tune into physical sensations to stimulate the vagus nerve and help regulate your nervous system. This approach is particularly relevant for trauma healing, as it offers a way to process and release trauma without having to relive the traumatic event.

Body awareness plays a central role in healing from trauma. Developing a keen sense of body awareness allows you to notice subtle changes in your physical state and take proactive steps to regulate your emotions. Techniques for enhancing body awareness include many of the practices we have already discussed, for example breath work and mindfulness meditation. Also invaluable are body-oriented relaxation exercises, which promote a sense of physiological and mental calm. In fact, the benefits of body awareness extend beyond emotional regulation; they also encompass physical well-being. By becoming more attuned to your body, you can reduce chronic pain, improve sleep, and enhance overall health.

Practical exercises in Somatic Experiencing can be life-changing. Grounding exercises, for instance, are simple yet powerful tools that help you stay connected to the present moment. One effective grounding exercise involves sitting in a chair with your feet flat on the ground. As you focus on the sensation of your feet touching the floor, feel the support of the chair beneath you. Take a few deep breaths and notice how your body feels. This exercise can help you anchor yourself in the present, reducing feelings of anxiety and overwhelm. Pendulation techniques are another valuable tool that are integral to somatic therapy. As you may recall, pendulation involves moving your attention between states of arousal and relaxation. This process increases body awareness and gradually expands our capacity to tolerate stress by shifting attention between sensations of discomfort or tension and sensations of ease or relaxation. The gentle back-and-forth movement between contrasting sensations in the body is a powerful way to practice embodied awareness, allowing us to stay present without becoming overwhelmed by stress or trauma-related feelings.

Practical Method for Practicing Pendulation

Begin by sitting or lying down in a comfortable, quiet space where you won't be interrupted for a few minutes. Close your eyes if it feels comfortable, and take a few deep breaths to settle into your body.

Bring your awareness inward and gently scan your body from head to toe, noticing any areas of tension, discomfort, or unease. This might be a tightness in your chest, a knot in your stomach, or a dull ache in your back. You don't need to fix or change anything—just notice it.

For example, you might notice a sense of tightness in your shoulders or heaviness in your chest. Focus on this area and allow yourself to feel it fully, while maintaining a sense of curiosity rather than judgment.

Now, shift your attention to another part of your body that feels neutral, relaxed, or even pleasant. This could be as subtle as a soft sensation in your feet, the gentle rise and fall of your belly as you breathe, or the weight of your hands resting in your lap. You may feel a soft warmth in your hands or the grounding sensation of your feet against the floor. Spend a moment focusing on this sensation of ease.

When you are ready, begin to gently pendulate, moving your awareness between the sensation of discomfort and the sensation of ease. Spend a few moments focusing on the uncomfortable area, then switch your attention to the area that feels neutral or pleasant. Keep moving back and forth at your own pace.

When focusing on discomfort, you might feel your shoulders' tension increase or pulse slightly. Allow yourself to feel the sensation without trying to change it.

When shifting to ease, notice how your body softens when you place your attention on the pleasant or neutral sensation, like the gentle warmth in your hands or the steadiness of your breath.

As you pendulate between these areas, you may start to notice shifts in sensation. The discomfort might lessen, or the ease may grow stronger. This process helps regulate your nervous system, allowing you to expand your capacity to stay present with both difficult and soothing sensations.

Continue this process for a few minutes, expanding your awareness of the sensations without getting overwhelmed by either. Over time, pendulation helps build resilience by teaching your nervous system that it can safely experience stress and then return to a place of calm.

After a few minutes of pendulating, return your focus to the neutral or pleasant sensation and let it fill your awareness. This will help ground you and leave you with a sense of calm. Take a few deep breaths and, when ready, slowly bring yourself back to the present moment.

Daily Routines for Vagal Nerve Health

Consistency is fundamental to sustaining and optimizing vagal tone. Just like building muscle through regular exercise, improving vagal tone requires systematic practice. Regular engagement with vagus nerve exercises will not only help with nervous system regulation but also builds resilience against stress and anxiety. Integrating these exercises into a daily regimen establishes a solid foundation for emotional and physiological equilibrium. Over time, this promotes adaptive stress responses, enabling a more efficient return to homeostasis following stress exposure.

Now, building a routine doesn't have to be overwhelming. You can start by identifying specific times during your day when you can dedicate a few minutes to these practices. Morning, midday, and evening are ideal times to integrate vagus nerve exercises. In the morning, begin with a few minutes of deep breathing exercises. This can set a calm tone for the day ahead. Sit comfortably, close your eyes, and take slow, deep breaths. Focus on the sensation of the air filling your lungs and then gently exhale.

By midday, you might start to feel the stress of the day building up. This is an excellent time for a quick mindfulness practice. Find a quiet spot, even if it's just your office chair, and spend a few minutes focusing on your breath or engaging in a brief body scan. This can help reset your nervous system, making you feel more centered and focused. These midday practices serve as a mental and emotional reset, helping you manage stress before it accumulates.

In the evening, incorporate relaxation techniques to wind down. You might try a gentle yoga session or a body scan before bed. Another element to consider in order to transition into a restful night's sleep is creating a bedtime routine that includes turning off electronic devices, dimming the lights, and spending a few minutes in a relaxing pose, such as Legs-Up-The-Wall. This can signal to your body that it's time to relax and prepare for sleep.

Thanks to the insistence of a good friend, I recently discovered the soothing benefits of using a Shakti Mat. Unsurprisingly, this has quickly become an integral part of my evening wind-down rituals. The Shakti Mat, also known as an acupressure mat, is a tool designed to promote relaxation, reduce stress, and restore balance the nervous system. However, don't be fooled – the initial discomfort deters many beginning practitioners! The mat is covered with small, pointed discs that apply a certain amount of pressure to specific points on the body, similar to acupuncture or acupressure. When you lie or stand on the mat, these pressure points stimulate your nervous system, helping to calm and reset your body. It also stimulates thousands of nerve endings in the skin, triggering the release of endorphins and oxytocin, the body's natural "feel-good" hormones. These chemicals help reduce stress and anxiety by activating the parasympathetic nervous system. This process is similar to the effects of massage or acupuncture, where targeted pressure signals the brain that it's safe to relax. Furthermore, the gentle pressure applied by the mat stimulates the vagus nerve, promoting vagal tone, therefore encouraging a state of relaxation and emotional resilience. This vagal stimulation lowers our heart rate, reduces cortisol (stress hormone) levels, and promotes mind and body restoration.

How to Use the Shakti Mat

Lying Down: Place the mat on a flat surface, lie down, and allow your body weight to press into the mat. Start with short sessions (5–10 minutes) and gradually increase to 20–40 minutes as your body becomes accustomed to the sensation.

Targeting Specific Areas: For tension in specific areas, such as the shoulders, lower back, or feet, you can adjust the mat's position or use it while sitting in a chair.

Shakti Mat Restorative Practices

Shavasana: This yogic "corpse pose" is highly effective when combined with a Shakti Mat for nervous system reset, particularly due to the combined benefits of deep relaxation and acupressure stimulation. By lying still and focusing on breath, shavasana helps calm the mind and body, facilitating a return to a balanced autonomic state. It aids in lowering heart rate, slowing breathing, and reducing cortisol levels.

Deep Breathing: While on the mat, practice slow, deep breathing to enhance relaxation and vagal stimulation. Breathe in for a count of 5-6 seconds and exhale for the same amount of time, creating a balanced, coherent breath cycle. Otherwise, you might choose to inhale for a count of 4-5, and exhale for a longer count (e.g., 6-8), as lengthening the exhalation helps activate the parasympathetic system, further enhancing the relaxation response promoted by the Shakti Mat.

When conscious breathwork is paired with use of the Shakti Mat, the benefits are amplified, accelerating and deepening a nervous system reset.

Chanting: Inhale deeply, and on the exhale, slowly chant "Om," allowing the sound to resonate. While doing this, focus on the vibration of the sound throughout your body.

"Om" sound meditation, also known as "Om chanting" or "Aum meditation," is a form of meditative practice that revolves around chanting or intoning the sacred syllable "Om" (or "Aum"). This sound is considered to be a primordial vibration, representing the essence of the universe in many spiritual traditions. The chant is synchronized with slow, deep inhalations and extended exhalations. The sound of the chant is elongated, allowing the body to relax with each exhalation. The vibration generated from chanting "Om" is believed to resonate through the body, particularly in the throat, chest, and abdominal area, stimulating the parasympathetic nervous system.

Humming: First, take a few deep breaths to relax. On the exhale, hum at a comfortable pitch, focusing on the vibration in your chest and throat. Let the hum last for the entirety of your exhale. Repeat for several breaths, allowing the sound to soothe your system.

Humming is a powerful technique for self-regulation and vagus nerve activation due to its effects on the parasympathetic nervous system. It causes vibrations in the throat, which directly stimulate the vagus. This activation instantly promotes relaxation, reducing the body's fight-or-flight response.

As it is an immediate fix and instantaneously soothing response to stress, humming can be particularly helpful during moments of emotional dysregulation to restore calm and balance.

Meditation: Combining meditation, whether independent or guided, with the practice of using a Shakti Mat creates a powerful evening wind-down routine. As you lie on the mat, the acupressure points activate the parasympathetic nervous system, while meditation enhances this effect by promoting mindfulness and calming mental chatter. Guided meditations that focus on deep breathing, body scanning, or relaxation help deepen the body's response to the mat's pressure, encouraging a deeper sense of release and calm. This combination not only reduces physical tension and stress but also helps prepare the mind and body for restful sleep by signalling safety and relaxation to the nervous system.

FOUR

PVT AND OTHER THERAPEUTIC APPROACHES

As WE MOVE FORWARD in our exploration of Polyvagal Theory, one thing is clear: this powerful method of viewing and addressing emotional blockages encompasses a variety of holistic healing approaches. As such, integrating PVT with other therapeutic practices will take our understanding of the nervous system's role in emotional regulation to a deeper level. You already know how crucial the autonomic responses are in shaping how we experience safety and threat. By weaving this into existing therapies—whether somatic work, trauma-informed care, or even cognitive-behavioral strategies—you will more effectively access your body's natural capacity for regulation. We will now explore further than simply managing symptoms by discussing powerful tools and techniques to work with our body's innate ability to restore balance.

Polyvagal Theory and EMDR

EMDR, developed by Francine Shapiro in the late 1980s, is an evidence-based therapy primarily used for treating trauma. Its origins trace back to Shapiro's discovery that certain eye movements could reduce the intensity of disturbing thoughts and memories. EMDR involves a structured eight-phase approach, which includes elements of cognitive-behavioral therapy along with bilateral stimulation, such as eye movements, taps, or sounds. The therapy aims to facilitate the brain's natural healing process, allowing us to reprocess traumatic memories and integrate them into our overall life narrative.

The basic mechanisms of EMDR revolve around the concept of adaptive information processing. Trauma can disrupt the brain's ability to process information, leading to the storage of traumatic memories in a fragmented and dysfunctional manner. EMDR helps to reprocess these memories, reducing their emotional charge and enabling more adaptive responses. The key components of an EMDR session include the identification of a specific traumatic memory, the use of bilateral stimulation to facilitate reprocessing, and the integration of new, more adaptive beliefs and emotions related to the memory. This process helps to desensitize us to the traumatic memory, reducing symptoms of PTSD and other trauma-related issues.

As Polyvagal Theory provides a framework for understanding the importance of neuroceptive safety, incorporating its principles with EMDR helps therapists create a safer and more supportive environment for EMDR sessions. Using these methods to enhancing neuroceptive safety ensures that the client's nervous system feels supported throughout the therapy process. This can be achieved by using vagal nerve exercises to prepare for and conclude EMDR sessions.

Combining Polyvagal Theory with EMDR can look like incorporating breathing exercises before starting an EMDR session. We've already explored how deep, diaphragmatic breathing can activate the vagus nerve, promoting relaxation and reducing anxiety. By starting the session with a few minutes of focused breathing, clients can enter a more regulated state, making the EMDR process more effective. Grounding techniques can also be used to manage heightened arousal during sessions. Simple practices like feeling the ground beneath your feet or holding a comforting object can help anchor you in the present moment, reducing the intensity of traumatic memories as they are processed.

Applying vagal nerve stimulation post-session is another valuable strategy. After an intense EMDR session, the nervous system may still be in a heightened state. Techniques such as humming, chanting, or gentle yoga help stimulate the vagus, promoting a return to a state of calm and balance. These practices will enhance the immediate effects of the therapy while supporting long-term nervous system regulation.

Cognitive-Behavioral Therapy (CBT) is one of the most widely used and effective forms of psychotherapy. It focuses on identifying and changing negative thought patterns and behaviors that contribute to emotional distress. At its core, CBT involves cognitive restructuring, behavioral activation, and exposure therapy. Cognitive restructuring aims to help you recognize and challenge distorted thoughts, replacing them with more balanced and realistic ones. Behavioral activation encourages you to engage in activities that bring pleasure and a sense of accomplishment, countering the inertia that often accompanies depression and anxiety. Meanwhile, exposure therapy allows us to gradually face and desensitize ourselves to feared situations or objects, reducing avoidance behaviors and increasing emotional resilience.

Adding PVT strategies to CBT practices can boost the effectiveness of therapy through its focus on addressing the physiological aspects of emotional regulation. By practising vagal nerve exercises into CBT, you can enhance your ability to regulate emotions and manage physiological responses while exploring conscious thought processes. For example, understanding how the vagus nerve affects your state of arousal can help you better manage anxiety during exposure tasks.

To effectively combine Polyvagal Theory with CBT, you can implement mindfulness and breathing exercises into therapy sessions. Before starting a CBT session, take a few minutes to practice diaphragmatic breathing, activating the vagus and promoting relaxation while reducing anxiety. During sessions, tapping into learned mindfulness practices (including grounding mantras) help us to stay present and focused. Simple techniques such as light breath work or partial body scans can help you remain connected with yourself and better manage emotional responses. Additionally, using vagal tone assessments will provide valuable insights into your progress. Monitoring changes in your HVR will help track improvements in vagal tone and emotional regulation, allowing for more tailored interventions during sessions. In sum, applying PVT principles alongside CBT addresses both cognitive and physiological aspects of emotional regulation, which enables us to achieve more effective and sustainable therapeutic outcomes.

Mindfulness and Polyvagal Theory

Mindfulness, at its core, is about being fully present in the moment, aware of your thoughts, emotions, and physical sensations without judgment. With its basic components including focused attention, body awareness, emotional regulation, and acceptance, this simple practice is profoundly impactful for mental health. By practising mindfulness exercises, you can cultivate a deeper connection with yourself and your surroundings. The benefits are extensive, ranging from reduced stress and anxiety to improved emotional regulation and overall well-being.

The practice of mindfulness comprises several key elements. First, we have focused attention, which is the ability to concentrate on a single point of reference such as breath, sounds, and visual objects. This focus helps to anchor your mind, reducing distractions and promoting a sense of calm. Body awareness allows us to tune into physical sensations, noticing areas of tension or relaxation. This heightened awareness can help you better understand how your body responds to stress and relaxation. Next, we have emotional regulation. By observing your emotions without judgment, you can learn to manage them more effectively, reducing the intensity of negative feelings and enhancing positive ones. Finally, acceptance is about embracing your experiences as they are, without trying to change or resist them. This attitude of acceptance helps us develop a sense of peace and resilience.

Polyvagal Theory complements mindfulness beautifully by providing a deeper understanding of how our autonomic nervous system influences our emotional and physiological states. When we practice mindfulness, we enhance our neuroceptive abilities, becoming more attuned to the subtle signals our body sends about safety and threat. This heightened awareness allows us to respond more effectively to stress, promoting a state of calm and relaxation. Additionally, mindfulness practices can improve vagal tone, the health of the vagus nerve, which is a central component when it comes to regulating our nervous system and developing resilience.

Combining mindfulness with Polyvagal principles can create a powerful restorative and healing practice. One excellent exercise is mindful breathing with a focus on vagal stimulation. Sit comfortably and close your eyes. Take slow, deep breaths, inhaling through your nose and exhaling through your mouth. As you breathe, visualize the breath traveling down to your abdomen, activating the vagus nerve and promoting relaxation. This practice will calm your mind while stimulating the vagus nerve, enhancing vagal tone and reducing stress.

Using Polyvagal Theory with Somatics

Somatic therapies focus on the body's role in processing and healing trauma. These therapies operate on the principle that the body stores traumatic memories and physical experiences, and by bringing awareness to these sensations, you can release stored tension and trauma. Somatic Experiencing, as we've discussed, is a foundational approach within this field. It emphasizes the importance of body awareness in trauma recovery and emotional regulation. The primary goal here is to help you reconnect with your body's sensations, enabling the release of pent-up energy and facilitating a return to a state of equilibrium.

Polyvagal Theory goes hand-in-hand with somatics, which is why combining them significantly enhances their effectiveness. Understanding how the vagus nerve influences your autonomic nervous system provides a valuable framework for these therapies. By incorporating vagal nerve exercises, you can enhance body awareness and promote a sense of safety. Polyvagal Theory also guides somatic interventions by helping therapists recognize the physiological states associated with trauma and stress. This insight allows for more targeted and effective therapeutic techniques, ensuring that interventions are tailored to the body's needs.

Grounding exercises are a powerful method in which PVT can be integrated into somatics. These help us stay connected to the present moment, reducing anxiety and promoting a sense of calm. One effective grounding technique involves standing barefoot on the ground, feeling the connection between your feet and the earth. As you stand, take slow, deep breaths, focusing on the sensation of the ground beneath you. This simple mindful practice allows us to bring our body and mind back to the present moment, activating the vagus through deep breathing, and enhancing our sense of stability and safety.

Pendulation techniques can also be used with vagal nerve awareness. A simple way to go about this is to start by focusing on a part of your body that feels tense or uncomfortable. Take time to notice the sensations and take a few deep breaths. Then shift your focus to a part of your body that feels relaxed or neutral. By alternating your attention between these areas, you can help your nervous system learn to move smoothly between different states, enhancing resilience and increasing your ability to manage stress.

Somatic healing therapies focus on bodily sensations and experiences, making them ideally suited to incorporate PVT principles. As trauma often leaves us stuck in a state of hyperarousal or hypoarousal, traditional talk therapies may be less effective, which is why somatic therapists can use PVT principles to help clients safely explore and release stored trauma in the body. Understanding how our nervous system shifts between states allows us to explore practices that promote ventral vagal activation. Therefore, with a greater awareness of vagus nerve function, somatic exercises can be more effectively used to calm the sympathetic fight-or-flight response or bring us out of dorsal vagal shutdown.

Integrating Polyvagal Theory into Talk Therapy

Talk therapy, commonly referred to as psychotherapy or counseling, is a fundamental pillar in the treatment of mental health. Simply put, it involves conversations with a trained therapist to explore thoughts, feelings, and behaviors. The key components of talk therapy consist of building a therapeutic relationship, setting goals, and using various techniques to promote insight, develop coping skills, and drive behavioral change. This approach provides a safe space for us to express emotions, understand our experiences, and develop strategies for managing life's challenges.

The combination of Polyvagal Theory with talk therapy holds much potential to enhance its effectiveness. One of the main advantages is creating a sense of safety within the therapeutic environment. When you feel safe, your autonomic nervous system can shift into a more regulated state, making it easier to engage in deep emotional work. Enhancing emotional regulation through Polyvagal-informed interventions is another important benefit. By understanding how your nervous system responds to stress and safety, your therapist can tailor interventions to better suit your needs. Guided imagery, grounding exercises, and mindful breathing can be added to sessions to help you manage emotional arousal. Moreover, using Polyvagal principles to guide therapeutic conversations keeps us attuned to our body's signals and allows us to adjust the pace and focus of the session accordingly. For example, if you notice signs of heightened arousal, your therapist might pause and guide you through a grounding exercise before continuing.

Vagal tone assessments are also useful to track therapy progress. Tools such as HRV monitors will help measure changes in vagal tone over time, indicating fluctuations and improvements in your nervous system regulation. These assessments can complement traditional therapeutic progress markers to provide a more holistic view of your well-being. By regularly monitoring your vagal tone, you and your therapist can make informed adjustments to your therapy plan, ensuring it continues to meet your evolving needs.

The Role of Art and Music Therapy in Vagal Stimulation

Art and music therapy offer unique pathways to healing that tap into the creative and expressive parts of ourselves. These approaches utilize the process of creating art to explore feelings, reconcile emotional conflicts, develop self-awareness, and manage behavior. Art therapy often involves drawing, painting, sculpting, or other forms of visual art. The act of creating is innate and freeing, allowing us to express emotions that might be difficult to verbalize. This creative process can be therapeutic, providing a non-verbal outlet for emotions and while creating a sense of accomplishment and self-discovery.

Music therapy, on the other hand, entails using music to address emotional, cognitive, and social needs. This can include listening to songs, playing instruments, singing, or composing music. The rhythm and melodies in music can have remarkable effects on the nervous system, promoting relaxation and emotional expression. As such, there is no doubt that music therapy helps in regulating emotions, reducing anxiety, and improving mood. Both visual arts and music provide safe spaces for emotional expression, which is a key factor in mental health. These artistic outlets allow us to explore and process emotions in a supportive and non-judgmental environment, while releasing subconscious baggage.

Polyvagal Theory enhances the effectiveness of art and music therapy by giving us a deeper understanding of how these activities can stimulate the vagus and promote neuroceptive safety. Engaging in creative expression tends to activate the ventral vagal complex, creating a sense of safety and social connection. This connection between creative expression and vagal tone offers a powerful tool for emotional regulation and trauma recovery, and can open our eyes to an entire new way of healing emotional wounds.

An artistic experience that focuses on vagal stimulation might lead us to engage in a drawing exercise, where we are mindful of our breath and the sensation of the pencil on the paper. This approach to creating art helps activate the vagus nerve and promote a state of inner calm. Similarly, in music therapy, we can use slow, rhythmic music to enhance vagal tone. Listening to calming music or playing a musical instrument with a focus on breath control will also stimulate the vagus, allowing a return to a calm and focus state. Another option might be to start an art therapy session with a few minutes of deep breathing to activate the vagus. Furthermore, as you engage in the creative process, you can add grounding techniques, such as feeling the texture of the materials or focusing on the colors and shapes. In music therapy, you might use humming or chanting before playing an instrument or singing. These creative outlets, when combined with Polyvagal Theory principles, provide unique and accessible ways to enhance neuroceptive safety while promoting emotional expression and regulation.

FIVE
HOLISTIC APPROACHES TO WELL-BEING AND VAGAL TONE

In our day-to-day high-stress environments, maintaining well-being through emotional equilibrium requires a comprehensive approach that supports both physical and mental health. In this chapter, we will explore how lifestyle choices impact our vagus nerve, directly influencing our nervous system and, therefore, the general state of our mind and body. We'll look into building daily routines comprised of small, impactful habits such as breath work, balanced nutrition, regular movement, and a wide-range of self-care tools, a combination which works miracles when it comes to improving vagal tone.

Nutrition for Vagal Health

The connection between diet and vagal tone reveals the significant impact that nutritional choices can have on maintaining optimal nervous system function. The influence of specific nutrients and dietary patterns on the health and efficiency of the vagus nerve is both complex and far-reaching. For instance, omega-3 fatty acids, predominantly found in fatty fish like salmon, are not only essential for the structural integrity of nerve cells but also play a central role in modulating vagal tone. These polyunsaturated fats have been extensively studied for their ability to enhance the parasympathetic nervous system's activity by reducing cellular inflammation, a key factor in preserving the health of the nervous system. The anti-inflammatory properties of omega-3s extend beyond basic nerve support, contributing to a more adaptive and resilient response to stress.

Moreover, the inclusion of anti-inflammatory foods such as berries, leafy greens, and nuts into the diet serves as a foundational strategy for bolstering vagal function. Chronic inflammation is a known detriment to vagal efficiency, often leading to dysregulation of the autonomic nervous system. Consuming plenty of fruits, vegetables, and whole grains is essential for supporting vagal health. These foods provide a range of vitamins, minerals, and antioxidants that help maintain the health of the nervous system. For instance, magnesium, found in dark leafy greens, nuts, and seeds, supports nerve function and helps to regulate muscle and nerve activity. Probiotics, found in fermented foods like yogurt, kimchi, and kefir, support gut health, which is closely linked to vagal pathways. The gut-brain connection is a crucial aspect of our overall health, and maintaining a healthy gut microbiome can positively influence vagal tone and emotional regulation. By prioritizing a diet rich in anti-inflammatory nutrients, we can actively reduce systemic inflammation, thereby supporting our vagus nerve's capacity to regulate physiological processes effectively.

To incorporate these nutrients into your daily diet, you can simply add fatty fish like salmon or sardines to your meals a few times a week. If you follow a plant-based diet, flaxseeds, chia seeds, and walnuts are excellent sources of omega-3s. Including magnesium-rich foods is also simple. Add a handful of nuts to your morning oatmeal or a serving of dark leafy greens to your dinner. Fermented foods can be a delicious addition to your diet as well. Try adding a spoonful of kimchi to your salad or having a serving of probiotic yogurt with your breakfast. These small changes can make a significant difference in supporting your vagal health.

One way to make these dietary changes more manageable is by including them in delicious and nutritious recipes. For instance, a salmon and quinoa bowl is a delicious meal that supports vagal health. Start by cooking a serving of quinoa and topping it with grilled salmon, a variety of colorful vegetables like bell peppers and spinach, and a sprinkle of flaxseeds. Drizzle with a lemon-tahini dressing for added flavor. For a quick and nutrient-packed breakfast, try a smoothie with spinach, banana, and probiotic yogurt. Blend these ingredients with a splash of almond milk and a tablespoon of chia seeds for a refreshing and energizing start to your day.

To help you plan your meals around nutrient-dense foods, following a weekly plan is a sure way to succeed. For example, you could start your week with a breakfast of overnight oats topped with berries and nuts. Then, enjoy a lunch of mixed greens with grilled chicken, avocado, and a side of fermented veggies. For dinner, try a stir-fry with tofu, broccoli, and bell peppers, served over brown rice. Snacks can include fresh fruit, a handful of almonds, or a serving of probiotic-rich kefir. Incorporating these dietary habits into your life will impact your vagal tone and emotional health. By making mindful choices about what you eat, you can nourish your body and support the function of your gut, brain, and nervous system. These small, consistent changes can certainly lead to significant improvements in your overall well-being, making you feel more balanced, resilient, and connected.

Sleep Hygiene: Enhancing Nervous System Recovery

Imagine waking up after a night of deep, restful sleep, feeling refreshed and ready to face the day. Quality sleep isn't a luxury - it is an absolute necessity for maintaining and improving vagal tone. When you sleep well, your body has the opportunity to restore and repair itself, including the vagus nerve. On the other hand, chronic sleep deprivation disrupts this balance, impairing vagal function and affecting overall well-being. Without adequate sleep, your body will struggle to manage stress, leading to increased anxiety, inflammation, and a weakened immune system.

Unfortunately, optimizing sleep hygiene is an often-overlooked factor in enhancing overall physiological balance. The relationship between sleep quality and the ANS is clear: disrupted sleep patterns can dysregulate the parasympathetic and sympathetic branches, directly impacting the vagus nerve's ability to restore homeostasis. A structured and consistent sleep routine, anchored in the principles of circadian biology, becomes essential. By maintaining regular sleep and wake times, even on weekends, you support the synchronization of your suprachiasmatic nucleus, which governs circadian rhythms. This consistency reinforces the natural ebb and flow of melatonin and cortisol, two key regulators of sleep-wake cycles that also influence the autonomic state.

Equal in its efficacy is the design of a pre-sleep routine that minimizes hyperarousal and supports the shift into ventral vagal dominance for rest and repair. Gentle somatic practices, such as restorative yoga or progressive muscle relaxation, downregulate sympathetic drive and promote parasympathetic recovery. The inclusion of ritualized self-soothing activities—like reading, warm baths, or listening to calming music—further prepares our nervous system for the descent into sleep by engaging the default mode network, nurturing reflection and releasing any residual tension.

Conversely, stimulating activities, particularly those involving exposure to blue light from screens, inhibit the natural secretion of melatonin by disrupting the retinal ganglion cells' response to light, thereby delaying the onset of sleep. This artificial interruption affects the HPA axis and keeps the body in a state of heightened alertness, perpetuating sympathetic dominance and inhibiting the vagus nerve's ability to regulate.

Consequently, optimizing your sleep environment is another essential step. Begin by eliminating external stimuli that could disrupt vagal signaling, such as ambient light and sound. Blackout curtains are useful for minimizing disruptions to circadian rhythms by blocking out artificial light, which can interfere with melatonin production and the body's sleep-wake cycle. Additionally, white noise machines or earplugs help mask erratic sounds that may trigger micro-arousals or sympathetic activation during the night.

Temperature regulation is another key factor, as cooler environments (ideally between 60-67°F/15-20°C) stimulate the parasympathetic system and facilitate the natural drop in core body temperature that occurs during sleep. This shift signals the body to enter a more relaxed state, encouraging deeper sleep stages where vagal tone is highest.

Also, investing in the right mattress and pillows tailored to your body's needs can influence autonomic function. Proper spinal alignment and support help reduce musculoskeletal tension that could otherwise keep the sympathetic nervous system engaged. By reducing physical discomfort, you will minimize the chances of nocturnal awakenings that fragment sleep and challenge the body's ability to maintain parasympathetic dominance.

Relaxation techniques play another important role in preparing your body and mind for sleep. Progressive muscle relaxation - tensing and then slowly relaxing each muscle group in your body – is a very calming exercise that is easy to practice. Start with your toes and work your way up to your head, paying close attention to the sensations of tension and relaxation. This will help release physical tension and promote a sense of calm.

Guided imagery is a highly effective therapeutic technique that leverages the power of the mind to induce a state of deep relaxation. To begin, close your eyes and consciously transport yourself to a tranquil environment—a pristine beach with gentle waves lapping at the shore, or a dense, peaceful forest bathed in dappled sunlight. Immerse yourself fully in this imagined setting, engaging all your senses to create a vivid, multi-sensory experience. Visualize the vibrant colors, inhale the soothing scents of saltwater or pine, listen to the rhythmic sounds of waves or rustling leaves, and feel the warmth of the sun or the coolness of the forest air on your skin. By fully embodying this serene environment, your mind and body can gradually unwind, promoting a deep sense of calm.

Similarly, a mindfulness meditation before bed is a particularly valuable tool to quiet the mind and alleviate the incessant flow of racing thoughts that often hinder restful sleep. As you settle into a comfortable position, direct your focus toward your breath—observing each inhale and exhale with gentle awareness. When distractions or wandering thoughts inevitably arise, acknowledge them without judgment and softly guide your attention back to the steady rhythm of your breathing. This practice will anchor you in the present moment and facilitate the transition from the busyness of the day to a calm state of mind, thereby easing the journey into restful sleep. These techniques, when practiced regularly, help to disconnect from daily stressors and easily enter a state of deep relaxation, paving the way for more restorative and uninterrupted sleep.

Sleep Hygiene Checklist

Evaluating and refining your sleep habits can become a more manageable task with the use of a checklist tailored to promote optimal rest. By following this checklist or using some of the items to create your own, you can establish a sleep routine and environment that promotes restful, rejuvenating sleep and supports your holistic health goals.

Set a Consistent Sleep Schedule

- Go to bed and wake up at the same time every day, even on weekends.
- Aim for 7-9 hours of sleep each night.

Create a Relaxing Bedtime Routine

- Wind down with calming activities like reading, taking a warm bath, or gentle stretching.
- Avoid stimulating activities or intense exercise close to bedtime.

Reduce Screen Time Before Bed

- Turn off electronic devices at least one hour before sleep.
- Consider using blue light filters on your devices if screen time is unavoidable.

Optimize Your Sleep Environment

- Keep your bedroom cool, dark, and quiet.
- Use blackout curtains to block out light and earplugs or a white noise machine to minimize noise.
- Invest in a comfortable mattress and supportive pillows.

Limit Caffeine and Heavy Meals

- Avoid caffeine, nicotine, and large meals at least 3-4 hours before bedtime.
- Opt for light snacks if you're hungry close to bedtime.

Incorporate Relaxation Techniques

- Practice deep breathing, progressive muscle relaxation, or mindfulness meditation to ease into sleep.
- Try guided imagery or soothing sounds to help calm your mind.

Get Regular Exercise

- Engage in regular physical activity during the day to promote better sleep.
- Avoid vigorous exercise close to bedtime, as it can be too stimulating.

Manage Light Exposure

- Get plenty of natural light during the day to regulate your sleep-wake cycle.
- Dim lights in the evening to signal to your body that it's time to wind down.

Avoid Napping Late in the Day

- Limit naps to 20-30 minutes and avoid napping in the late afternoon or evening.

Limit Alcohol Before Bed

- Avoid alcohol close to bedtime, as it can disrupt your sleep cycle and reduce sleep quality.

Physical Exercise and Vagal Tone

There is no denying that physical exercise plays an important role in enhancing vagal tone and overall health, particularly within the scope of PVT, which aims to support a balanced and resilient autonomic nervous system.

During aerobic exercises such as running, swimming, or cycling, the body's demand for oxygen and energy increases, leading to an elevated heart rate and enhanced circulation. As the cardiovascular system works harder, the sympathetic nervous system dominates to support this heightened state of activity. However, the true benefit for vagal tone emerges during the cooldown phase, when the body transitions from a state of exertion back to rest. Here, the vagus nerve facilitates a swift and efficient reduction in heart rate and blood pressure, signaling the body to shift back into parasympathetic dominance. This process, known as cardiac vagal modulation, is a key indicator of vagal tone. The more efficiently your body can transition from high-intensity activity to a relaxed state, the stronger and more adaptive your vagal response becomes.

While aerobic exercise is often highlighted for its cardiovascular benefits, strength training also plays an important role in enhancing vagal tone and nervous system health. Resistance exercises, such as weightlifting, promote muscle growth and hypertrophy, which, in turn, leads to increased metabolic efficiency and improved muscle oxygenation. Additionally, strength training induces a reduction in systemic inflammation, partly due to the release of anti-inflammatory cytokines known as myokines during muscle contractions. This reduction in inflammation is an important aspect as chronic inflammation can impair vagal tone, leading to dysregulation of the ANS and contributing to conditions such as anxiety, depression, and cardiovascular disease. By reducing inflammation, strength training supports the overall health of the vagus nerve and its ability to regulate bodily functions.

Beyond individual benefits, combining aerobic and strength training exercises has even more impact on enhancing vagal tone. Regular engagement in these two types of activities not only strengthens the vagus nerve but also improves heart rate variability, a key marker of autonomic balance.

For those knowledgeable in the field, it's important to recognize that optimizing vagal tone through exercise is not only focused on physical exertion, but is also about balancing intensity, recovery, and consistency. Tailoring an exercise regimen that incorporates both aerobic and resistance training, along with mindful cooldowns and adequate rest, will undoubtedly impact the health of your vagus nerve.

Creating a structured workout routine is an excellent way to help you maintain consistency and achieve better results. A weekly aerobic exercise plan might include three to five sessions of moderate to vigorous aerobic activity, such as 30 minutes of running, cycling, or swimming. For yoga, a beginner-friendly routine could involve practicing for 20 to 30 minutes, three to four times a week, focusing on poses that promote relaxation and deep breathing. A simple strength training circuit could include exercises like squats, lunges, push-ups, and dumbbell rows, performed in sets of 10-15 repetitions, two to three times a week.

We all know that staying motivated and consistent with exercise routines can often be challenging; however, setting small, realistic, attainable goals, such as committing to a 10-minute walk each day or attending a yoga class once a week, is a proven method to develop this new habit. As you build confidence and see progress, gradually increase the intensity and duration of your workouts. Finding an exercise buddy or joining a support group can also boost motivation. Working out with a friend or participating in group fitness classes provides accountability and makes exercise more enjoyable. Tracking your progress and celebrating milestones is another effective strategy. Keep a journal or use a fitness app to record your workouts, noting improvements in your endurance and strength. Remember to reward yourself for reaching milestones, whether it's treating yourself to a new workout outfit or enjoying a relaxing spa day!

The Role of Social Connections in Nervous System Regulation

Picture this: You walk into a room filled with familiar faces, the kind where even before a word is spoken, the warmth of the space wraps around you. The laughter, the eye contact, the shared smiles—they create an invisible web of connection that instantly puts your body at ease. In that moment, something powerful is happening within your autonomic nervous system. This isn't just a fleeting mood boost; it's the activation of your ventral vagal complex, the part of your nervous system that thrives on safety, trust, and social engagement.

As Polyvagal Theory teaches us, the ventral vagal complex is our gateway to connection, signaling to the body that it's safe to let its guard down. In this state, your vagus nerve gets to work, subtly adjusting your heart rate, calming your breath, and shifting you out of a defensive state. You might feel your muscles relax, your breath deepen—all signs that your body is entering a state of regulation. These small, meaningful moments of connection are certainly pleasant, but they also happen to be essential. In fact, they help reinforce the pathways in your nervous system that promote resilience, building your capacity to respond calmly in stressful situations. Over time, the strength of these social bonds tunes your vagal tone, creating an internal rhythm of safety and ease that supports your mental and physical health. This is the silent, powerful role of social connection in shaping how we experience both the world around us and the world within.

While this ventral vagal activation promotes relaxation, it also further strengthens our capacity for social bonding. In contrast, the absence of such connections—whether through loneliness, social isolation, or chronic stress—can lead to a significant reduction in vagal tone. Prolonged isolation can be, for some, an emotional burden; for all of us, however, it is a physiological stressor that disrupts the balance of our autonomic nervous system. This dysregulation can trigger a cascade of effects, including elevated cortisol levels, increased heart rate, and a heightened stress response, all of which make it more challenging to manage emotions and cope with daily stressors. Over time, this can lead to a vicious cycle where the lack of social engagement further weakens vagal tone, contributing to feelings of anxiety, depression, and a reduced ability to bounce back from adversity.

Supportive and healthy relationships are a pillar of both emotional and physical well-being. Having people you can turn to during times of stress provides emotional support that can buffer against anxiety and depression. The simple act of talking to a friend about your worries can reduce stress hormones and promote a sense of relief. These relationships also bolster your resilience, giving you the strength to cope with life's challenges. Knowing that someone has your back can make you feel more confident and capable of handling difficult situations. Furthermore, supportive relationships enhance mental health by reducing feelings of isolation and creating a sense of belonging. The physiological benefits of supportive relationships are equally significant. Research consistently demonstrates that individuals with strong social networks experience lower rates of chronic illnesses, such as cardiovascular disease and diabetes, and enjoy better overall health outcomes. These benefits are partly due to the influence of positive social interactions on the immune system, which can boost immunity and reduce inflammation—factors that are critical in preventing and managing chronic diseases. Additionally, it has been shown that people with strong social ties are more likely to engage in health-promoting behaviors, such as regular exercise and balanced nutrition, which further contributes to their physical well-being.

Building and maintaining social connections requires effort, but the rewards are well worth it. Start by joining clubs or groups that align with your interests. Whether it's a book club, a hiking group, or a volunteer organization, engaging in activities you enjoy with others can create a strong foundation for lasting relationships. Volunteering is another excellent way to connect with like-minded individuals while giving back to your community. It offers the dual benefit of helping others and enhancing your own well-being. By dedicating your time and skills to help others, you align yourself with like-minded individuals who value service and community. This brings about a sense of purpose and enriches your life by expanding your social network and contributing to your community's well-being. The reciprocity inherent in volunteering —where both the giver and the receiver benefit—can enhance your own sense of happiness and fulfillment, as research consistently shows that acts of kindness boost psychological health and promote a positive self-image.

Additionally, nurturing existing relationships is just as important as building new ones. Regular contact with friends and family, even through small gestures like a quick text, a thoughtful message, or a brief phone call, reinforces the bonds that anchor your social life. Scheduling regular meet-ups—whether it's a monthly coffee date with a friend or a weekly video chat with family—provides a dependable rhythm of connection, ensuring that these relationships are continuously nour-ished. These deliberate efforts, though they may seem small, strengthen your social ties. Over time, they contribute to a support network that enhances your overall well-being, offering emotional support, compan-ionship, and a shared sense of life's journey – not to mention contributing to vagal tone.

Self-Assessment Tools for Social Engagement

When it comes to social connections, determining your level of engage-ment with others can help you identify areas for improvement, and a self-assessment questionnaire that explores your current interpersonal relationships can be a helpful starting point. The following self-assessment tool is designed to help you evaluate your current level of social engagement, identify strengths and areas for growth, and develop strategies to enhance your social well-being. Take your time to reflect on each question, and use your answers as a guide for making meaningful changes.

1. Frequency of Interactions

How OFTEN DO you communicate with friends or family members (in person, via phone, text, or social media)?
- ☐ Daily
- ☐ Several times a week
- ☐ Weekly
- ☐ Monthly
- ☐ Rarely/Never

REFLECTION: Is this frequency aligned with your desired level of connection? If not, what could you change?

2. Quality of Relationships

Do you feel understood and supported by those you regularly interact with?
- ☐ Always
- ☐ Often
- ☐ Sometimes
- ☐ Rarely
- ☐ Never

REFLECTION: Consider the quality of your most important relationships. Are there ways you could improve communication or strengthen these bonds?

3. Diversity of Social Interactions

Do you engage with a variety of social groups (e.g., family, friends, coworkers, community groups)?
- ☐ Yes, regularly
- ☐ Yes, but infrequently
- ☐ No

REFLECTION: Would expanding your social circles add value to your life? What steps could you take to meet new people?

4. Participation in Group Activities

Do you participate in group activities that you enjoy (e.g., sports teams, book clubs, hobby groups)?
- ☐ Yes, regularly
- ☐ Occasionally
- ☐ Rarely/Never

REFLECTION: Are there activities or hobbies you love that you could share with others? How might this enhance your social life?

5. Volunteering and Community Involvement

ARE you involved in volunteering or community service?
- ☐ Yes, regularly
- ☐ Occasionally
- ☐ No

REFLECTION: Volunteering can be a fulfilling way to connect with like-minded people. Are there causes or organizations you feel passionate about?

6. Social Support Network

Do you have people you can turn to for emotional support during challenging times?
   ☐ Yes, several people
   ☐ A few people
   ☐ Not really

REFLECTION: If you feel your support network is lacking, consider how you might strengthen or expand it.

7. Barriers to Social Engagement

Do you experience social anxiety, shyness, or other challenges that hinder your social interactions?
   ☐ Yes, often
   ☐ Occasionally
   ☐ Rarely/Never

REFLECTION: Identify specific situations where you feel anxious. What coping strategies could help you manage these feelings?

8. Managing Social Anxiety

Have you tried deep breathing exercises or mindfulness techniques to calm your nerves before social interactions?
   ☐ Yes, regularly
   ☐ Sometimes
   ☐ No, but I'm interested

ACTION STEP: Practice deep breathing before your next social interaction. Inhale deeply for 4 counts, hold for 4, and exhale for 6. Notice any changes in your anxiety levels.

9. Taking Small Steps

ARE you willing to take small, manageable steps to increase your social engagement (e.g., attending a social event for a short time, initiating one-on-one conversations)?

☐ Yes, I'm ready
☐ I need more preparation
☐ Not at the moment

ACTION STEP: Choose a small, manageable social goal to work on this week, such as staying at an event for 15 minutes or reaching out to someone for a coffee chat.

10. Building Confidence Over Time

ARE you committed to gradually expanding your social comfort zone over time?

☐ Yes, I'm committed
☐ I'm hesitant but willing to try
☐ No, not ready yet

ACTION STEP: Track your progress with each small step. Reflect on how your confidence grows as you gradually increase your social interactions.

Using Your Results

- What aspects of your social engagement are you satisfied with? Celebrate these as strengths.
- Which areas could benefit from more attention? Set specific, achievable goals to improve your social connections.
- Based on your reflections, create a plan to enhance your social engagement. Include small, actionable steps that align

with your comfort level and build confidence over time.
- Revisit this self-assessment periodically to track your progress and make adjustments as needed.

ENHANCING your social network is a journey that will require self-awareness, intentional effort, and patience. Deepening existing relationships is equally important; make an effort to be present and attentive during interactions. Listen actively, ask open-ended questions, and show genuine interest in the other person's life. Expressing appreciation and gratitude can also strengthen your bonds. Let your friends and family know how much they mean to you and how their support positively impacts your life. These gestures, while simple, are sure to deepen your connections and generate a sense of mutual understanding and support.

Creating a Holistic Wellness Plan

Creating a holistic wellness plan allows us to weave together diverse aspects of our life to cultivate a state of complete well-being—one that goes beyond the absence of illness to embrace physical vitality, emotional resilience, and social connectedness. This approach acknowledges that true health is multifaceted, requiring the integration of physical, mental, emotional, and social dimensions. Each component helps maintain a balanced, healthy lifestyle, where the mind and body are in harmony, and relationships provide meaningful support.

For starters, social health is, once again, the often-underestimated pillar of holistic wellness. This emphasizes the importance of relationships, community involvement, and a sense of belonging. Strong social connections provide emotional support, reduce feelings of loneliness, and contribute to a longer lifespan. Positive relationships can buffer against stress, offering a source of comfort and resilience in challenging times. The quality of social interactions directly impacts mental health, influencing everything from our stress levels to self-esteem. When social bonds are strong, they contribute to a healthier mind and body, reinforcing the idea that well-being is not just an individual pursuit but a collective one.

Physical health is the foundation of a holistic wellness plan, encompassing regular exercise, a balanced diet, and adequate sleep. Exercise not only strengthens muscles and improves cardiovascular health, but it also enhances brain function, boosting mood-regulating neurotransmitters like serotonin and dopamine. A nutrient-rich diet fuels the body's systems, supporting everything from immune function to cognitive performance. Proper sleep, often overlooked, is essential for cellular repair, hormone regulation, and mental clarity. Together, these elements keep the body physiologically strong and resilient, creating a solid base for overall well-being. Physical health is deeply intertwined with mental and emotional health, as regular exercise, proper nutrition, and restful sleep are known to reduce stress, alleviate symptoms of anxiety and depression, and promote a sense of vitality and energy.

Mental and emotional health focuses on the mind's well-being, which helps in managing stress, maintaining mental clarity, and fostering emotional resilience. This aspect of wellness includes practices like mindfulness, meditation, and relaxation techniques that help regulate the nervous system and enhance vagal tone. These practices reduce the impact of stressors and improve our ability to respond to challenges with calmness and clarity. Emotional well-being is closely linked to physical health, as chronic stress and negative emotions can lead to inflammation, hormonal imbalances, and a weakened immune system. Conversely, maintaining a healthy mental and emotional state supports the body's ability to heal and thrive, as per the interconnected nature of mind and body. The body and mind are not separate entities; rather, they exist in a dynamic relationship where each affects the other. For instance, regular physical activity stimulates the production of endocannabinoids, which improve mood and reduce pain perception. Similarly, a diet rich in omega-3 fatty acids supports brain health and can help manage depression. Meanwhile, chronic stress—if left unchecked—can lead to physical ailments such as hypertension, gastrointestinal issues, and a weakened immune system. By addressing all aspects of well-being—physical, mental, emotional, and social—a holistic wellness plan ensures that these interconnected systems are working together in harmony, leading to a more balanced, fulfilling, and healthy life.

To create a personalized wellness plan, you can begin by assessing your current overall health status. Take a moment to reflect on how you feel physically, emotionally, and socially. Identify areas where you might need improvement. Next, set specific, achievable goals. These goals should be realistic and tailored to your individual needs. For example, if you struggle with sleep, a goal might be to establish a consistent bedtime routine. If you feel socially isolated, a goal could be to join a local club or group.

Once you have determined your goals, create a balanced routine that includes all aspects of wellness. If you have a tendency to be inactive, start by scheduling regular exercise sessions, such as morning walks or evening yoga classes. Think about making small changes to your eating habits, perhaps beginning with nutritious snacks and meals that include a variety of fruits, vegetables, whole grains, and lean proteins. Establish a consistent sleep schedule to ensure you get enough rest each night. Integrate mindfulness practices into your daily routine. This could be as simple as taking a few minutes each day to focus on your breath or practicing a guided meditation. Lastly, make time for social activities. Schedule regular meet-ups with friends and family, and look for opportunities to get involved in your community.

For a busy professional, a wellness plan might include a quick morning workout, packing healthy lunches, and setting aside time each evening for relaxation and reflection. A stay-at-home parent might incorporate family walks, prepare balanced meals, and schedule playdates or parent groups for social interaction. Someone recovering from trauma might focus on gentle exercises, nutrient-rich foods that support healing, and mindfulness practices to manage stress and anxiety.

Staying accountable and motivated can be challenging, but there are several strategies to help. Keeping a wellness journal or using a health app to monitor your activities and reflect on your achievements are excellent ways to track your progress. Finding accountability partners, such as friends or family members who share similar goals, can provide support and encouragement. Adjusting goals and routines as needed is also important. Life is dynamic, and your wellness plan should be flexible enough to adapt to changing circumstances. If you find that a particular goal is no longer serving you, don't hesitate to modify it or set a new one. Finally, keep in mind that putting these strategies into motion and sprinkling bits of positive changes to your daily life will lead to a more balanced and fulfilling existence. It is a most rewarding form of self-care, supporting you to thrive in all areas of your life.

Self-Care for Vagal Health

Taking care of yourself is far from being a mere indulgence; it is an essential practice for maintaining and enhancing your vagal tone, especially once you begin to unravel the complexities of your autonomic nervous system. Regular and intentional self-care practices influence the efficiency and responsiveness of your nervous system. By prioritizing self-care, you engage in activities that directly modulate your autonomic nervous system, helping to shift your body from a sympathetic state to a parasympathetic state, thereby promoting physiological calm and homeostasis. This regulation is key for managing chronic stressors of modern life, reducing anxiety, and enhancing emotional health.

A well-regulated nervous system allows for greater flexibility in responding to stress, enabling a return to baseline more swiftly after stressful events. This neurobiological resilience forms the bedrock of mental and emotional stability, which in turn supports physical health by reducing the burden of stress-related disorders such as hypertension, insomnia, and gastrointestinal issues. By consistently dedicating time to self-care—whether through practices like mindful breathing, meditation, regular physical activity, or social connection—you are reinforcing the health and resilience of your entire nervous system.

Different types of self-care practices contribute to vagal health in various ways. Physical self-care includes activities that nourish and care for your body such as exercise, proper nutrition, and adequate sleep. Engaging in physical activities like walking, yoga, or swimming can activate the vagus, promoting relaxation and reducing stress. Emotional self-care revolves around practices that help you manage your emotions and maintain mental clarity. Social self-care is about spending time with loved ones, participating in group activities, and volunteering to enhance your sense of connection and support.

Adding self-care practices to your daily routine can have a significant impact on your life. A morning self-care routine could include a few minutes of deep breathing or meditation to set a positive tone for the day. Follow this with a healthy breakfast that includes nutrient-dense foods to fuel your body and mind. In the evening, winding down with a relaxing activity such as reading a book, taking a warm bath, or practicing gentle stretches. Weekend self-care activities can be more leisurely and fulfilling, such as spending time in nature, engaging in a hobby, or having a spa day. These practices allow you to recharge mind and body, and make the most of your time off.

Of course, prioritizing self-care can be challenging, especially when life gets busy. Identifying and addressing barriers to self-care is an important first step. Common obstacles include lack of time, feelings of guilt, or not knowing where to start. To overcome these barriers, start by acknowledging that self-care is not selfish but necessary for your well-being. Schedule self-care activities into your calendar as you would any other important appointment. Make self-care a non-negotiable part of your daily routine by setting reminders and creating rituals that you look forward to. Finding support and resources for self-care can also be helpful. Join a self-care group, seek advice from friends or professionals, and use apps or books that offer guidance and inspiration.

Embracing self-care practices can truly transform your life. To make self-care more accessible - just like the other practices we have explored - break it down into small, manageable steps. Instead of trying to overhaul your entire routine, start with one or two elements that resonate with you. For example, you could start your days with a five-minute body scan sequence or set aside time to connect with a friend each week. Gradually, you can build on these practices, creating a comprehensive self-care routine that supports your overall well-being.

SIX

SELF-ASSESSMENT TOOLS FOR NERVOUS SYSTEM STATES

IMAGINE SETTLING into your favorite cozy chair, a warm cup of tea in hand, as you take a few intentional moments to check in with yourself. As you breathe deeply, you begin to notice the subtle sensations within your body—perhaps a slight tension in your shoulders, the gentle rise and fall of your chest, or the lingering emotions just beneath the surface. This mindful awareness, this act of tuning into your body's signals, is a window into the current state of your nervous system. Understanding and identifying fluctuations in your nervous system—whether you're experiencing the calm and connection of a ventral vagal state, the alertness and tension of sympathetic activation, or the withdrawal and numbness of dorsal vagal shutdown—is essential for navigating your emotional landscape and managing stress.

Recognizing is about much more than labeling your experience; it provides an essential framework for understanding the complex interactions between your emotions, physical sensations, and behaviors. For instance, if you find yourself feeling inexplicably anxious or overwhelmed in certain situations, it could be a sign of sympathetic activation—your body's fight-or-flight response taking the reins. On the other hand, moments of profound calm and connection are indicative of a well-regulated ventral vagal state, where social engagement and relaxation are possible. Conversely, the heavy, disconnected feeling that can accompany extreme stress or trauma may point to a dorsal vagal shut-down, where your nervous system conserves energy by pulling back from the external world. By cultivating this awareness, you will empower yourself to make informed, compassionate choices about how to respond to your body's cues. This might mean engaging in practices that support ventral vagal activation, or gently easing out of sympathetic overdrive. Understanding your nervous system then becomes a personal-ized guide to emotional regulation, offering you the tools to manage stress more effectively and to live with greater emotional resilience.

Recap: Our Nervous System States

As we've covered much ground in the area of PVT, let's just take a moment to step back and revisit the main aspects of our nervous system states. This recap is intended as a quick reference for those who wish to reinforce their understanding. If you feel that you are now very familiar with these concepts and eager to dive into the practical exercises, feel free to skip ahead to the next section. Otherwise, take a minute to refresh your memory and ensure that you are well-versed on these notions before pursuing practical application.

Firstly, we have the ventral vagal state, which is often described as safe and social. When you are in this state, you feel grounded and connected to yourself and others. Your heart rate is steady, your breathing is relaxed, and you can engage in social interactions with ease. This state is characterized by feelings of safety, trust, and positive social engagement. You might find yourself enjoying a conversation with a friend, feeling at peace while reading a book, or simply appreciating a quiet moment of solitude. In this state, your body is optimized for rest and digestion, with blood flow directed towards your digestive system and your immune system functioning efficiently.

In contrast, the sympathetic state is our "fight or flight" mode. This state is triggered when our body perceives a threat, real or imagined. Heart rate increases, muscles tense, and you might feel a surge of adren-aline. Common indicators include sweating, rapid breathing, and a heightened sense of alertness. Anxiety is a hallmark of this state, and you may find it challenging to focus or relax. The body redirects resources to your muscles and limbs, preparing you to confront or escape perceived danger. While this state can be beneficial in short bursts, chronic activation can lead to health issues such as high blood pressure and weakened immune function.

Finally, we have the dorsal vagal shutdown state, which is the body's most primitive defense mechanism. Activated when the sympathetic branch is overwhelmed, this state is characterized by a significant reduction in heart rate, blood pressure, and movement. You might feel emotionally numb, disconnected, or detached from your surroundings. Fatigue and a sense of hopelessness are common in this state. It's as if your body has hit the "off" switch to protect you from overwhelming stress. While this response can be adaptive in life-threatening situations, chronic shutdown can lead to depression and a sense of isolation.

Self-Assessment Toolbox

Deepening your awareness of your nervous system states involves honing the ability to attune to the subtle signals your body sends. This process, often referred to as interoception, helps us understand the interplay between physical sensations and emotional states. As such, techniques that enhance body awareness serve as useful tools in this endeavor, allowing us to cultivate a nuanced understanding of our internal landscape. A good starting point is to observe specific physiological markers such as the rhythm of your heartbeat, the degree of muscle tension, and the pattern of your breath. Each of these signals offers precious insight into the state of your autonomic nervous system, reflecting whether you are in a mode of relaxation, stress, or somewhere in between.

For instance, a racing heart or shallow breathing may indicate sympathetic arousal, while a relaxed posture and steady breath could signal parasympathetic activation. As you notice areas of discomfort or tension—perhaps a tightness in the shoulders or a clenching in the gut—allow yourself to explore these sensations without judgment, considering what they reveal about your current emotional and physiological state.

Mindfulness practices, such as breath-focused meditation or body scanning, further refine this awareness. A body scan, where you systematically bring attention to each part of your body from head to toe, can illuminate areas of unconscious tension or holding patterns that might otherwise go unnoticed. These practices enhance our ability to detect shifts in our nervous system and promote a greater sense of embodied presence, grounding us in the moment.

To deepen this beautiful connection between physical and emotional experiences, you can engage in reflective self-inquiry. Questions like "What is my body communicating to me right now?" or "How does this physical sensation correlate with my current emotional state?" can allow for a more integrated understanding of your inner experience. Over time, these practices build a sophisticated awareness of how your nervous system responds to various stimuli, enabling you to proactively manage stress.

So, in order to engage in effective self-regulation and optimize well-being, it is important to develop a nuanced understanding of your nervous system's state at any given moment. This will involve recognizing your emotional and physiological responses while systematically assessing them with precision. For those well-versed in nervous system dynamics, a detailed self-assessment checklist can serve as an indispensable tool in identifying whether you're operating from a ventral vagal state, experiencing sympathetic activation, or slipping into a dorsal vagal shutdown. As we now know, each of these states deeply impacts our behavior, emotions, and overall health, and being able to distinguish between them is essential for informed self-care.

Practical Self-Assessment Checklist for Identifying Nervous System States

1. Ventral Vagal State: The Zone of Safety and Social Engagement

When in this state, the vagus nerve efficiently regulates heart rate and promotes a balanced response to the environment, enabling healthy social interactions and emotional resilience.

Emotional Indicators:

I feel safe and secure in my environment.

I experience ease and joy in social interactions.

I am able to stay present and engaged with others.

Physical Indicators:

My breathing is steady and deep, with a smooth rhythm.

My body feels relaxed, with little to no muscle tension.
I have a stable, comfortable heart rate.

Cognitive Indicators:

I can focus clearly and make decisions without feeling overwhelmed.
I experience a sense of purpose and clarity in my thoughts.

2. Sympathetic Activation: The Fight-or-Flight Response

While this response is necessary for survival, chronic activation can lead to anxiety, restlessness, and a range of stress-related symptoms.

Emotional Indicators:

I feel anxious, on edge, or easily irritated.
I have a heightened sense of alertness, as if constantly scanning for danger.
I find it difficult to relax, even in familiar environments.

Physical Indicators:

My heart is racing, and I can feel my pulse in my chest or neck.
I notice muscle tension, particularly in my jaw, shoulders, or stomach.
My breathing is shallow, rapid, and sometimes feels constricted.

Cognitive Indicators:

My thoughts are fast-paced, often jumping from one worry to another.
I struggle with concentration and may find it hard to complete tasks.

3. Dorsal Vagal Shutdown: The State of Disconnection and Conservation

In this state, your body conserves energy by minimizing metabolic activity, often manifesting as depression or emotional numbness.

Emotional Indicators:

I feel emotionally numb, as if I am disconnected from my feelings.
I experience a pervasive sense of hopelessness or apathy.
I feel detached from others, as if I am observing life from a distance.

Physical Indicators:

I am constantly fatigued, with little energy to engage in daily activities.
My body feels heavy or slow, and I may have difficulty moving.

My breathing is shallow, with a sense of constriction or difficulty in taking deep breaths.

Cognitive Indicators:

My thoughts are slow and repetitive, often focused on themes of despair or worthlessness.

I find it difficult to concentrate, and my mind feels foggy or blank.

BY USING THIS SIMPLE CHECKLIST, you will learn to more accurately identify which state your nervous system is in, allowing you to tailor your self-care practices accordingly. For instance, recognizing that you are in (or shifting towards) a sympathetic state might prompt you to engage in calming activities such as deep diaphragmatic breathing or grounding exercises. If you identify with dorsal vagal shutdown symptoms, it may be beneficial to seek gentle stimulation, like light physical movement or engaging with a supportive friend, to gradually re-engage your system.

Understanding your fluctuating nervous system states will also sharpen your ability to detect triggers. It will enable you to develop strategies to prevent emotional escalation, as well as gently shift toward more adaptive states. This informed approach allows for more effective interventions and supports long-term resilience in the face of life's challenges.

Tools for Tracking Vagal Tone

As incredible as it may seem, it is possible to start every day with a practice that offers a snapshot of your nervous system's adaptability – yes, that's correct: a diagnostic tool for your long-term health. As we've discussed earlier on, tracking vagal tone, typically measured through heart rate variability (HRV), provides a nuanced insight into the functioning of your vagus nerve. Unlike the fleeting fluctuations of stress or mood, vagal tone serves as a stable biomarker of your body's ability to maintain homeostasis. High vagal tone reflects parasympathetic dominance, indicating a flexible and resilient nervous system capable of quickly adapting to stressors, while low vagal tone signals sympathetic overactivity, often linked to chronic stress, systemic inflammation, and a host of physical and mental health issues, including anxiety, depression, and cardiovascular problems.

Tracking vagal tone is a powerful way to understand how your body responds to both stress-inducing stimuli and recovery techniques. By regularly monitoring HRV, you can observe the subtleties of your body's response to everything from exercise, diet, and sleep quality, to emotional stressors or various restorative practices. This offers invaluable feedback on the efficacy of interventions, allowing you to fine-tune your wellness regimen. For example, if your vagal tone remains consistently low despite implementing relaxation techniques, it may suggest deeper underlying issues—such as dysregulated circadian rhythms or persistent low-grade inflammation—that warrant further exploration.

The relationship between vagal tone and emotional regulation is especially notable. Those of us with higher vagal tone exhibit greater emotional resilience, experiencing more rapid recovery from stress and a greater ability to remain calm and composed in the face of challenge. This adaptability, often called vagal flexibility, is a reflection of our capacity to move fluidly between sympathetic arousal and parasympathetic restoration. Advanced practitioners of nervous system health can use vagal tone tracking to identify personal triggers that might otherwise go unnoticed. For instance, subtle drops in vagal tone may correlate with factors like skipped meditative practices, disruptions in sleep, or even brief but intense interpersonal conflicts.

Tracking vagal tone with precision requires the use of tools that can reliably assess HRV. For professionals and individuals deeply invested in understanding vagal tone, there are several advanced devices and methods that go beyond basic consumer wearables. Electrocardiogram (ECG) monitors, like the Polar H10 chest strap or BioHarness, provide a gold standard for HRV measurement due to their high sensitivity and direct measurement of heart electrical activity. These devices capture detailed variations in the intervals between heartbeats (R-R intervals), offering precise data on parasympathetic regulation. While wrist-based trackers like the Whoop Strap and Oura Ring are widely used, they rely on photoplethysmography (PPG), which, though less precise than ECG, provides a convenient method of tracking trends in HRV alongside other indicators like resting heart rate, sleep quality, and recovery.

For those seeking more nuanced insights, breathing rate monitors such as the Spire Stone or Leaf Therapeutics offer complementary data by tracking respiratory cycles and their relationship to vagal activity. Monitoring respiratory sinus arrhythmia (RSA)—the natural increase and decrease in heart rate that occurs during breathing—can provide additional information about vagal tone and its influence on the respiratory system.

Integrating multiple sources of data will help us develop a comprehensive view of our vagal tone. Many advanced HRV monitors, such as Elite HRV or Kubios HRV, pair with mobile applications that allow you to analyze long-term trends in vagal tone, offering insights into how stress, exercise, sleep, and emotional states affect our autonomic nervous system. These platforms can break down high-frequency HRV components, specifically related to parasympathetic activity, which directly reflects vagal influence. They also allow users to compare baseline readings with those during stress-inducing activities or recovery periods, providing a clearer picture of how resilient the vagal pathways are under various conditions.

Maximizing the accuracy and utility of these tools requires methodical application. For instance, when using a chest strap HRV monitor, ensure it is positioned correctly and used during controlled conditions, such as immediately upon waking or after structured relaxation practices, to reduce confounding variables like dehydration or external stressors. It's also essential to standardize data collection times—ideally taking morning HRV readings before eating or engaging in physical activity—to maintain consistency and improve the reliability of long-term trend analysis. Advanced users can also explore vagal biofeedback tools like HeartMath or EmWave, which provide real-time HRV biofeedback, which helps consciously regulate vagal tone through paced breathing and relaxation techniques.

If you find yourself interested in continuous, real-time monitoring, devices such as Biostrap or Firstbeat offer 24/7 tracking, with detailed breakdowns of HRV patterns in response to daily activities, sleep phases, and stressors. The granularity of this data allows for an in-depth understanding of how vagal tone fluctuates throughout the day and can guide personalized interventions aimed at improving autonomic balance.

Ultimately, understanding and improving vagal tone through HRV monitoring is not just about observing single metrics, but about gaining insights into systemic patterns—the interplay between stress, recovery, and overall nervous system health. This holistic perspective gives us the knowledge to target interventions and implement more refined adjustments in our lifestyle or stress management techniques.

Journaling to Reflect on Nervous System States

Journaling offers another powerful way to reflect on and understand your nervous system states. By putting your thoughts and feelings on paper, you enhance self-awareness and gain emotional clarity. This simple act of writing can help you connect the dots between your experiences and your body's responses. Journaling also aids in nervous system regulation by providing a space to process emotions and identify patterns that might otherwise go unnoticed.

When journaling about your day, you will create a record of your emotional and physical states, enabling you to track the impact of different situations and to notice trends over time. For example, you might discover that certain environments or interactions consistently trigger anxiety, while others promote calm and relaxation. Understanding your triggers and responses will aid in developing strategies to manage your nervous system more effectively. Moreover, writing about your experiences will lead you to release pent-up emotions, reducing stress and promoting a sense of relief.

Like many other well-being rituals, a successful journaling practice requires consistency, dedication, and a few practical strategies. Set aside a specific time each day for journaling, whether it's in the morning with your coffee or in the evening before bed. Creating a comfortable and peaceful journaling space can enhance the experience. Choose a quiet spot with minimal distractions and add elements that promote relaxation, such as soft lighting or calming music. Using journaling apps or physical journals can also help you stay consistent. Some people prefer the tactile experience of writing by hand, while others find digital journaling more convenient; choose the method that works best for you.

Self-Assessment Worksheets for Daily Monitoring

Regular self-assessment is like a daily check-in with your mind and body, supporting self-awareness and emotional regulation. As you will find with the worksheets provided hereafter, taking a few moments each day to reflect on your current state will help you detect early signs of stress and dysregulation, allowing you to address them before they escalate. Using these worksheets effectively requires consistency and attention to detail. Begin by filling out the daily mood and state tracking worksheet each morning and evening. In the morning, take a few moments to note how you feel upon waking, including your mood, energy levels, and any physical sensations. In the evening, reflect on your day, noting any significant events, emotional shifts, and physical symptoms.

When using the symptom and trigger identification worksheet, try to be as specific as possible. Note the exact nature of the symptom, such as "tightness in chest" or "racing thoughts," and the context in which it occurred. Identifying triggers might require some reflection, so consider factors like your environment, interactions with others, and any recent stressors. Over time, this worksheet can help you uncover patterns and develop targeted strategies for managing triggers.

The stress and relaxation response worksheet can be particularly insightful when used after practicing relaxation techniques. Take a few moments to describe the stressor you encountered and how your body responded. Then, note the relaxation technique you used, such as deep breathing or progressive muscle relaxation, and describe how your body and mind felt afterward. This reflection can help you identify the most effective techniques for managing stress and promoting relaxation.

IDENTIFYING areas that need change or improvement begins with your self-assessment findings. Look at the patterns and trends you've documented in your self-assessment worksheets or journals. Are there specific times of day when you feel more anxious or stressed? Are there particular activities that consistently improve your mood? Use this information to pinpoint areas that could benefit from change. For example, if you notice that your anxiety peaks in the late afternoon, a mindfulness practice or a short walk during that time will to help manage your stress levels.

Regular check-ins with yourself will help you learn to identify areas that need change or improvement. Once you've begun using these tools on a regular basis, you will need to adjust your practices based on the information derived from the self-assessments. This connection between self-assessment and personalized routines ensures that you are addressing your unique needs, which is likely to lead to better emotional regulation and reduced stress – basically, a more focused, grounded, and present version of yourself. The routine adjustments you choose to put in place can be small or significant, but know that each one plays a role in supporting your overall health. The key is to start small, be consistent, and regularly check in with yourself to ensure that your routines are meeting your needs.

DAILY PVT MOOD TRACKER

Date: _____

Time of Day: _____

1. Emotional State

Circle or highlight one or more emotions that apply, or write in your own.

- Calm / Grounded
- Anxious / Hypervigilant
- Happy / Content
- Sad / Grief
- Angry / Frustrated
- Disconnected / Numb
- Overwhelmed / Panicked
- Peaceful / Relaxed
- Curious / Engaged
- Irritable / Agitated
- Other: _____

2. Physical Sensations

Note any physical symptoms, such as tightness, pain, tension, or ease in the body.

Neck/Shoulders:

_____

Chest/Heart:

_____

Stomach/Gut:

_____

Breathing: (Deep, shallow, tight, easy)

_____

Hands/Feet: (Cold, warm, tingling, sweaty, grounded)

_____

Other Body Areas:

_____

3. Autonomic Nervous System State

Check which state you feel closest to based on your experience, following Polyvagal Theory's autonomic states.

☐ **Ventral Vagal State** (Connected, calm, safe, engaged with the world)

☐ **Sympathetic Activation** (Fight/flight, anxious, restless, on edge)

☐ **Dorsal Vagal State** (Shutdown, disconnected, low energy, numb)

4. Energy Level

Rate your energy on a scale of 1 to 10, where 1 is completely drained, and 10 is fully energized.

Energy Rating: ____ / 10

5. Mental Clarity and Focus

Rate your ability to focus and think clearly on a scale of 1 to 10, where 1 is foggy/unfocused and 10 is sharp and clear.

Clarity Rating: ____ / 10

6. Significant Events or Triggers

Note any significant events, interactions, or stressors that may have impacted your mood or state today.

_____

_____

_____

_____

_____

_____

_____

_____

_____

_____

_____

_____

7. Response to Events

How did your nervous system respond? Did you notice physiological reactions such as heart racing, shallow breathing, numbness, or a shift in energy?

_____

_____

_____

_____

_____

_____

_____

_____

_____

_____

_____

_____

8. Self-Regulation Practices

What self-regulation tools did you use today to manage your state?
Include breathing techniques, movement, grounding exercises, etc.

Breathing Exercises (e.g., diaphragmatic, physiological sigh, box breathing):

_____
_____
_____
_____
_____
_____
_____
_____
_____
_____
_____
_____

Movement (e.g., walking, yoga, stretching):

_____

_____

_____

_____

_____

_____

_____

_____

_____

_____

_____

Grounding Techniques (e.g., noticing surroundings, touch, cold water):

_____

_____

_____

_____

_____

_____

_____

_____

_____

_____

_____

_____

Meditation or Mindfulness:

_____

_____

_____

_____

_____

_____

_____

_____

_____

_____

_____

_____

Other (e.g., connection with a friend, creative expression, music):

_____

_____

_____

_____

_____

_____

_____

_____

_____

_____

_____

_____

9. Overall Mood Shift Over the Day

Looking back over the day, how did your mood and physical sensations change?

_____

_____

_____

_____

_____

_____

_____

_____

_____

_____

_____

_____

_____

10. Vagal Tone Awareness

Note any moments when you felt more grounded, connected, or relaxed, reflecting an increase in vagal tone. Describe what you did or experienced at those moments.

_____

_____

_____

_____

_____

_____

_____

_____

_____

_____

_____

_____

11. Observations and Reflections

Any other insights about your emotional and physical state, nervous system responses, or patterns you've noticed today.

_____

_____

_____

_____

_____

_____

_____

_____

_____

_____

_____

_____

End of Day Summary:

Overall Mood Rating (1–10): ____

Dominant ANS State:
Ventral Vagal / Sympathetic / Dorsal Vagal

Key Trigger or Event:

_____

_____

_____

_____

_____

_____

_____

_____

_____

_____

_____

_____

Self-Regulation Success (What worked well today?)

_____

_____

_____

_____

_____

_____

_____

_____

_____

_____

_____

_____

_____

What could I improve tomorrow?

_____

_____

_____

_____

_____

_____

_____

_____

_____

_____

_____

_____

SYMPTOM AND TRIGGER
IDENTIFICATION WORKSHEET

Date: _____

Symptoms:

_____

_____

_____

_____

_____

_____

_____

_____

_____

_____

_____

_____

_____

Trigger (what happened before the symptom occurred?):

_____

_____

_____

_____

_____

_____

_____

_____

_____

_____

_____

_____

Coping strategy used:

_____

_____

_____

_____

_____

_____

_____

_____

_____

_____

_____

_____

Effectiveness: 1 2 3 4 5 6 7 8 9 10

Notes/insights:

_____

_____

_____

_____

_____

_____

_____

_____

_____

_____

_____

_____

Instructions:

Note the specific physical, emotional, or mental symptom you experienced (e.g., headache, anxiety, muscle tension, irritability).

Severity (1-10): Rate the intensity of the symptom on a scale of 1 (mild) to 10 (severe).

Trigger: Identify any potential triggers or events that occurred before the symptom began. Consider environmental factors, emotional stressors, or physical activity (e.g., stress from a conversation, lack of sleep, exposure to loud noises).

Coping Strategy Used: Record any strategies you used to manage the symptom (e.g., deep breathing, meditation, a walk, talking to a friend).

Effectiveness (1-10): Rate how effective the coping strategy was on a scale of 1 (not effective) to 10 (extremely effective).

Notes/Insights: Write down any additional observations or *thoughts, such as how the trigger might be avoided, whether the symptom worsened or improved after a certain action, or new coping strategies to try.*

STRESS AND RELAXATION RESPONSE WORKSHEET

Step 1: Identify the Stressor

Describe a stressful situation you encountered. Be specific—what was the stressor, and how did it make you feel emotionally?

Date: _____

Stressful Situation/Trigger:

(e.g., work deadline, argument, unexpected event)

_____

_____

_____

_____

_____

_____

_____

_____

_____

_____

_____

_____

Emotional Response:

(e.g., anxiety, frustration, overwhelm)

_____

_____

_____

_____

_____

_____

_____

_____

_____

_____

_____

_____

Step 2: Record Your Body's Initial Stress Response

Note how your body physically responded to the stress. Pay attention to sensations, changes in breathing, or muscle tension.

_____

_____

_____

_____

_____

_____

_____

_____

_____

_____

_____

_____

Body's Stress Response:

(e.g., shallow breathing, tight shoulders, racing heart, sweaty palms)

_____

_____

_____

_____

_____

_____

_____

_____

_____

_____

_____

_____

Mind's Stress Response:

(e.g., racing thoughts, difficulty focusing, negative thinking)

_____

_____

_____

_____

_____

_____

_____

_____

_____

_____

_____

_____

Step 3: Choose and Practice a Relaxation Technique

Write down the relaxation technique you used to calm your mind and body.

_____

_____

_____

_____

_____

_____

_____

_____

_____

_____

_____

_____

Relaxation Technique Used:

(e.g., deep breathing, progressive muscle relaxation, guided meditation, visualization)

\
_____

_____

_____

_____

_____

_____

_____

_____

_____

_____

_____

_____

Step 4: Observe Your Body's Response After the Relaxation Technique

Reflect on how your body and mind felt after practicing the relaxation technique. Focus on changes in physical sensations, emotional shifts, and mental clarity.

_____

_____

_____

_____

_____

_____

_____

_____

_____

_____

_____

_____

Body's Response After Relaxation:

(e.g., slower breathing, reduced muscle tension, heart rate slowed)

_____

_____

_____

_____

_____

_____

_____

_____

_____

_____

_____

Mind's Response After Relaxation:

(e.g., calmness, clearer thoughts, improved focus)

_____

_____

_____

_____

_____

_____

_____

_____

_____

_____

_____

_____

Step 5: Evaluate the Effectiveness

Based on your experience, evaluate how effective the relaxation technique was in helping you manage the stress. Use a scale from 1 (not effective) to 5 (very effective).

Effectiveness Rating:

1 ☐ 2 ☐ 3 ☐ 4 ☐ 5 ☐

Additional Thoughts/Notes:

Did you feel more relaxed? Was there anything surprising about your response?

_____

_____

_____

_____

_____

_____

_____

_____

_____

_____

_____

Step 6: Action Plan for Future Stress

How might you adjust or use this relaxation technique next time you face a similar stressor?

_____

_____

_____

_____

_____

_____

_____

_____

_____

_____

_____

Plan for Future Stressful Situations:

_____

_____

_____

_____

_____

_____

_____

_____

_____

_____

_____

_____

DAILY JOURNALING PROMPTS FOR EMOTIONAL AWARENESS

Use this worksheet to reflect on your emotional state and gain insights into how daily experiences influence your emotions and nervous system. Take a few minutes each day to journal your thoughts and track patterns, triggers, and progress.

1. How did I feel today?

Describe your overall emotional state. Were there any dominant feelings such as happiness, sadness, anxiety, or calm?

2. What moments brought me joy or stress?

List specific events, interactions, or thoughts that evoked feelings of joy, peace, or excitement. Similarly, note any moments of stress, frustration, or tension.

3. What events or interactions triggered strong emotions today?

Identify key triggers that led to intense emotions, whether positive or negative. Consider both external (people, situations) and internal (thoughts, memories) factors.

4. How did my body respond to these triggers?

Reflect on how your body physically reacted to emotional triggers. Did you notice changes in heart rate, muscle tension, breathing, or gut sensations? Describe how your body felt during these moments.

5. Did I use any strategies to manage my emotions or stress today?

Think about any coping mechanisms you used when faced with emotional challenges. This might include deep breathing, exercise, taking a break, or talking to someone. What worked well for you today?

6. Were there moments when I felt grounded or calm?

Reflect on any periods of the day when you felt relaxed, present, or at ease. What contributed to these feelings? Were you practicing mindfulness, engaging in a hobby, or connecting with others?

7. Have I noticed any changes in my emotional responses over the past week?

Look back on the past few days or week. Have you seen any shifts in how you respond to situations emotionally? Are there patterns emerging that you weren't aware of before?

8. What triggers are becoming more recognizable to me?

As you observe your emotional patterns, which triggers have you started to identify more clearly? Are you becoming more aware of what sets off strong emotional or physiological responses?

9. How has my nervous system reacted overall today?

Tune into your nervous system. Did you feel more in **fight-or-flight**, **freeze**, or **rest-and-digest** mode throughout the day? Did your nervous system calm down or become more activated at certain times?

10. What strategies have been effective in managing my stress or emotional responses recently?

Review any tools, techniques, or habits that have helped you navigate stress or strong emotions. Are there practices, like meditation or breathing exercises, that consistently help regulate your nervous system?

11. What small steps can I take tomorrow to support my emotional well-being?

Based on your reflection today, what intentional actions can you take tomorrow to nurture your emotional health? Think of realistic, gentle strategies that can help maintain balance in your nervous system.

OVERCOMING OBSTACLES

Picture this: You're seated in a bustling café, where the ambient hum of conversations, clinking cups, and the comforting aroma of freshly brewed coffee permeate the air. As you take a sip of your latte, you might not consciously realize that your ventral vagal complex is at work, inducing a sense of safety and readiness to engage socially. Subtle cues in the environment—a friendly smile from the barista, the familiar warmth of your drink, and the predictability of the setting—trigger a parasympathetic response, gently modulating your heart rate, calming your breath, and allowing your muscles to release tension. This seemingly ordinary experience is a demonstration of how your autonomic nervous system, guided by neuroception, continually assesses safety and threat. Through the Polyvagal lens, we can understand how our nervous system dynamically shifts between states, influenced not just by conscious perception but by subconscious processing of cues from our environment. This everyday moment beautifully illustrates the impact of autonomic regulation on our ability to navigate the complexities of modern life, and manage stress with greater nuance and awareness.

Tackling Obstacles in Self-Regulation

Navigating the complexities of nervous system regulation, particularly through the lens of Polyvagal Theory, requires more than just a basic understanding of the vagus nerve—it demands an intentional, nuanced approach to recognizing and responding to subtle shifts in autonomic state. One of the most significant challenges lies in the integration of consistent self-regulation practices within the constraints of modern life. The constant demands of work, family, and social obligations often result in fragmented time and diminished capacity for sustained self-awareness. This lack of consistency can impair the neural circuits that support the regular practice of vagal toning exercises, such as breathwork or mindfulness, making it harder to maintain the flexibility and resilience needed for nervous system regulation.

Equally critical, however, is the emotional inertia that arises from deeply ingrained autonomic patterns. These familiar physiological and emotional responses, even if maladaptive, are often rooted in survival strategies developed over time, creating subconscious resistance to change. The neuroception of safety, as described by Dr. Porges, is elusive in this state; venturing beyond these entrenched patterns can feel destabilizing, making it difficult to engage in interventions that challenge your body's long-established autonomic habits.

Another complication is the difficulty in accurately detecting state transitions. Without a finely attuned awareness of subtle shifts—from ventral vagal calm to sympathetic mobilization, or from sympathetic arousal to dorsal vagal shutdown—we may struggle to implement the most appropriate interventions at the right moment. This lack of interoceptive clarity impairs timely self-regulation and often leads to the escalation of stress responses before a calming or grounding technique can be employed. The ability to track these transitions in real time is essential for effective nervous system regulation, yet it requires a high level of body awareness and practice.

To effectively address the challenges of maintaining consistent self-regulation practices, it's essential to integrate intentional time management strategies that align with your body's natural rhythms and the state of your autonomic nervous system. Rather than simply breaking your day into segments, attune to moments where your ventral vagal state is more accessible, ensuring that self-regulation practices occur during times when you can engage fully with minimal resistance. For instance, using early morning or evening wind-down periods, when the body is naturally more primed for parasympathetic activation, can amplify the impact of practices like diaphragmatic breathing or safe place visualizations.

Aim for strategic intervals of neuroceptive recalibration throughout the day. Incorporate somatic titration or pendulation exercises to promote vagal tone, even in high-demand environments. Instead of rigidly adhering to clock-based schedules, experiment with micro-interventions—two-minute pauses for co-regulatory actions such as focused exhalation, humming, or a brief body scan. These are ideally woven into transition moments, such as before or after meetings or during natural lulls in activity, to avoid further sympathetic arousal.

Consistency in these practices enhances the flexibility of the autonomic ladder, making way for a more robust vagal tone. This approach moves beyond simple habit-building into the territory of neuroplasticity, supporting long-term shifts in your capacity to self-regulate. Additionally, you will recall that digital tools such as heart rate variability trackers can offer real-time biofeedback, allowing you to adjust your interventions dynamically based on physiological data, ensuring that each practice is responsive to your current autonomic state rather than being a static routine. Finally, setting neuroceptive, rather than productivity-based goals, such as tracking subtle shifts in interoceptive awareness or moments of felt safety, can reinforce positive reinforcement pathways and encourage sustainable progress.

Next, we have emotional resistance to change which is a complex, adaptive response that often reflects underlying nervous system patterns shaped by past experiences. Rooted in the neuroceptive processes of Polyvagal Theory, resistance can emerge as a protective mechanism when the autonomic nervous system perceives uncertainty or change as a threat, even when it's not consciously recognized as dangerous. Instead of pushing through resistance, it is important to approach it with compassionate curiosity, acknowledging that these responses are natural attempts by your nervous system to maintain a sense of safety.

Recognizing the role of the dorsal vagal state or sympathetic activation in emotional resistance allows us to create a strategy for change that won't overwhelm our system. Instead of pushing past discomfort, it's more effective to engage in titration—breaking the change process into small, manageable steps that allow for gradual neuroceptive recalibration. By gently stretching the window of tolerance, small, non-threatening actions enable the nervous system to rewire and adapt without triggering a defensive response. Setting incremental, measurable goals will allow our ventral vagal system to remain engaged.

Incorporating self-compassion practices such as mindfulness, grounding, or interoceptive exercises will improve resilience as your body navigates discomfort. Compassionate self-talk is powerful as it activates the ventral vagal pathway, helping to diffuse the autonomic response to perceived threats. Moreover, surrounding yourself with co-regulating relationships—trusted friends, family, or a therapist—can provide essential external support, facilitating safe social engagement that reinforces vagal tone. Sharing your journey of change within these relationships will further enhance your polyvagal network, allowing for mutual attunement and emotional validation, which are critical for sustaining momentum through difficult emotional terrain.

When setbacks and relapses occur, handle them with patience and kindness. Everyone experiences setbacks; they are a natural part of the process. Simply revisit your initial goals and adjust them as necessary. Sometimes, taking a step back and simplifying your routine can help you regain momentum. Staying motivated can be challenging, but exploring a variety of practices can keep things interesting. Try new exercises or alternate between different techniques to prevent monotony. If you still find yourself struggling, don't hesitate to seek additional support. Therapists, support groups, or even online communities can provide the guidance and encouragement you need. In the end, recognizing your personal obstacles and planning and employing practical strategies to overcome them will enhance your ability to regulate your nervous system with PVT principles.

Overcoming Potential Barriers

Whether you are a practitioner attempting to apply Polyvagal Theory principles to improve your health or a therapist supporting clients through this process, challenges are inevitable. Even with a deep understanding of holistic health, there are numerous scenarios in which we can end up feeling stuck, therefore hindering our progress. In order to be better prepared to embark on this polyvagal healing venture, below is a list of common obstacles, along with practical exercises we have previously explored and helpful strategies to address each one.

1. Disconnection or Dissociation (Dorsal Vagal Shutdown)

Obstacle: Those of us with trauma histories may frequently dissociate or shut down, making it difficult to engage the ventral vagal complex or even sense our body's signals.
Practical Exercises:
Titration with Interoception: Start with very small, manageable steps in body awareness. Guide yourself or clients to notice neutral or mildly positive sensations, like the feeling of their feet on the ground or the gentle rise and fall of their breath. Use short, timed intervals to help clients stay connected without becoming overwhelmed.

Orienting to Safety: Encourage them to look around the room and identify objects that signal safety (e.g., noticing the color of a wall or the texture of a chair). This practice gently engages the ventral vagal pathway by activating the visual and sensory systems without forcing introspection too soon.

2. Overwhelming Emotional Responses (Sympathetic Overactivation)

Obstacle: Some of us may experience overwhelming fear, anxiety, or anger, leading to sympathetic hyperarousal that is difficult to downregulate.
Practical Exercises:
Grounding Through Movement: Encourage the person to engage in slow, rhythmic movements like gentle rocking or walking. Movement helps discharge excess sympathetic energy and invites the body back into a state of regulation. This rhythmic motion can signal safety to the body while reducing the intensity of the emotional response.

Guided Resonant Breathing: Lead client in resonant breathing (5–6 breaths per minute) to regulate heart rate variability. This technique directly stimulates the vagus nerve and can bring the body out of a state of sympathetic overdrive.

3. Resistance to Feeling Safe or Trusting the Process

Obstacle: Those who have lived in chronic stress or trauma may find it difficult to feel safe or trust the therapeutic process, as their neuroception is skewed toward perceiving danger.

Practical Exercises:

Vocal Prosody Practice: Use gentle vocalization exercises (humming, chanting, or speaking in a calm, melodic tone) during sessions. This practice not only stimulates the vagus nerve but also demonstrates a safe, co-regulated environment. Encourage clients to hum softly with you to activate their own vagal pathways.

Incremental Exposure to Comfort: Start by helping the client identify neutral or mildly pleasant experiences. Avoid jumping directly into deep relaxation or meditation, which can feel threatening to some clients. Gradually increase the length and depth of safe, soothing exercises as trust builds.

4. Difficulty with Emotional Awareness or Expression

Obstacle: Some individuals may have difficulty identifying or expressing their emotions due to past trauma, cultural conditioning, or dorsal vagal shutdown.

Practical Exercises:

Emotion Mapping: Have clients map where they feel different emotions in their body. For example, "Where do you feel sadness?" or "Where do you notice anger?" This allows them to connect with bodily sensations and gain insight into their emotional state without needing to verbalize it immediately.

Use of Imagery: Guide clients through a visualization exercise where they imagine a safe, calming space. Encourage them to notice the sensations in their body as they imagine themselves in this environment. This can help clients gently reconnect with emotions in a controlled, non-verbal way.

5. Challenging Client-Provider Co-regulation

Obstacle: Co-regulation may be difficult when clients struggle to feel safe or if the practitioner's own nervous system is dysregulated.

Practical Exercises:

Practitioner Self-Regulation: Practitioners should practice self-regulation exercises before and during sessions. Simple tools like diaphragmatic breathing or grounding techniques (e.g., feeling the weight of the body in the chair) can ensure that the practitioner is maintaining their own ventral vagal tone. This creates a safe and co-regulated environment for the client.

Pausing to Re-establish Connection: If the session begins to feel dysregulated, pause and invite the client to take a few breaths or check in with their body. Reflect back any non-verbal cues you notice (e.g., "I see your shoulders are tense; what do they feel like right now?"). This pause allows both the practitioner and the client to recalibrate their nervous systems.

6. Hypervigilance or Difficulty Letting Go of Control

Obstacle: Those who are hypervigilant due to trauma may find it difficult to relax or relinquish control, constantly scanning for threats.

Practical Exercises:

Orienting Exercise: Encourage clients to notice and label their environment with curiosity. This allows them to engage the ventral vagal system by orienting to safety cues, rather than constantly scanning for danger. For instance, ask, "What do you notice in the room right now? Can you find three things that feel comforting or neutral to look at?"

Controlled Exhale Breathing: Guide clients in breathing exercises that emphasize the exhale, as this activates the parasympathetic system. A practice like inhaling for 4 counts, holding for 2, and exhaling for 6 counts can help clients slowly release tension and restore a sense of control.

7. Limited Ability to Stay Present in the Body

Obstacle: Some may find it difficult to stay present with bodily sensations, especially if they've experienced dissociation or numbness.

Practical Exercises:

Somatic Anchoring: Start with small, localized sensations, like the feeling of hands on the lap or the sensation of the feet pressing into the floor. These "anchors" help the client gradually build capacity to stay connected to their body without feeling overwhelmed. Over time, encourage clients to widen their awareness to include more parts of their body.

Mindful Touch or Object Focus: Allow the client to hold an object (e.g., a soft pillow, a textured ball) and focus on its physical qualities (temperature, texture, shape). This creates a safe, tangible focus for bodily awareness, encouraging presence in the moment.

8. Overwhelm from Complex Trauma Histories

Obstacle: Clients with complex trauma histories may become easily overwhelmed by emotions or physical sensations during somatic work.

Practical Exercises:

Safe Place Visualization: Before engaging in deeper somatic work, guide clients through a visualization of a safe space (real or imagined) where they feel calm and in control. This creates a mental and emotional refuge they can return to if they start to feel overwhelmed during body-based exercises.

Somatic Resourcing: Help the client identify somatic resources—areas of the body that feel neutral, pleasant, or strong. For example, a client may feel safe in the soles of their feet or the strength of their hands. When overwhelm occurs, guide the client to focus on these body resources to ground and re-establish a sense of safety.

Creating a Supportive Environment for Healing

Within our Polyvagal context, the relationship between environment and nervous system regulation is a nuanced yet essential factor in optimizing the healing process. Beyond the basic understanding of how external surroundings impact our emotional states, creating an intentional environment aligns directly with supporting ventral vagal activation, which is key to fostering states of safety, connection, and well-being. Disorganized, chaotic, or overly stimulating environments can act as low-grade stressors, potentially keeping the sympathetic or dorsal vagal pathways active, thus perpetuating a state of heightened vigilance or shutdown. Conversely, a well-structured space can create a neuroceptive "safe zone," which primes the nervous system for parasympathetic engagement, reducing baseline stress and supporting a sense of groundedness. A therapeutic space becomes an external extension of our neuroceptive processes. So, when curated thoughtfully, our physical environment can reinforce neuroception of safety, facilitating access to the ventral vagal complex and promoting our social engagement system.

The design of such an environment involves more than simple decluttering. Organizing the space should prioritize minimizing stimuli that could provoke sensory overload. This might include reducing harsh or unnecessary sounds, or removing visual clutter that draws constant attention, which can inadvertently activate subcortical threat detection circuits. For instance, incorporating biophilic design principles—elements of nature like plants or water features—can engage the ventral vagal system through soft fascination, which is a form of non-taxing, restorative attention. Natural elements help to down-regulate sympathetic arousal while promoting cognitive and emotional replenishment.

Lighting also plays an important role. Given that the visual system is one of the most energy-intensive in terms of neural processing, using lighting that mimics natural circadian rhythms helps signal safety to our nervous system. Warm light spectrums, particularly in the evening, mirror the calming effects of sunset, encouraging melatonin production and lowering cortisol levels, thus preparing the body for rest. This synchrony with circadian biology can enhance recovery from stress by stabilizing autonomic rhythms.

Moreover, sensory input, such as scent, has a direct line to the limbic system, which governs emotional regulation. By diffusing essential oils such as lavender or bergamot, which have been shown in clinical studies to lower heart rate variability and increase vagal tone, the environment can further cue the brain to shift out of defense and into a more ventral vagal state. Even the choice of textures in furniture, such as soft, natural fibers, can contribute to the somatic experience of comfort and safety, enhancing interoceptive awareness and deepening the relaxation response.

Next, setting clear boundaries around personal space and time plays a significant role, particularly to maintain an environment conducive to nervous system regulation and vagal tone enhancement. From a Polyvagal Theory perspective, intentionally creating a space dedicated to relaxation or mindfulness serves as a powerful neuroceptive cue, signaling safety and facilitating a shift from sympathetic arousal to parasympathetic states. This physical space, though it need not be elaborate, should be designed with sensory attunement in mind—textures, lighting, and objects that promote a sense of calm and safety for your body. For example, a soft blanket or dim, warm lighting can engage the social engagement system, reinforcing cues of safety.

Equally important is establishing clear temporal boundaries. Allocating uninterrupted time for mindfulness or vagal stimulation practices can reinforce to your nervous system the consistency and predictability needed for recalibration. This structure helps maintain neurophysiological flexibility, which is essential for emotional regulation. And, don't forget that communicating these boundaries effectively to those around you is also most important. Whether with family, colleagues, or friends, expressing your need for undisturbed periods can create a support system that respects the co-regulatory process, allowing you to focus on your inner work without the interference of external stressors. This goes a long way in enhancing your practice and creating an environment of mutual respect, where others learn to respect your rhythms and needs.

Before we move on to social support, let's take a moment to discuss boundaries as a whole. Personal boundaries, when consciously and skilfully established, influence how we regulate our autonomic states and, by extension, how we engage in relationships. They work to prevent overwhelming social and environmental stimuli, thus maintaining autonomic balance and facilitating effective co-regulation with others. By intentionally regulating our own nervous system and respecting our needs for space, rest, and emotional safety, we allow for more authentic and fulfilling connections that support long-term resilience.

Social boundaries are essential for nervous system recovery, particularly in maintaining the capacity for effective co-regulation, a dynamic process at the heart of Polyvagal Theory. Co-regulation refers to the reciprocal, moment-to-moment interaction in which we help regulate each other's autonomic states, often unconsciously, through subtle social cues such as eye contact, facial expressions, tone of voice, and physical proximity. These nonverbal signals are mediated by the ventral vagal complex, which governs social engagement. However, co-regulation is mostly beneficial when both parties are able to remain within their window of tolerance, or emotional and physiological range of stability, without becoming overwhelmed.

In the context of Polyvagal Theory, effective co-regulation depends on our ability to move fluidly between autonomic arousal and rest. The latter is the state in which social engagement is possible because the nervous system perceives safety. However, when our nervous system becomes dysregulated—shifting into sympathetic activation or dorsal vagal shutdown—the ability to co-regulate diminishes, as these defensive states disrupt the natural flow of social engagement cues. In such cases, recognizing the signs of dysregulation becomes most important, as it allows for the conscious setting of social boundaries to protect our nervous system from further stress.

Therefore, boundaries in this context are not simply about limiting external demands, but about creating safe, predictable spaces that allow for autonomic recovery. When we feel overwhelmed, our capacity for co-regulation diminishes, leading to the potential for misattunement with others, where one person's nervous system inadvertently triggers further dysregulation in another. To prevent this, it is essential to set boundaries such as limiting time in overstimulating environments, disengaging from emotionally intense conversations, or pausing interactions when sensing autonomic shifts can provide the space needed to reset and return to a ventral vagal state. These actions protect our ability to engage in healthy co-regulation once autonomic balance is restored.

Moreover, neuroception, or the nervous system's subconscious evaluation of safety and danger, plays a pivotal role in co-regulation. When neuroception detects threat, even in subtle ways, it disrupts the capacity for mutual regulation. Healthy boundaries can act as buffers that maintain a sense of safety within social interactions, ensuring that the nervous system remains within the ventral vagal zone where co-regulation is possible. For those of us healing from trauma or chronic stress, where our nervous system may be more prone to perceiving threat, boundaries offer a way to modulate exposure to stressors and reduce the likelihood of entering dysregulated states.

By creating autonomic flexibility through setting healthy boundaries, we can engage in co-regulation from a place of calm rather than distress, facilitating deeper connection and mutual healing. However, the ability to co-regulate effectively is contingent upon our ability to recognize when dysregulation arises and to establish boundaries that protect our need for autonomic recovery. Below is an overview of types boundaries and their importance in nervous system health.

Identifying Autonomic Shifts

Begin by becoming acutely aware of your autonomic state during social interactions. As you work on this, you will begin to notice when you move from a ventral vagal state into sympathetic arousal (fight/flight) or dorsal vagal shutdown (freeze). This requires finely tuned interoception, where you sense internal cues such as increased heart rate, shallow breathing, or dissociation. These shifts indicate that boundaries may need to be reinforced or adjusted to maintain regulation.

Assertive Communication

Healthy boundaries go hand in hand with clear communication. When your nervous system signals that you're nearing dysregulation, it's essential to articulate your needs in a way that promotes understanding and mutual respect. For example, if a social interaction becomes overwhelming, saying, "I need a moment to pause and reset," reinforces your boundary while signaling to the other person that you're prioritizing self-regulation. This encourages a form of co-regulation where the other party can adjust their behavior to maintain a safe, supportive dynamic.

Time-Based Boundaries

Social exhaustion often results from overstaying in sympathetic or dorsal vagal states without adequate recovery time. Set clear time limits for social engagements, especially if you're recovering from trauma or nervous system dysregulation. For example, after a prolonged interaction, taking 5–10 minutes alone to engage in vagal toning practices like deep diaphragmatic breathing or physiological sighs can prevent autonomic fatigue and support quicker recovery. Everyone has a different social battery capacity, and the amount of energy we are able to dispense is influenced by many factors that fluctuate constantly. Therefore, it is beneficial to practice self-awareness exercises and get to know our limits to avoid overstimulation, which leads to fatigue and is harmful to our nervous system.

Emotional Boundaries

The ventral vagal system thrives on safety cues, and emotional boundaries ensure that we don't overextend ourselves emotionally, which could push us into dysregulation. Emotional boundaries can be established by limiting exposure to emotionally taxing conversations or environments that trigger a neuroceptive threat response. For example, if someone repeatedly shares distressing news, kindly expressing that you're not in a space to process heavy emotions can prevent sympathetic activation and preserve your ability to maintain a regulated state. The foundational principles of successful **c**o-regulation are deeply rooted in values of safety, mutual attunement, empathy, and respect. So, if your boundaries are ignored or disrespected, it is a sign that this person or group is not a "safe" social option for emotional well-being and is unlikely to contribute to your inner peace (shift to ventral vagal state) through co-regulation.

Co-Regulation Boundaries

Co-regulation requires a balance between receiving support and offering it. It's essential to be mindful of how much emotional energy you expend in trying to regulate others. Overextending in this regard can lead to your own dysregulation. Set limits on how much you invest in co-regulating others, especially in relationships where the reciprocity is uneven. To maintain healthy co-regulation, consider gently stepping back when you notice signs of compassion fatigue or emotional depletion, allowing space for your own recovery.

Practical Tips for Setting Boundaries

Start with Self-Regulation: Use self-regulation practices to ensure that you are in a ventral vagal state before setting or enforcing a boundary. Practices such as vagal breathing or progressive muscle relaxation will help you tap into your social engagement system and communicate boundaries from a place of calm rather than reactivity.

Use "I" Statements: When setting boundaries, frame your needs in terms of your own experience. For example, "I feel overwhelmed and need to take a break" signals your internal state without blaming or shaming the other person. This approach reduces the likelihood of triggering a defensive reaction and promotes smoother co-regulation.

Non-Verbal Cues: Since the vagus nerve also plays a role in facial expression and vocal tone, be mindful of your non-verbal communication when setting boundaries. A calm, warm tone and relaxed facial expression will help maintain a ventral vagal state in both you and the person you're interacting with, creating an atmosphere of safety.

Regular Check-Ins: In long-term relationships or work environments, establish regular check-ins to assess how boundaries are working. This practice can help adjust boundaries as needed, ensuring ongoing regulation and reducing the risk of burnout or dorsal vagal collapse.

IN THE NEXT CHAPTER, we will explore how to build a supportive community for healing. You will learn how to find and form support groups, share your journey with others, and use online platforms for community support. This chapter will provide practical tips and real-life examples to help you create a strong support network that enriches your emotional health goals and well-being.

EIGHT
BUILDING A SUPPORTIVE
COMMUNITY FOR HEALING

IMAGINE yourself attending a homey neighborhood gathering on a warm summer evening. A soft hum of conversation weaves through the air, punctuated by bursts of laughter that ripple like waves across the room. The scent of fresh food mingles with the sound of clinking glasses, and as you glance around, you catch familiar faces, their expressions soft and welcoming. You're wrapped in an atmosphere of ease—your body naturally relaxes, your shoulders drop, and a gentle smile plays across your lips. There's a tangible sense of connection, a warmth that radiates not just from the room but from within you. Every shared glance, every nod of understanding, sends a message of safety to your nervous system, grounding you in the moment.

As we are now aware of, this isn't merely an enjoyable social event—it is an act of deep healing. In these moments of effortless connection, your ventral vagal system is fully engaged. Your body senses safety, allowing you to feel open, present, and attuned to the people around you. The smiles and laughter are not just fleeting exchanges; they are signals that your nervous system absorbs, reinforcing feelings of belonging and emotional resilience. This gathering becomes a peaceful retreat for your body and mind, where co-regulation happens naturally, gently easing any tension and filling you with a sense of calm and wholeness.

Social connections and community support can profoundly affect our emotional and physiological well-being. The role of community in healing is firmly established in our biology. When we feel connected to others, our body can better manage stress, reducing the physiological burden that chronic stress places on your system. Scientific evidence also supports the benefits of community involvement. Studies have shown that those who are part of a supportive community experience lower levels of anxiety and depression. In fact, research published in the journal *Psychological Science* found that social support is linked to improved immune function and better overall health outcomes. The presence of a supportive network can buffer against the negative effects of stress, providing a sense of security and stability. This is particularly important for women, who often juggle multiple roles and responsibilities. The emotional and psychological benefits of community support can lead to tangible improvements in physical health, such as reduced inflammation, enhanced immune responses and, of course, improved vagal tone.

We have touched on co-regulation in the previous chapter, as it is a key concept in understanding the healing power of community. Briefly, it refers to the process through which we regulate our nervous system through social interactions. When you are with someone who is calm and supportive, your nervous system can sync with theirs, promoting a state of safety. This phenomenon is not just psychological; it has a physiological basis. For example, a study in *Developmental Psychobiology* found that infants' heart rates synchronize with their caregivers', illustrating the profound impact of co-regulation from an early age. As adults, this same principle applies. Positive social interactions can help stabilize your emotional state, making it easier to navigate stressful situations. Co-regulation enhances emotional stability, providing a shared space where feelings of safety and connection can flourish.

The importance of a trauma-informed community cannot be overstated, especially for trauma survivors. This is your tribe - a community who understands the complexities of your experiences and provides a compassionate, supportive environment. Characteristics of such a community include empathy, patience, and a non-judgmental attitude. This approach allows us to express our feelings and experiences without fear of being misunderstood or judged. You should also note that the benefits of a trauma-informed community extend beyond emotional support. They include practical assistance, such as helping with daily tasks or providing resources for professional help. This holistic approach supports trauma recovery by addressing both emotional and practical needs.

Reflection Section: How Community Enhances Healing

Take a moment to reflect on your own experiences with community support. Consider the following questions and jot down your thoughts in a journal:

- When have you felt the most supported by others?
- How did this support impact your emotional and physical well-being?
- Are there specific individuals or groups who provide you with a sense of safety and connection?
- How do you contribute to the emotional well-being of others within your community, and how does this influence your own healing?
- What feelings arise when you think about asking for support, and how do they impact your ability to seek help?
- Reflect on a time when you felt disconnected from your community. How did this affect your sense of safety and regulation?
- In what ways can you create boundaries within your community to protect your own well-being while still nurturing meaningful connections?
- What steps can you take to strengthen these connections or seek out new supportive communities?

Reflecting on these questions will help you recognize the value of community in your healing journey. It is also likely to guide you in creating deeper, more meaningful connections that contribute to your healing goals.

Finding or Forming Support Groups

Navigating the world of support groups can feel daunting, but it doesn't have to be. Finding a group that aligns with your needs and interests is the first step. Start by checking local community centers and mental health organizations. These places often host or can direct you to support groups tailored to a variety of needs. Libraries and hospitals can also be valuable resources. They frequently offer or advertise support programs, especially those focusing on mental health and trauma recovery.

Online directories and resources are another excellent way to find support groups. Websites like Psychology Today and Healthline have comprehensive lists of support groups categorized by specific issues, such as PTSD, anxiety, or chronic illness. These directories often include reviews and detailed descriptions, helping you gauge which group might be the best fit. Social media platforms are also easily accessible and host various support communities. Searching specific hashtags or joining relevant groups on Facebook, Reddit, or specialized forums can connect you with like-minded individuals. Keep in mind to consider the privacy and security of online groups, ensuring they have clear guidelines and are moderated effectively.

Evaluating the suitability of a support group is the next important step. Attend a few meetings or observe interactions within the community to get a sense of the group dynamics. Consider how members interact with one another and how the facilitator manages the sessions. It's important to feel comfortable and safe. Look for groups that encourage open, respectful dialogue and have a structured format. If you find yourself feeling more anxious or uncomfortable after attending, it might be worth exploring other options. Otherwise, you can combine one-on-one therapy sessions alongside your group meetings to ensure that you are on a path that suits your needs. Remember, it is essential that the group aligns with your personal values and goals.

Forming a new support group is another option that can be incredibly empowering and beneficial. When you create a group, you have the freedom to tailor it to meet specific needs and interests. This can be particularly helpful if you find existing groups don't fully address your concerns. Starting a new group provides opportunities for leadership and community building, while supporting a sense of ownership and commitment among members. It can also fill gaps in available resources, offering a unique space for people with similar experiences to come together and support one another.

To do this, begin by identifying the group's purpose and goals. Clearly define what you hope to achieve, whether it's sharing experiences, learning new coping strategies, or simply providing a safe space for open discussion. Next, find and invite potential members. Reach out to your network, use social media, or post flyers in community centers. Make sure to communicate the group's purpose and what new members can expect. Establish meeting times, locations, and formats that are convenient for most participants. Decide whether meetings will be in-person or virtual, and how often they will occur.

As you move through this process, you will want to create group guidelines and expectations as these are vital for maintaining a productive and supportive environment. Set clear rules about confidentiality, respectful communication, and participation. This helps ensure that everyone feels safe and valued. You can also choose to encourage members to contribute to these guidelines, which creates a sense of collective responsibility. Make sure to revisit and adjust these rules as the group evolves, keeping them relevant and effective.

Facilitating effective group meetings requires active listening and empathetic communication. As a facilitator, your role will be to guide discussions, ensuring everyone has a chance to speak. Use open-ended questions to encourage deeper conversations and validate each person's experiences. Techniques like reflective listening, where you paraphrase what someone has said to confirm understanding, can enhance communication and trust. Managing group dynamics and conflicts is another unavoidable aspect. Address any issues promptly and fairly, promoting a harmonious environment. Encourage members to express their feelings and perspectives while maintaining respect for others.

Incorporate engaging activities and discussions to keep meetings dynamic and meaningful. Icebreakers can help new members feel comfortable, while structured activities like sharing circles or themed discussions can provide focus. Introducing mindfulness exercises or brief relaxation techniques can also be beneficial, helping members to center themselves and reduce stress. Keeping the group engaged and connected through varied activities can enhance the overall experience, making each meeting something members look forward to.

Exercise: Starting Your Own Support Group

To help you get started with forming your support group – assuming you feel that this is right for you at this point in time - try this exercise. Begin by writing down the purpose and goals of your group. Consider what specific needs you want to address and what outcomes you hope to achieve. Next, list potential members and how you will invite them. Think about the logistics—where and when you will meet, and whether the meetings will be in-person or virtual. Finally, draft a set of guidelines and expectations for your group. Reflect on how you will facilitate meetings, including strategies for active listening and managing group dynamics. Use this exercise as a plan to create a supportive and effective community tailored to your needs.

Sharing Your Journey with Others

Sharing your healing journey can be a profoundly transformative experience, both for you and those who hear your story. When we open up about our experiences, we often find emotional relief and validation. It can be incredibly therapeutic to voice the struggles and triumphs we've faced along the way. This openness creates a space of empowered vulnerability, where others feel inspired to take steps in their own healing. Your story can be a source of hope and encouragement, showing that recovery is possible and that we are not alone in our struggles.

When sharing your personal experiences, it is important to focus on personal growth and resilience. Highlight the progress you've made through mistakes, challenges, and lessons learned. This shift from merely recounting hardships to showcasing your strength and adaptability can be empowering for both you and your listeners. Always be mindful of triggers and sensitivities, as sharing too much too quickly can be overwhelming for you and your audience. As per habitual healthy communication conventions, use "I" statements to express your feelings and experiences. For instance, saying "I felt overwhelmed when..." rather than "People overwhelm me..." keeps the focus on your own experience and makes your story more relatable and less accusatory.

Vulnerability plays a critical role in building deep and meaningful connections. When you are open and honest about your struggles and progress, you invite others to do the same. This mutual vulnerability fosters trust and understanding, creating a safe space where everyone feels valued and heard. Sharing your journey not only helps you but also encourages others to be vulnerable, which can lead to stronger, more supportive relationships. For example, a trauma survivor might share their story in a support group, detailing how they managed their anxiety through specific techniques. This act of sharing can inspire others in the group to open up about their own challenges and coping mechanisms.

Consider the case of client X – let's call her Olivia – who, like many others, decided to document her healing process on social media. Initially hesitant, she started by posting about her daily struggles with anxiety and the small victories she achieved using Polyvagal techniques. Slowly but surely, Olivia's posts garnered a following of individuals who found comfort and inspiration in her journey. Naturally, they began to share their own experiences in the comments, forming a supportive network where everyone felt seen and heard. Olivia's openness and vulnerability helped her begin to heal, while also providing a platform for others to support one another.

Sharing your journey will be more than a recount of past events, as it will allow you to create a narrative of resilience and growth that can benefit both yourself and others. As such, take note that in a trauma healing community, the way we communicate is vital. In this space, mutual respect and the ability to truly listen to others with an open mind are foundational principles. "We don't know what we don't know"—and this mindset reminds us to approach every conversation without judgment, as we cannot fully understand another's experience until we take the time to hear it (perhaps not even then). However, our only job is to listen attentively and remain open in order to create an environment where everyone feels safe to share their story. Whether through a support group, social media, or personal conversations, your story has the power to inspire healing and transformation while hearing and holding space for others. In this way, your personal journey becomes part of a powerful shared experience that encourages mutual connection, respect, and collective growth.

Shared Experience and Connection

In the quiet moments of our lives, when we sit and reflect on our experiences, we often find that our deepest sense of connection comes from shared experiences. Recognizing and sharing these common experiences can forge powerful bonds of empathy and understanding. When you share your story and listen to others, you create a space where mutual support flourishes. This shared vulnerability reduces feelings of isolation, reminding us that we are not alone in our struggles. The role of empathy in these connections cannot be overstated. Empathy allows us to step into someone else's shoes, to feel their emotions and understand their perspective. This deep understanding builds trust and creates a most supportive community.

Creating a supportive and connected group requires intention and effort, which starts with encouraging open and honest communication. When members feel safe to express their true feelings and experiences, deeper connections form. This openness can be facilitated through regular group bonding activities. Simple acts like sharing a meal, going for a walk together, or participating in a group project can strengthen bonds. Icebreakers and group exercises can also help build rapport, especially in the early stages of forming a group. Activities like sharing circles or storytelling sessions allow members to share their stories in a structured and supportive environment.

Inclusivity and diversity are another important aspect to consider when trying to build a sense of shared experience and connection. A group that embraces diverse perspectives and experiences will be richer and more supportive. Understanding and respecting these differences creates an environment where everyone feels valued. Ensure that all voices are heard and all members feel welcome, which might involve actively seeking out diverse members, being mindful of cultural differences, and creating an environment that celebrates rather than just tolerates diversity.

Activities that promote connection can be varied and engaging. Group mindfulness and relaxation exercises can help members tune into their bodies and minds to instil a collective sense of calm and connection. Sharing circles, where each person takes a turn to speak while others listen, can provide a safe space for expressing feelings and experiences. Storytelling sessions allow members to share personal stories, which promotes empathy and understanding. Collaborative projects, like community service activities, can also strengthen bonds. Working together towards a common goal inevitably creates a sense of unity and shared purpose.

Perhaps this could look like a group of women gathering for a weekly mindfulness session. They start with a simple breathing exercise, focusing on their breath and tuning into their bodies. This shared practice creates a sense of calm and connection. They then move into a sharing circle, where each woman takes a turn to share her experiences and feelings. The others listen with empathy and understanding, creating a supportive and non-judgmental space. After sharing, they work together on a community project, perhaps organizing a charity event or a local clean-up. These activities slowly build a bond of connection and trust, while also providing a sense of purpose and accomplishment.

Creating a supportive community is a powerful tool for healing, especially as it supports ventral vagal activation and co-regulation. Through shared experiences, open communication, inclusivity, and engaging activities, we can unite to heal and assist each other in co-regulation. This safety and connection will activate our ventral vagal state, creating an atmosphere of calm, groundedness, and social engagement, which (as we know), is essential for emotional and physiological well-being. By building a community that uplifts and supports one another, you will create an environment that enhances individual healing and strengthens collective resilience and growth.

CONCLUSION

As WE REACH the final pages of this handbook, I would like us to take a moment to reflect on the knowledge we've gathered, as well as the transformation this understanding has the potential to spark in our lives.

The principles of Polyvagal Theory—so carefully dissected throughout this book—are so much more than theoretical constructs. They are living, dynamic processes that govern the most fundamental aspects of our existence: how we feel safe, how we connect with ourselves and others, and how we navigate both joy and hardship.

The journey toward vagal healing is not a linear one. Much like the breath itself—cycling through expansion and contraction, activation and rest—the spiralling path of nervous system healing invites us to revisit familiar terrain with fresh insight, deeper awareness, and new tools. It is a process of continuous growth, one that asks us to honor our body's wisdom, attune to its signals, and cultivate a relationship of compassion with ourselves.

By now, you have explored the many workings of the vagus nerve, from its role in regulating autonomic states to its remarkable impact on emotional resilience, social engagement, and overall well-being. You've learned how neuroception, the body's innate ability to detect safety or danger, operates beneath the surface of consciousness, shaping our interactions and reactions in ways we might never have understood before. Perhaps you've also discovered new, practical ways to restore balance—

whether through breathwork, movement, social connection, or mindful attention to the body.

Yet, beyond the technicalities and exercises lies the deeper promise of this work: the opportunity to shift the way we experience the world and ourselves. In healing our vagus nerve, we are not just addressing physiological imbalances; we are reclaiming our capacity for aliveness. We are learning how to live in a way that is both open to connection and grounded in safety. This is the heart of Polyvagal healing—a movement toward a life that is not merely reactive, but responsive, purposeful, and deeply connected.

As you continue to integrate Polyvagal principles, remember that this process calls for patience and self-compassion. Healing, especially from trauma, is not something to be rushed or forced. The nervous system requires careful attention, gradual adjustment, and consistent care. There will be moments when you feel firmly rooted in a ventral vagal state, fully present and engaged in life. And there will be moments when old patterns resurface—when the sympathetic fight/flight response rears its head or when dorsal vagal shutdown pulls you into withdrawal. However, these challenging episodes are not failures - far from it! They are unique opportunities for growth, a chance to catch yourself and apply the knowledge and practices learned within these pages. These are precious experiences, where you will find comfort in noticing a shift within, and empower yourself through the proper use of an effective restorative technique at the most opportune moment. Fluctuations are part of the nervous system's natural rhythm, a reminder that healing is cyclical. When triggers arise, remember to meet them with curiosity rather than frustration. Instead of asking, "Why am I still feeling this way?" shift the question to, "What is my body trying to communicate? How can I support it now?" This gentle, inquisitive stance opens the door to deeper understanding and trust in your own capacity for healing.

One of the most important lessons Polyvagal Theory offers us is the recognition that healing does not happen in isolation. As social beings, we are wired for connection; our nervous systems crave attunement with others. Co-regulation is a vital tool in this work; during moments of dysregulation, we can lean on our trusted relationships to find balance. In turn, our presence, our tone of voice, our eye contact, and our calm can offer that same gift to others.

But co-regulation is not just about finding safety in community; it's about cultivating the courage to show up authentically, with all our vulnerability. Healing through Polyvagal principles encourages us to move beyond the fear of being seen, to embrace the discomfort of connection, and to allow ourselves to be soothed and strengthened by the presence of others. When we do this, we begin to create a ripple effect—our own regulated nervous system becomes a road to safety for those around us, and their safety reinforces our own.

With the knowledge of PVT in hand, you are now equipped with a new lens through which to view your life, your body, and your relationships. You may find that situations you once approached with fear or frustration now elicit a softer, more compassionate response. You may notice that the subtle signals your body sends throughout the day—tension in your chest, a quickening pulse, or the ease of a deep breath—are invitations to pause, tune in, and respond with care. Use this newfound awareness as a guide for living fully and intentionally. By understanding your nervous system, you gain access to a deeper sense of embodied wisdom—a wisdom that teaches you how to protect your energy, how to nourish your connections, and how to create a life that supports your ongoing growth. As you step forward from this book, remember that this is only the beginning. Each practice you engage with —each breath, each boundary, each moment of mindful presence—will build resilience. Over time, these small acts of self-care and connection will accumulate into important shifts in how you experience yourself and the world around you.

And so, I invite you to carry this Polyvagal wisdom as you navigate the complexities of life. When challenges arise, as they inevitably will, trust in the strength of your nervous system. Know that you possess sufficient knowledge and tools to recalibrate and return to safety. You have learned to honor the language of your body, and that is an incredible gift.

May this handbook be your companion, an important asset and most reliable resource on your journey toward wholeness. The path ahead is a promising one, filled with resilience, renewal, and endless possibility.

POSTSCRIPT

I'd love to hear your thoughts...!

As an independent author with a small marketing budget, **reviews** are my livelihood on this platform. If you enjoyed this book, I would truly appreciate it if you left your honest feedback.

You can do this by clicking the link to *The Complete Somatic Therapy & Polyvagal Theory Toolbox* on www.amazon.com.

Additionally, you can jump in and join our well-being community via https://www.facebook.com/groups/theemeraldsociety, or contact me directly at ydgardens@emeraldsocpublishing.com.

I personally read every single review, and it truly warms my heart to hear from my readers.

With Kindness,
  Yas

GLOSSARY

Autonomic Nervous System (ANS)

The part of the nervous system responsible for controlling involuntary bodily functions, including heart rate, digestion, respiratory rate, and reflexes. It is divided into the sympathetic, parasympathetic, and enteric nervous systems.

Allostasis

The process by which the body maintains stability and balance through change, especially in response to stressors or challenges. It involves the dynamic adjustment of physiological systems (like heart rate, hormone levels, or immune responses) to anticipate and adapt to varying demands. This process helps the body cope with stress, but chronic or excessive allostatic load—when the body is constantly adapting—can lead to wear and tear, contributing to health problems.

Vagus Nerve

The longest cranial nerve in the body, extending from the brainstem to the abdomen, influencing heart rate, digestion, mood, and other functions. It plays a crucial role in the parasympathetic nervous system.

Polyvagal Theory

A theory developed by Dr. Stephen Porges that explains how the vagus nerve impacts emotional regulation, social connection, and fear response. It describes how the ANS adapts to stress and safety.

Sympathetic Nervous System
Part of the ANS responsible for the "fight or flight" response, preparing the body to respond to perceived threats by increasing heart rate, dilating pupils, and redirecting blood flow to muscles.

Parasympathetic Nervous System
The "rest and digest" system of the ANS, which conserves energy by slowing the heart rate, enhancing digestion, and promoting relaxation.

Dorsal Vagal Complex (DVC)
The part of the vagus nerve associated with immobilization, freeze responses, and conservation of energy under stress.

Ventral Vagal Complex (VVC)
The part of the vagus nerve linked to social engagement, calm states, and the regulation of heart and breathing rates in safe environments.

Social Engagement System
A concept within polyvagal theory describing how the ventral vagal complex allows for social interaction, communication, and connection when feeling safe.

Fight or Flight Response
An automatic physiological reaction to an event perceived as stressful or frightening, triggered by the sympathetic nervous system.

Freeze Response
A state of immobilization often associated with high levels of fear or trauma, mediated by the dorsal vagal complex.

Neuroception
A term coined by Dr. Stephen Porges, referring to the unconscious assessment of safety, danger, or life threat in the environment, which influences the autonomic state.

Co-Regulation

A process where two or more individuals influence and regulate each other's physiological states, often seen in healthy social bonds.

Self-Regulation

The ability to manage one's emotional, physiological, and behavioral responses, especially during stressful situations.

Heart Rate Variability (HRV)

A measure of the variation in time between heartbeats, often used as an indicator of autonomic nervous system balance and vagal tone.

Vagal Tone

A measure of the activity of the vagus nerve, often associated with the body's ability to regulate heart rate, digestion, and emotional states.

Myelination

The process by which nerve fibers are covered with a protective myelin sheath, enhancing signal transmission speed and efficiency, particularly relevant to the vagus nerve.

Trauma

An emotional response to a deeply distressing or disturbing experience that can dysregulate the autonomic nervous system and impact vagal function.

Somatic Experiencing

A therapeutic approach to healing trauma by focusing on bodily sensations, often used to help regulate the autonomic nervous system and vagus nerve function.

Breathwork

Techniques involving controlled breathing to stimulate the vagus nerve, enhance relaxation, and regulate the autonomic nervous system.

Tonic Immobility

A survival response characterized by a state of physical inactivity or paralysis, often triggered in extreme fear or trauma and linked to dorsal vagal activation.

Biofeedback

A technique that teaches individuals to control physiological processes, such as heart rate, through feedback, often used to enhance vagal tone.

Resilience

The ability to recover from stress or adversity, often involving efficient autonomic nervous system regulation and a well-functioning vagus nerve.

Mind-Body Connection

The interrelationship between mental, emotional, and physical health, particularly relevant in the context of vagal nerve function and polyvagal theory.

Safety Cues

Environmental or interpersonal signals that indicate safety, activating the ventral vagal complex and promoting relaxation and social engagement.

Stress Response

The body's reaction to any demand or challenge, often involving sympathetic activation and vagal nerve modulation.

THE EMERALD
S O C I E T Y

JOIN OUR TRIBE

The Complete Somatic Therapy & Polyvagal Theory Toolbox

VOLUME I REFERENCES

• *Breathing: the legacy of Wilhelm Reich* https://www.sciencedirect.com/science/article/pii/S1360859299800291
• *How Does Somatic Experiencing Therapy Work?* https://www.verywellmind.com/what-is-somatic-experiencing-5204186
• *Post-traumatic stress disorder: the neurobiological impact ...* https://www.ncbi.nlm.nih.gov/pmc/articles/PMC3182008/
• *What is CBT vs. Somatic Therapy? - North Carolina ...* https://www.nccenterforresiliency.com/somatic-articles/what-is-cbt-vs-somatic-therapy/
• *Post-traumatic stress disorder: the neurobiological impact ...* https://www.ncbi.nlm.nih.gov/pmc/articles/PMC3182008/
• *Body Awareness: How to Deepen Your Connection with ...* https://www.healthline.com/health/mind-body/body-awareness
• *Breathing to reduce stress - Better Health Channel* https://www.betterhealth.vic.gov.au/health/healthyliving/breathing-to-reduce-stress
• *5 Incredible Stories of Self-healing and Transformation* https://somaticmovementcenter.com/healing/
• *Body Scan Meditation: Benefits and How to Do It* https://www.verywellmind.com/body-scan-meditation-why-and-how-3144782
• *Buddhist Antecedents to the Body Scan Meditation* https://www.buddhismuskunde.uni-hamburg.de/pdf/5-personen/analayo/buddhistantecedentsbodyscan.pdf
• *Bodysensing: Learn to Listen to Your Body in Meditation* https://www.yogajournal.com/meditation/meditation-classes/bodysensing-learn-listen-body-meditation/
• *Evoking calm: Practicing mindfulness in daily life helps* https://www.health.harvard.edu/blog/evoking-calm-practicing-mindfulness-in-daily-life-helps-202110142617
• *Effects of Mindfulness on Psychological Health: A Review ...* https://www.ncbi.nlm.nih.gov/pmc/articles/PMC3679190/
• *30 Grounding Techniques to Quiet Distressing Thoughts* https://www.healthline.com/health/grounding-techniques
• *Effect of breathwork on stress and mental health - Nature* https://www.nature.com/articles/s41598-022-27247-y
• *How nature benefits mental health* https://www.mind.org.uk/information-support/tips-for-everyday-living/nature-and-mental-health/how-nature-benefits-mental-health/
• *Impact of dance therapy on adults with psychological trauma* https://www.ncbi.nlm.nih.gov/pmc/articles/PMC10334851/
• *Yoga For Emotional Release: 8 Postures For Peace* https://www.brettlarkin.com/yoga-for-emotional-release/
• *Effectiveness of Dance Movement Therapy in the ...* https://www.frontiersin.org/articles/10.3389/fpsyg.2019.00936/full
• *5 Ways to Make Your Home a Healing Space* https://www.psychologytoday.com/us/blog/how-healing-works/202005/5-ways-make-your-home-healing-space
• *The Benefits of Somatic Movement* https://totalsomatics.com/the-benefits-of-somatic-movement/#:~:text=Somatic%20movement%20helps%20to%20alleviate,system%2C%20breathing%20and%20heart%20rate.

• *Trauma Recovery: Stages and 7 Things to Consider* https://www.healthline.com/health/mental-health/trauma-recovery
• *Integrating Somatic Learning into Everyday Life* https://www.jstor.org/stable/1585773
• *Somatic Awareness Journaling: A simple daily practice to ...* https://kristyarbon.com/somatic-awareness-journaling/
• *7 deep breathing exercises to help you calm anxiety* https://www.calm.com/blog/breathing-exercises-for-anxiety#:~:text=The%204%2D7%2D8%20breathing%20technique%20is%20a%20method%20that,a%20state%20of%20deep%20relaxation.
• *Mindfulness-Based Interventions for Anxiety and Depression* https://www.ncbi.nlm.nih.gov/pmc/articles/PMC5679245/
• *Real Stories of SE* https://traumahealing.org/real-stories-of-se/
• *The Importance of the Outdoor Environment for the Recovery ...* https://www.ncbi.nlm.nih.gov/pmc/articles/PMC9915437/#:~:text=(1)%20Background%3A%20Research%20has,as%20part%20of%20their%20treatment.
• *Somatic Experiencing Therapy: 10 Best Exercises & ...* https://positivepsychology.com/somatic-experiencing/
• *Polyvagal Theory Explained (& 18 Exercises & Resources)* https://positivepsychology.com/polyvagal-theory/
• *On The Importance of Titration for Trauma Healing (10 Benefits)* https://www.new-synapse.com/aps/wordpress/?p=1842
• *Somatic Mindfulness: What Is My Body Tellin...- GoodTherapy* https://www.goodtherapy.org/blog/somatic-mindfulness-what-is-my-body-telling-me-and-should-i-listen-0619185/#:
• *Efficacy of journaling in the management of mental illness:* https://www.ncbi.nlm.nih.gov/pmc/articles/PMC8935176/
• *Mind/Body Awareness Writing Exercises* https://www.fammed.wisc.edu/files/webfm-uploads/documents/outreach/im/handout_mbs_workbook.pdf
• *100+ Self-Care Journal Prompts for Healing and Reflection* https://blog.gratefulness.me/self-care-journal-prompts/
• *Writing Therapy: How to Write and Journal Therapeutically* https://positivepsychology.com/writing-therapy/
• *Body Scan Meditation: Benefits and How to Do It* https://www.verywellmind.com/body-scan-meditation-why-and-how-3144782
• *30 Grounding Techniques to Quiet Distressing Thoughts* https://www.healthline.com/health/grounding-techniques
• *Body- and Movement-Oriented Interventions for ...* https://www.ncbi.nlm.nih.gov/pmc/articles/PMC6973294/
• *Breathwork for Healing Trauma: 3 Popular Techniques ...* https://www.othership.us/resources/breathwork-for-healing-trauma
• *The Role of Community Support in Mental Health Recovery:* https://www.fundamentalchange.life/the-role-of-community-support-in-mental-health-recovery
• *What Is Online Group Therapy? Plus, How to Find it* https://www.healthline.com/health/mental-health/online-group-therapy
• *Guide to Starting a Support Group* https://iocdf.org/ocd-finding-help/supportgroups/how-to-start-a-support-group/
• *How To Set Social Media Boundaries To Protect Your Mental Health:*

https://mindfulhealthsolutions.com/how-to-set-social-media-boundaries-to-protect-your-mental-health/

• *Somatic Therapy: Benefits, Types And Efficacy – Forbes Health*

https://www.forbes.com/health/mind/somatic-therapy/#:

• *10 Somatic Interventions Explained*

https://integrativepsych.co/new-blog/somatic-therapy-explained-methods

• *Somatic experiencing – effectiveness and key factors*

https://www.ncbi.nlm.nih.gov/pmc/articles/PMC8276649/

Integrating Somatic Practices into Everyday Life — Repose https://byrepose.com/journal/integrating-somatic-practices-into-everyday-life

VOLUME II REFERENCES

- *Stephen W. Porges, PhD | Polyvagal Theory* https://www.stephenporges.com/
- *Neuroanatomy, Cranial Nerve 10 (Vagus Nerve) - StatPearls* https://www.ncbi.nlm.nih.gov/books/NBK537171/
- *Neuroception: How your body detects threat before you* https://apolloneuro.com/blogs/news/neuroception-how-your-body-detects-threat-before-you?srsltid=AfmBOop-BqmWFHEPOYeTEMkHmBVVgGRoW4OQoXLoye-EuVrXp796wR6UI
- *Vagal tone and the physiological regulation of emotion* https://pubmed.ncbi.nlm.nih.gov/7984159/
- *Post-traumatic stress disorder: the neurobiological impact ...* https://www.ncbi.nlm.nih.gov/pmc/articles/PMC3182008/
- *Dorsal Vagal Shutdown and the Polyvagal Ladder* https://www.neurosparkhealth.com/blog/understanding-dorsal-vagal-shutdown-a-deep-dive-into-the-bodys-response-to-trauma.html
- *Hypervigilance in PTSD and Other Disorders* https://www.verywellmind.com/hypervigilance-2797363
- *The Polyvagal Theory: Neurophysiological Foundations of ...* https://www.ncbi.nlm.nih.gov/pmc/articles/PMC3490536/
- *Diaphragmatic Breathing Exercises and Your Vagus Nerve* https://www.psychologytoday.com/us/blog/the-athletes-way/201705/diaphragmatic-breathing-exercises-and-your-vagus-nerve
- *The Effects of Mindfulness and Meditation on Vagally ...* https://www.ncbi.nlm.nih.gov/pmc/articles/PMC8243562/
- *5 Poses for Vagus Nerve Regulation* https://www.clinicalyogainstitute.com/post/5-poses-for-vagus-nerve-regulation
- *Somatic Experiencing: Supporting Trauma Resolution and ...* https://traumahealing.org/
- *Polyvagal Theory and EMDR Therapy* https://maibergerinstitute.com/polyvagal-theory-emdr/
- *CBT Treatment for Stress and Rumination* https://bayareacbtcenter.com/stress-rumination/
- *8 Vagus Nerve Stimulation Exercises That Help You Relax* https://www.parsleyhealth.com/blog/how-to-stimulate-vagus-nerve-exercises/

- *Somatic Experiencing, Polyvagal Theory And Trauma* https://global.sacap.e-du.za/blog/applied-psychology/somatic-experiencing-polyvagal-theory-and-trauma/
- *Linking the Vagus Nerve and Gut Health* https://wisemindnutrition.-com/blog/linking-vagus-nerve-gut-health
- *Transcutaneous Vagus Nerve Stimulation Could Improve …* https://www.ncbi.nlm.nih.gov/pmc/articles/PMC9599790/
- *Exercise activates vagal induction of dopamine and …* https://www.ncbi.nlm.nih.gov/pmc/articles/PMC6334665/
- *Social connections drive the 'upward spiral' of positive …* https://www.sci-encedaily.com/releases/2013/05/130509123537.htm
- *Polyvagal Theory: A Ladder of Nervous States* https://khironclinics.-com/blog/polyvagal-theory-a-ladder-of-nervous-states/
- *What Is Vagal Tone and How to Improve Yours* https://drruscio.com/vagal-tone/
- *7 Ways to Stimulate Your Vagus Nerve and Why It Matters* https://www.everydayhealth.com/neurology/ways-to-stimulate-your-vagus-nerve-and-why-it-matters/
- *Mental Health Benefits of Journaling* https://www.webmd.com/mental-health/mental-health-benefits-of-journaling
- *Polyvagal Theory Explained (& 18 Exercises & Resources)* https://posi-tivepsychology.com/polyvagal-theory/
- *Creating visual explanations improves learning - PMC* https://www.ncbi.nlm.nih.gov/pmc/articles/PMC5256450/
- *Polyvagal Theory Explained (& 18 Exercises & Resources)* https://posi-tivepsychology.com/polyvagal-theory/
- *What is Self-Regulation? (+95 Skills and Strategies)* https://positivepsycholo-gy.com/self-regulation/
- *The Ubiquity of Trauma and the Role of Community Healing* https://www.psychologytoday.com/us/blog/beyond-mental-health/202310/the-ubiquity-of-trauma-and-the-role-of-community-healing
- *Why We Can't Heal Alone: The Crucial Role of Co-Regulation …* https://annieauyoga.com/why-we-cant-heal-alone-the-crucial-role-of-co-regulation-in-trauma-healing/#:~:text=Co%2Dregulation%20pro-vides%20a%20secure,within%20a%20more%20compassionate%20context.
- https://bemovedtherapy.com/a-little-intro-to-polyvagal-theory-and-the-vagus-nerve/

- *The 5 Best Online PTSD Support Groups* https://www.healthline.com/health/mental-health/ptsd-online-support-group
- *16 Facilitation Techniques and Their Benefits | Indeed.com* https://www.indeed.com/career-advice/career-development/facilitation-techniques

Printed in Great Britain
by Amazon

59295442R00219